Men

xxxx

BETTY CAMPBELL BEATY

WINGED LIFE

BETTY CAMPBELL BEATY

WINGED LIFE

A BIOGRAPHY OF
DAVID BEATY
MBE DFC*

Airlife
England

For our daughters, Sue, Carole and Karen.

He who binds to himself a joy,
Doth the winged life destroy
But he who kisses the joy as it flies,
Lives in Eternity's sunrise.

William Blake

Copyright © 2001 Betty Campbell Beaty

First published in the UK in 2001
by Airlife Publishing Ltd

British Library Cataloguing-in-Publication Data
 A catalogue record for this book
 is available from the British Library

ISBN 1 84037 243 5

Typeset by Phoenix Typesetting, Ilkley, West Yorkshire
Printed in England by Biddles Ltd., Guildford and King's Lynn.

Airlife Publishing Ltd

101 Longden Road, Shrewsbury, SY3 9EB England.
E-mail: airlife@airlifebooks.com
Website: www.airlifebooks.com

ACKNOWLEDGEMENTS

I am deeply indebted to so many individuals and institutions who helped me in the compilation of this biography.

Among them, Sir Alec Atkinson KCB, DFC, David's lifelong friend who wrote the foreword, read the manuscript, and encouraged me with his enthusiasm; Gina Alexander of the British Airline Pilots' Association for information on David's civil flying; Wing Comander Sid Banks DFC, Legion of Honour, who checked the RAF chapters; Captain Ken Beere who gave so much time to discussing the book, to reading the manuscript, to putting it on disk, to organising the index; Bonny Beere who tamed the computer; Stephen Garnett of This England who read the first manuscript and made valuable editorial suggestions; Bob Denwood, for his unique information on U-boats; Mrs Alix Donald who allowed me to use her husband's photograph and loaned me a print of the commemorative stamp in his honour; Captain Jack Frost DFC for valuable information on U-boat sinkings and armament; Flight Lieutenant Jim Glazebrook DFC, who patiently answered my queries, and allowed me to use his Wartime History of 206 Squadron, to quote from his vivid account of the sinking of U575 as well as to use his collection of photographs; Wing Commander J.C. Graham DFC* for his recollections of the Azores and for finding extra information for me from The Public Record Office, and for checking the chapters on 206 Squadron; Peter Gunn whose history of 206 will soon be published and who was generous in answering my queries; Captain Peter Harris RN, CBE, who obtained more information from the Navy on U575; Roy Haycock who checked the manuscript for any aviation errors, advised on photographs and visited The Imperial War Museum on my behalf; Jo Johnston, the widow of David's navigator for her description of the crew's return from the Baltic; Brenda Laird for loaning me her late husband Peter's log-books and photographs; Kingswood School and John Lewis of the Kingswood Association of former pupils for his co-operation; Frank McManus, David's radio operator on many flights, who has allowed me to quote from his book; Squadron Leader John Martin DFC, AFC, commander of A Flight 206 for his permission to quote from the letters which he wrote to his aunt in 1945 while trooping to India; Members of the George Cross Island Association; The Overseas Development Administration; the British Embassy at Quito, Ecuador; Captain Alan Smith M.R.Ae.S., the tireless secretary of 206 Squadron Association who put me in touch with many helpful members; Wing Commander Tom Cross the present commander and serving members of 206 Squadron; Wing Commander Spooner DSO*, DFC* for the splendid account he sent me of Force K and the Special Flight operations in Malta and for allowing me the use of his descriptions and his photographs; Charles Wildblood, David's school friend for his story of David's unconventional arrival at Charles' wedding; David's sisters, Kathleen and Margaret, who gave me descriptions of their Ceylon childhood; our daughters for their tremendous support, their enthusiasm and their valuable suggestions; my editor at Airlife, Peter Coles, for his patience and forbearance as well as his editorial skills; and David himself for keeping a meticulous diary even in the heat of the Malta battle and the D-Day landings, for the inspiration of his life which he lived so fully and so courageously.

FOREWORD

by

Sir Alec Atkinson KCB, DFC

I first met David Beaty over seventy years ago when we both arrived as new boys at Kingswood School, a Methodist school founded by John Wesley at Kingswood, Bristol, in 1748, but later moved to Bath. Both David and I had fathers who were Methodist Ministers, his father being a missionary in Ceylon. We soon became friends and eventually fellow prefects. By 1938, we had both won scholarships to Oxford colleges. His was to Merton College where he read Modern History and was soon appointed Editor of *Cherwell*, a well-established university magazine.

Over all the years I knew David, despite his eventful life and solid achievements, he remained the same modest, friendly, thoughtful and quietly determined person that I had known at the start. Fortunately, he never lost his sense of fun. It might have been said of him as Boswell, Dr Johnson's biographer, said of the lawyer Oliver Edwards, that he tried in his time to be a philosopher but somehow 'cheerfulness kept on breaking in'. Throughout his life David had a strong moral sense and, at core, was a serious-minded and tireless searcher of truth. He constantly set himself aims which would be difficult to achieve, but never spared himself in the attempt. In the outcome, he developed an unusually potent mixture of moral and physical courage and was never content to be swayed by the conventional wisdom or the fashion of the moment. Through his ideally happy marriage to Betty, now his biographer, whom he first met when she was a wartime WAAF officer, he became the centre of a devoted family which it was always a joy and an inspiration to visit.

As can be seen from this biography, alongside a wealth of other interests and experiences, David's post-university career fell into four main phases. First he became a highly decorated Coastal Command pilot who played an important part in the Battle of the Atlantic, and in the Mediterranean during the siege of Malta; then a BOAC pilot who helped to investigate the practicalities of civil air-to-air refuelling and to develop the post-war transatlantic service; then a novelist concentrating on aviation themes whose experience as a pilot in war and peace combined with his gifts as a writer brought the true stamp of authenticity to his work; and finally a pioneer in examining the significance of human factors in aircraft accidents. His sustained efforts in this area led to significant improvements in accident investigation and in airline safety. Large airlines worldwide now recognise in their pilot training the need to address the problems which David exposed so clearly in *The Human Factor in Aircraft Accidents* (1969) and *The Naked Pilot* (1991). This has been a crucial development and David it was who led the way.

Throughout his adult life, David seemed to attract difficult and perplexing challenges which he never failed to face up to with courage and painstaking effort. His close collaboration with Betty in all his literary activities together with her own professional experience as an author make her uniquely qualified to tell the story of his life. She herself shared the values he held so dear and she tells the gripping story of their life together with such immediacy that events of long ago seem to the reader to be happening now. This remarkable and moving record will be treasured by all who knew them, as well as by the many others who first come to know them through this book.

CONTENTS

The Pilots and the Wonder Plane

At 17.56 GMT on 26 October 1952, Captain Harry Foote lined up the blue-and-white Comet 1 G-ALYZ on Runway 16 at Ciampino Airport and called for the before-take-off check. He was bound for Cairo and Johannesburg. He was proud of his aircraft, proud to be its captain. The BOAC Comet Fleet was an élitist group, for the Comet was a wonder plane, the first jet airliner in the world.

The night was pitch dark and raining. The wipers clanked across the windows to reveal muzzy blobs of runway lights, but there was no horizon. Trim was set to neutral and the flaps lowered to fifteen degrees. The four Ghost engines were opened up to full power and rpm checked at 10,250 on all engines. Fuel flows, engine temperatures and pressures were reported correct.

Captain Foote released the brakes. The heavily loaded Yoke Zebra moved slowly into the damp darkness.

The de Havilland Comet was sleek and streamlined with its engines sunk into the wings. Orders had come in from all over the world and it was set to be a money-spinner.

The Comet gave a banshee wail when it flew, but inside the cabin all was quiet and vibration free. Yoke Zebra began gathering speed down the slippery runway. The needle on the airspeed indicator crept round the dial – 60,70,75 knots.

80 knots . . . the speed laid down in the BOAC training manual to lift the nosewheel. Exactly as he had been instructed, Foote eased the control column back.

The nosewheel came off the ground. The speed built up to 112 knots, the already calculated 'unstick' speed. Again Foote moved the control column back, this time to lift the aircraft off the runway.

Yoke Zebra inched off the ground. Foote called, 'Undercarriage up!'

At that instant, the port wing dropped violently. The aircraft swung left, then began juddering. Twice Captain Foote tried to correct on the

11

control column, but the juddering worsened. Instead of rising, Yoke Zebra bounced back on the runway.

It was as though she were bewitched. Everything appeared perfectly normal – but the aircraft simply would not fly. And they were rapidly approaching the red boundary lights at the end of the runway.

Horrified, Foote's only thought then was to save his passengers. He slammed back the throttles and tried to stop.

Seconds later, Yoke Zebra was sliding over rough ground. There came the terrible sound of tearing metal. Both undercarriage legs were wrenched off. The wing broke. The aircraft came to a graunching halt.

Suddenly there was silence. The ominous reek of kerosene was everywhere. But immediately the crew sprang into action, shepherding all the passengers out safely. The kerosene did not ignite. There was no fire. The first officer was injured but no passenger.

There was an immediate outcry. Nothing could be wrong with the wonder plane. Hardly had the pieces been picked up from the ground, let alone examined, than the Ministry of Civil Aviation and BOAC issued a joint statement saying they and de Havilland were satisfied that neither the engines nor the aircraft were to blame.

At the subsequent Inquiry, Foote was found to have got the nose too high, as a result of which, too much drag developed for Yoke Zebra to become airborne. Blame was therefore attributed to him.

He was posted to Yorks, the oldest BOAC aeroplane. They were frequently used to carry freight and exotic animals such as monkeys, leopards and elephants. Wide publicity in the newspapers highlighted his punishment and the vindication of the wonder plane.

Confidence in the Comet had thus been preserved in overseas buyers. One such was Captain Charles Pentland, then Operations Manager of Canadian Pacific Airlines. Less than two months after the Foote Inquiry, he arrived in England to take possession of CPA's new Comet, *Empress of Hawaii*.

By chance, David Beaty, who had just brought in the Constellation service from New York, bumped into him in London. They knew each other well. Pentland, a tough, harsh-voiced Canadian with a rare Clark Gable grin, had been Chief Training Captain with BOAC and had taught David's generation of ex-RAF officers to become airline pilots. He had taught them well. David had alternately resented and admired him. But always trusted him.

Of him, David wrote in *The Water Jump*, 'As a result of his and Bill May's efforts, the BOAC safety record over the Atlantic was the finest in the world.'

Captain Pentland was on his way to Hatfield, where he received instruction on the Comet. He was particularly shown 'the Foote take-off', being warned against getting the aircraft into that nose-high attitude.

On Sunday, 1 March 1953, Captain Pentland took off in the new Comet from London Airport, with four crew and six technicians, and flew without incident to Beirut, bound for India.

Fog obscured Karachi, so he diverted to Nawabshab airport, returning to Karachi when the fog cleared.

Tuesday was a hot dark night. In the early hours, at maximum all-up weight, Captain Pentland prepared for take-off for Calcutta.

The *Empress of Hawaii* sped a reported 3,270 yards down the runway and smashed through a barbed wire boundary fence. Her wheels were torn off in a road culvert. She slid on her belly over the sandy ground, hit the twenty-foot embankment and burst into flames. All on board were killed. Four hours later, the fire still burned.

The Accident Investigation was carried out by the Pakistan Government, assisted by British Inspectors. The report was kept confidential but the finding was almost a carbon copy of the Rome accident report. The crash was caused by the nose of the aircraft being lifted too high. There were headlines in the papers, 'Pilot erred and Comet was wrecked.'

Foote was convinced that, if only he had been listened to, the Karachi accident would never have happened and that he had been unfairly blamed. David, who knew both men well, agreed with him. He knew they would never disobey The Book, and realised there must be some other reason for the two crashes.

Two months later, in May 1953, Maurice Haddon, Captain of Comet Yoke Victor was about to board the crew car waiting outside their hotel in Bangkok. The BOAC crews were popular guests and all the staff had come to wave them off.

As Haddon swung himself inside the car, one of the four gold bars on the epaulette of his uniform fell off. Remembering the old Siamese superstition that, if any part of a warrior's armour falls off before he goes into battle, he will be killed, the staff were dismayed.

But Yoke Victor's take-off and flight were smooth and swift. So swift that they flashed past Harry Foote in his lumbering York twenty thousand feet below. Twenty minutes after Yoke Victor landed at Dum Dum airport, Foote came into Operations and had a chat with Haddon who was making up his flight plan to Delhi.

At 10.59 GMT, as Foote and his crew were getting into the transport for the Calcutta hotel where they were night-stopping, Captain

13

Haddon, his five crew and thirty-seven passengers took off in Yoke Victor.

At 11.02 Haddon contacted Area Control. 'Departed Calcutta 10.59. Estimated time of arrival Palam 13.20. Climbing to 32,000ft.'

An hour later, when Foote and his crew reached their hotel, they heard a rumour that Area Control had lost contact with Yoke Victor.

Foote said immediately, 'It will have crashed.'

Next day, BOAC issued a statement saying they did not consider Yoke Victor to be lost, that it might have landed elsewhere, that other aircraft would be keeping a look-out and that a York freighter had taken off at first light to search.

That York freighter was Harry Foote in his punishment aircraft. He sighted the wreckage at the village of Jangipara, twenty-five miles west of Calcutta. Thus, ironically, the pilot who had been demoted from the wonder plane now flew round its wreck.

The mystery of these tragic events and his own conviction that the pilots had been wrongly blamed, sharpened David's resolve to begin the study of hitherto unrecognised human factors in aircraft accidents, a study to which he devoted much of his life.

CHAPTER ONE

CEYLON CHILDHOOD

That life began in a concrete bungalow above Hatton, a small town set in a rough valley of the Central Highlands of Ceylon, at the foot of the sacred mountain of Adam's Peak. A railway line cuts through the valley, serving the gem mines and the tea plantations that rib the lower slopes of the mountain range in a glistening dark chenille green.

In 1906 when David's father, the Reverend Stanley Beaty, took up his appointment as Methodist Minister for the sprawling central circuit, Hatton prospered, at least on the surface. Poverty was confined to the Tamils working on the tea estates and there were fine Victorian public buildings flying the Union Jack, proclaiming an Empire on which the sun would never set.

Here in the small concrete manse, the Reverend Stanley Beaty awaited the arrival of his bride-to-be, May Horne. Like him, she came from a well-known family in Carlisle. The Beatys owned a large printing works in Carlisle, which was now being run with disastrous results by his three argumentative brothers. The family claimed descent from Dr William Beattie, the author and biographer of the poet Thomas Campbell. Dr Beattie, after practising medicine in Edinburgh and London, was summoned to attend the Duke of Clarence (William IV) and his family, travelling with them through the Courts of Europe. His only remuneration for fourteen years service was a canteen of silver plate and a letter certifying him to be 'a perfect gentleman'. The family also claimed, although the Reverend Beaty regretfully cast honest doubt on this, descent from Admiral Nelson's medical attendant at Trafalgar.

May was a brown-eyed, gentle girl, dominated by her older more vivacious sister, but with a hidden strength of her own She and the Reverend Beaty had met at a church social, playing a game in which the man spun a plate calling a girl's name and, if she fancied the man in question, she had to rush out and catch the plate before it fell. May, shy at first but certainly fancying the good looking theology student, had held back, till, egged on by her merrier friends, she had darted

15

out, caught the plate in the nick of time, and their courtship had begun.

It was not entirely smooth. The Reverend Beaty's family were staunch Methodists. The Hornes were staunch Presbyterians and, although the difference to anyone else might seem academic, it was not so to the families in question. Although the couple became engaged, it was not until May 'converted' to Methodism that the Hornes' unstinted approval could be given: then, after a three-year engagement May booked her passage to Ceylon.

She brought her bridal gown with her. There were three other young brides on the voyage and, when the boat docked in Colombo, all three stepped eagerly down the gangway to meet their impatient fiancés waiting below. But May stayed in her cabin. Only when the Reverend Beaty hurried up anxiously to seek her out would she greet him, and let him coax her ashore.

After a Methodist wedding in Colombo, the Reverend Beaty and his young wife took up residence in the Hatton Methodist Mission House, a square concrete bungalow on a hilltop close to the tea plantations, and there they raised their family of three daughters and one son, David.

At the birth of each daughter the Beatys' servants, even the ones who were Christian converts, expressed their deep disappointment, the cook by going out onto the balcony and spitting, the rest by moaning and beating a slow sad drum.

The birth of David on 28 March 1919 saved the day. It was greeted with loud acclamation. Fireworks were lit in the garden and all around the valley, and a new ayah chosen, Sugathi, a young Tamil girl from Hatton.

She quickly consulted the star-wise-man, who made a picture of her new charge's twenty-eight star mansions on a palm leaf and thus cast his horoscope. She was dismayed to be told that because of the journey of the sun and moon through Mars he would be concerned with war. But, as her disapproving employers pointed out, the war to end wars had finished four months before. There would never be another. And in any case, the whole family were Methodists dedicated to peace.

Twenty-six years later, another World War had just ended, Sugathi was a mother herself with a home of her own, and fireworks of a different sort were ripping open the overcast when David, now an RAF Squadron Leader, lowered his Liberator aircraft into the approach at Ratmanala airfield in the land of his birth. It was September 1945, and he had certainly been concerned with war. He had completed four tours of operations in the hottest theatres of the conflict, been awarded the DFC for the sinking of a U-boat, the Bar to it for bringing home

16

David's father with his motorbike doing parish rounds through the jungle.

The manse at Hatton where David was born. His father is about to mount his horse to visit outlying villages.

across the North Sea a Liberator severely crippled in his attack on a German battleship. Sandwiched between tours attacking German U-boats and battleships had been a tour as a test pilot and a tour in Malta during the most perilous period of the island's siege.

Now a Flight Commander of the illustrious 206 Squadron, he and the Station Commander were familiarising themselves with the route for 206's latest assignment; that of bringing the troops home from the Far East, and ferrying others to trouble spots in the Middle East.

As the Liberator's wheels touched down, a tropical storm was bursting, one of the several which had enlivened the long flight via Castel Benito, Heliopolis and Karachi. But apart from signs of war in the hastily constructed airfield, outside its barbed wire Ceylon was unchanged and as he remembered it in his childhood.

It had been a reasonably happy childhood and Sugathi had been his stability. She was warm and loving, and until the age of three David would have nothing to do with his mother, although they later became very close. Mrs Beaty had many duties to perform for the missionary community, which was strong and lively and full of zeal to convert the heathen. Their social life was a less ostentatious and simpler version of the colonial life lived by the tea planters and the diplomatic servants of the crown. There were tennis and croquet parties, cricket matches, picnics, church outings and musical evenings round the piano, but, the Methodists then being strong on temperance, no drinking of alcohol. Unlike the planters and the servants of the crown, the missionaries' social life was subordinate to work. They ran classes for the children of the plantations, held meetings, open-air and indoor services and made strenuous efforts to improve the tea workers' living conditions.

Although the pay of missionaries was very small, the Beatys kept six servants. All of them, from Apu, the head boy and general facilitator, to Matteiah, the youngest, a punkah wallah and David's particular friend, were loyal and hard working and they were grateful that the Reverend Beaty never tried to take advantage of their relationship by insisting they convert to Christianity.

He was a man of courage and a natural administrator. He travelled from village to village negotiating the difficult roads on a motorbike and sidecar and occasionally on horseback or pedal cycle, teaching and preaching. Usually he went alone because the native population avoided the jungle at night, where not only predatory animals, pumas and leopards, and wild boar and the occasional rogue elephant roamed, but evil spirits.

When the monsoon rains came, the roads became cataracts of floodwater and impassable, and he couldn't return until the next morning.

His daughter, Margaret, can still remember waiting anxiously with her mother and sisters throughout stormy nights for the puttering of the motor bike engine up the steep slope to the bungalow.

She can also remember that her father was a disciplinarian, on one occasion caning all three girls in turn for the offence of coaxing Sugathi to take them for a walk into the nearby tea gardens where they did nothing more daring than skip up and down among the scented bushes.

The Reverend Beaty took his work very seriously. His great rivalry was not with the Buddhists and Hindus, with whom he got on well; in fact, together, all three priests had fervently rung the bells announcing peace with Germany at the end of World War One. The Reverend Beaty's rivalry was with the Roman Catholics, whom the Methodists felt had an unfair advantage with their rosary beads and crucifixes, holy water, incense and fine impressive robes, not to mention their ritual, their confessions and absolutions.

The Methodists were worried not only about the Roman Catholics and the heathen practices of the native population, but also about the drunkenness of the British. Besides the notorious drinking habits and womanising of the planters, British sailors putting into the ports of Colombo or Trincomalee and making straight for the arak taverns were regularly to be seen on the docksides, drunk and robbed and often seriously injured.

The young Mrs Beaty, who shared her husband's courage, established and served in a milk bar they set up in a rough shanty street on the Colombo dockside. The milk bar was intended to be a rival to the arak taverns, and to wean the British seamen away from arak, the fiery and powerful distillation of coconuts. But although the milk bar was used by sailors seeking a sympathetic female shoulder to cry on, they were not tempted by the milk, and having told Mrs Beaty of their homesickness and sorrows and their suspicions about their wives, they soon found their way to the arak taverns. So in the end the milk bar failed for lack of support.

Setting high standards of courage for themselves, the Beatys demanded the same from their children. They told them of a fellow missionary whose little daughter had died of smallpox. How brave the child had been and how at her funeral, her parents had shed not a tear but praised the Lord for taking her to Him so early in life, singing songs of joy all the way to the graveside and back again.

At the age of three, sent by his father with a message to his mother who was at the far end of the garden, David found his path barred by a prowling leopard. Frightened, he rushed back to his father, who told him to return to the spot where he would probably find that the

David and his ayah, Sugathi.

David riding one of the
elephants helping to build
Kingswood School at
Kandy.

leopard had gone or if it hadn't, he must walk round it. He must never be afraid.

The leopard had gone, but only a little further along the path was a hooded cobra. A return visit to his father elicited the same instructions. Go back, if it hasn't gone, walk straight past it. Never be afraid. Instructions which, inculcated in the child, perhaps echoed down the years and became the courage that characterised the man.

Those years with all the family together were the most secure. The children were largely in ignorance of the perils that beset the community. The Reverend Beaty suffered from malaria, which recurred all his life, and he lost the sight of one eye, but the inconvenience was never referred to. David's closest sister, Mamie, was bitten by a rabid dog and had to be taken to Colombo, their nearest hospital, every week for painful anti-rabies injections into her stomach. Two young children of close colleagues died of dysentery. The wife of one missionary simply disappeared. She walked out of the house one morning and was never seen again. She boarded no ship. She made no contact with her family in England. Her body was never found, and after a while her name was never mentioned. Strange, swiftly fatal diseases were everywhere. A nearby village suffered an epidemic of the plague. It was ringed in a wall of corrugated iron, and the surviving inhabitants evacuated. Scorpions crept into slippers and, apart from the benign rat snake that lived under the bath, there were many different varieties of snakes and stinging insects.

But the air was sweetly scented with bougainvillea and cannas and the smell of the tea gardens. There were brilliantly coloured birds, the bulbul, the blue-tailed bee-eater, parrots and the 'fire thief', and myriads of butterflies strangely flying in their thousands against the wind. Exotic fruit was plentiful – mangoes and mangosteens, rambutans and pineapple, guavas and papaws, melons and bullock's hearts and fifty varieties of banana. The food was cooked with delicious spices and the bungalow cleaned by apparently willing servants.

While Sugathi taught the children the songs and colourful legends of Ceylon, which was the venue of the sixth and seventh voyages of Sinbad in the *Arabian Nights*, Mrs Beaty taught her children to tell the time and to sing hymns to her accompaniment on the piano. It was a potent mixture of cultures. Meanwhile David taught himself to read from the Gamages catalogues, which he always went around clutching. He had a red pedal car in mind.

The family made a brief trip to England when David was two, because Grandfather Beaty had died. England had still not recovered from World War One. It was a gloomy visit. But when they returned

The Beaty family. The Revd and Mrs Beaty, Kath, Margaret, Mamie and David.

The red car.

to Ceylon, the Beatys left behind in Carlisle the two older girls, Kathleen and Margaret, aged nine and eight, at a dreadful boarding school reminiscent of Charlotte Bronte's Lowood and which they remember with horror. Mamie stayed with her aunt who eventually rescued the two older girls.

David remembered little of the journey except leaving behind his weeping sisters and being thankful that such a fate had not befallen him. In all he made three round trips between Ceylon and England

David and Edgar Small (later Klopinger).

before he was ten, and on the second of these he acquired the little red pedal car.

The family brought Sugathi with them each time. Those were not the days of overt colour prejudice. But few inhabitants of Britain had seen a brown skin. The local children were fascinated by her exotic beauty. They rushed to follow and admire her whenever she came out, addressing her respectfully as 'Chocolate Lady'.

When David was five the Reverend Beaty was appointed the Chairman of the South Ceylon District of the Methodist Church and the family moved to Colombo. There the smell was of the Indian Ocean, the sounds were of the chugging of a lemonade factory close by and the whistle and rattle of the trains that ran along the railway line at the bottom of the garden between the manse and the sea.

The Reverend Beaty was allowed a car and a chauffeur instead of the old motorbike and sidecar. There were many more social activities. David met other missionaries and their families. In particular, the Reverend Small, a gaunt austere minister, his rather inscrutable German wife and a son by her first marriage, Edgar, whom the

23

Reverend Small had adopted and to whom he was devoted. The two boys became staunch friends, exploring the edges of the jungle, climbing the rocks, swimming in the tranquil lakes called 'tanks' or in the clear blue sea off Mount Lavinia, playing cricket and riding elephants and watching the buffaloes, threshing the paddy fields, trampling out the grain.

A few years later, the Reverend Beaty, having served in Ceylon since 1906, set sail for service in England, accompanied by his wife and four children. Edgar and his parents waved them off from the quayside. That was the last the two boys saw of each other for over sixty years.

CHAPTER TWO

SCHOOLDAYS

Shortly after they returned to England the Reverend Beaty received a long letter from the Reverend Small. The tone of the letter was sad but resigned. He was now living alone. His wife, wishing Edgar to be educated in Germany, had returned there with him. He did not say whether or not she was ever expected back, but mindful of the uncertainty and unrest in Germany, the devaluation of the mark, the extreme political parties that were holding demonstrations, the Reverend Small was deeply worried.

Meanwhile the Reverend Beaty became Minister at Somerset Road Methodist Church, Handsworth Wood, Birmingham. David and his sister Mamie were sent to Soho Hill High School for Girls (boys accepted till ten), a strict establishment, humiliatingly female as far as David was concerned, and far too stern for Mamie.

David's teacher was Mrs Kimberley, a forbidding lady dressed from throat to toe in black bombazine, her large bosom festooned in jet necklaces, her pince-nez spectacles secured with black moire ribbon. To enforce discipline she carried a solid cylindrical black ruler, which she had no hesitation in using. The name of Mrs Kimberley early entered the Beaty family lexicon of monsters, and yet when a child stole in order to buy sweets and gifts to win friends, she was kind and surprisingly perceptive.

Out of school, once they had become used to the clammy cold of England and the noise and dirt of Birmingham, they were happy. The family was for the time being together, and the manse was a large comfortable Victorian house. Their neighbours were an elderly couple, Walter and Marion, with no children of their own, but with an accomplished maid called Bertha. Bertha's expertise was in cooking and in reciting doggerel rhymes culled from gravestones, especially children's gravestones, which Mamie and David loved to hear. The little girl whose chair was empty because of eating too much

The Hall House Committee.

watermelon, and another from over-indulgence in spearmint were great favourites. As were:

> 'Grim death to please his liquorish palate,
> Has taken my Lettice to put in his sallat.'

But their number one favourite was:

> 'Here lies the body of Mary Gwynne,
> Who was so very pure within,
> She cracked the shell of her earthly skin,
> And hatched herself a cherubim.'

Untiringly reciting rhymes and telling strange stories, Bertha, and her employers too, set about making the Beaty family's stay in England as enjoyable as possible. The congregation also accepted the Reverend Beaty's ministrations with enthusiasm and generosity. The family was the recipient of Christmas hampers and birthday presents. But there was born in the children, especially David, an intense dislike of being receivers, of any form of dependence, and of living in a house that was never theirs. Their especial dislike was when the Circuit Stewards came round, which they did with monotonous regularity, to inspect their property. And although Mrs Beaty always made sure it was in perfect order and there were never any complaints or criticisms, it somehow made them feel the objects of charity.

When the Reverend Beaty returned to Ceylon, he did so on his own. The family scattered. To be close to the children, his mother stayed for a while with her older sister Meg, a good looking, very strong minded woman who now ran a dame school for her own three children and those of friends. Mrs Beaty took Mamie and Margaret with her to Aunt Meg's in Guisborough. Kathleen, at sixteen, had been accepted for nursing training at The Children's Hospital, Windermere, and on a brief home visit from there had met and captivated an ardent young theology student, Max Woodward, an old boy of Kingswood School (to which David was to try to gain entry) who after only two brief meetings, both in the company of other people, had begged her parents to allow them to be engaged. They refused to allow an engagement on such a slender acquaintance, but as Max had decided to be a missionary in Ceylon they consented to the exchange of letters. David sat the entrance examination for Kingswood School, and was offered a place.

Buying his uniform and impedimenta was expensive and worrying for David's mother. But she promised the last day treat of a visit to the cinema before he went to school. First, however, she had to attend an afternoon talk at the Mothers' Union. David sat through it impatiently. Then at the end of the talk it was announced that there would be a silver collection, ironically for the Mission Field. As Mrs Beaty only had one single silver coin in her purse, the florin to buy the cinema tickets and an ice-cream, she had to put that in the collecting plate and the pre-school treat was cancelled.

School was a whole new world. Kingswood, built on the shoulder of Lansdown Hill, had been established in 1748 by John Wesley, the founder of Methodism. Of Kingswood he said that he wanted a school 'that would not disgrace the Apostolic Age'. Strict rules were laid down. The children had to rise at four. They were to work at their lessons every day of the year except Sundays. Christmas was eventually permitted to be a holiday and, later, Boxing Day. But the children must never play.

Although its philosophy and timetable were by that time ameliorated, especially when A.B. Sackett took over as headmaster from the stern H.A. Wootton, Kingswood still embodied much of Wesley's teaching and was at first open only to the sons of Ministers. David never forgot one exasperated master shouting at his class, 'Remember, you are all the sons of intelligent paupers.'

27

The stated aim of the school was to develop the student's sense of responsibility through discipline and scholarship. The fees were small, about £40 a year, the discipline strict, but the teaching good.

The headmaster, A.B. Sackett, was a much-respected figure. A sensitive, imaginative man and an ardent lover of natural beauty, he had shown great bravery as an infantry captain during World War One, serving at Gallipoli and on the Western Front. He was awarded the Military Cross for his leadership in an attack on the German front line. As a result of the injuries he sustained in France, his left leg had been amputated. His approach down the polished corridors was made more theatrically fearful by the heavy thud of his artificial limb. After several years as headmaster, he had reluctantly re-introduced the cane as a last resort, but he was known to be just and rarely did he administer punishment himself.

David was creative and highly intelligent, but clumsy and untidy. He used to say that with hindsight he recognised he had a laterality problem bordering on dyslexia which made it difficult for him to master simple tasks, such as tying shoelaces and knotting ties. For years he had to ask another boy to tie his tie before going down to breakfast. But that problem probably started him on the study of laterality and eventually that of human factors.

At school he made friends but liked and needed solitude. He read avidly. He began to write short stories. One story was particularly vivid – *Crude Rope.* It was based on fact, which as a child he had pieced together from the overheard whispers of adults. It concerned five young Tamil men awaiting execution in the grim prison at Kandy, which David had seen many times as a boy. It had been one of the Reverend Beaty's duties to visit the condemned men, three of whom were Christians, and decades afterwards, recalling their deaths, he would still be overcome with emotion. Round this event David had written his short story, a strangely macabre and compassionate one for a young boy and one which perhaps made him so emphatically opposed as he was all his life to capital punishment, bombarding successive Home Secretaries with letters and telegrams.

Apart from sloppiness in his clothes and a horrendously untidy desk, he didn't fall foul of the powers-that-be at Kingswood except on the occasion of the headmaster's gooseberries. David was small and slight and therefore, on occasion, bullied.

Judson, a particularly hefty and sadistic bully had a small gang of equally hefty and sadistic followers. Apart from whipping the legs of small boys with wet towels in the changing rooms, they used to lurk in the gardens on a Sunday afternoon, when the headmaster's garden was open for pupils to stroll in. That privilege was usually taken up by the boys from abroad who had no parents to visit them on Sundays and no parents at hand to complain to.

David was wandering in the school gardens adjoining that of the headmaster when Judson and co. leaped out from the bushes, knocked him down and banged his head on the ground several times. They then vanished, just as a posse of David's classmates emerged from the head-master's garden. His classmates immediately offered practical comfort in the shape of a handful of unripe gooseberries, which they had feloniously picked in the sacred garden.

David bit one in two, found it as sour as vinegar and immediately spat it out.

Later, at supper, the headmaster rose to announce an unscheduled address. He then proceeded to harangue all the boys on the twin sub-jects of gross ingratitude and common theft. To wit, some ungrateful boys had so abused the generous privilege of being allowed to stroll in the headmaster's garden that they had used that privilege to steal his gooseberries.

Mr Sackett ended his peroration by bellowing, 'Now stand up those boys who ate the headmaster's gooseberries.'

A great moral debate went on in David's head, one that presaged many throughout his life. He had not strictly speaking stolen anything. He did not in fact like unripe gooseberries at the best of times. And he had not been inside the headmaster's garden nor actually plucked the forbidden fruit. But the wording of the indictment was 'who ate' and, like Adam, he had eaten.

Besides, the miscreants were his friends and comforters. He stood up, and was duly punished.

But punishment, and bullying and homesickness notwithstanding, David embraced the all-male atmosphere of the school, finding it a refreshing change from a family which, like Oliver Cromwell's, had too many females. When the holidays came and he went to his aunt's, he gruffly insisted that his mother and everyone else addressed him as Beaty, never by his Christian name. He played rugby with great verve and courage and was chosen for the lower school team. His great rival was Monkey Wright, who subsequently played for England.

To his profound disgust David was also chosen to play Lavinia in the school production of *Androcles and the Lion*, and, to his embar-rassment, was praised by the reviewer of the local Bath paper as a female lead of considerable promise. Briefly, several of the older boys appeared to see him in a totally different light. They suspended all bullying and instead issued invitations to tea and crumpets, to outings on whole holidays and other favours: a change which David, being of an innocent disposition, was only later in life able to explain to himself.

*　　*　　*

Life at Kingswood was Spartan. The building was old and cold, the paint above the few hot-water radiators worn away by small fingers seeking their almost non-existent heat. Apart from twice-weekly 'extras', the food consisted of porridge and bread for breakfast, a greasy mince stew for their midday meal, rock buns and cocoa for the last meal of the day, supper.

The meals were served and the school cleaned by young local girls to whom the boys were not allowed to speak, and in the slang of the school, the girls were known as 'dumbs'. The greasy mince stew was known as 'cat's spew'.

The boys were also forbidden to speak to the girls of The King's School, situated just a little lower down the hill. The pupils there were the daughters of Service officers. Dressed becomingly in straw boaters, gym slips and neat blazers, the girls marched by the walls of Kingswood in chattering enticing crocodiles, as the boys peeped over wistfully.

David also stared up wistfully that term as the huge silver shape of the R101 slid out of the clouds above the train rattling him back to school on a dark October evening. The R101 was on its much heralded but fatal maiden flight scheduled for Egypt and India, but already being beaten by wind and weather before its crash at Beauvais. It was a ship and an enterprise and an environment which would one day be of intense interest to David, and the route it had embarked upon one that he himself would often fly. But at the time, he would simply have liked to be in what seemed like freedom up there instead of returning to the confines of school.

Academically, Kingswood did him well. David was taught English by a young and lively teacher, John Maw, who recognised the depth of his imagination and intelligence. He also recognised David's lack of sophistication and of any form of deviousness or manipulation. He once said that David was a mixture of Chinese sage and Glaxo baby. Mr Maw encouraged David's literary efforts, praising his short stories, a collection of which he had begun to assemble at the age of ten.

When Mr Maw married an attractive and highly intelligent young lady called Gulie, they used to invite David and some of the other boys

David on holiday at Cleeve Prior with Kath.

Staying at the Wildbloods' Welsh cottage.

for evenings when they discussed literature and philosophy, drank coffee sweetened with special brightly coloured sugar crystals, which seemed the acme of sophistication, and set the world to rights. Gulie possessed both charm and a keen mind, was interested in civics and women's rights and eventually became Mayor of Bath. But best of all for the boys at Kingswood, she was motherly and perceptive, ameliorating the harsher aspects of Sackett's all-male world

The least serious lesson was music. The music master, Percy Hancox, was a kindly and eccentric bachelor whose friendships in his student days had given him sufficient influence in the top ranks of the music profession to enable him to attract world-famous musicians to perform at the school for less than their standard fees. He was, however, by no means a natural disciplinarian. Baited by some of the musically unreceptive boys, many of his lessons ended in uproar with Mr Hancox using his conductor's wooden baton as a cane, and making the class bend over. But he was too kindly to let the punishment hurt, and the discipline never improved.

There was occasional escape. His friend and classmate Charlie Wildblood's mother came to Bath to take Charlie out to lunch or tea. Being kind and compassionate, she frequently asked David to join them. She was an English teacher and David delighted in her knowledge of literature and the sharpness of her argument and wit.

He delighted too in the company of his friend Alec Atkinson, with whom he spent whole holidays cycling around the Cotswolds. Alec was to become a fighter pilot and then a very senior civil servant and a staunch lifelong friend. Another friend was Dick Posnett, a keen sportsman and an excellent hurdler who in 1940 was to win the 120 yards hurdles for Cambridge against Oxford. After service in Uganda, he eventually became Governor of Bermuda, but was a little too democratic to please the wealthier residents there.

Mrs Wildblood, as well as his mother, visited David when he was in the sanatorium, following an operation on a scrotum abscess. With the stoicism which was natural to him and reinforced by the school ethos, David had endured great pain but not told anyone, until a young under-matron, noticing he was walking like a crippled old man, took it upon herself to find out why.

David spent a holiday afterwards with the Wildbloods at a little cottage they had in the Welsh mountains, which he loved. But in general, holidays were anticipated with mixed feelings, for they held their own particular dread. Apart from his mother's sister, Aunt Meg, and her husband Uncle Cam, most of David's relatives were dragooned in various degrees of unwillingness to accept the Reverend Beaty's children.

It was an unwillingness matched by David's own to go to stay with them. His uncles and aunts, many of whom he had never seen in his life before, had been strictly and frugally brought up in the Methodist or Presbyterian church. Some of them had been missionaries themselves. Children were to be seen and not heard. And with their tiny salaries, they had their own problems and difficulties, so an extra guest at the table was not always welcome.

On one occasion, David was due to go and stay with a particularly strict and pious aunt on his way to his Aunt Meg, when he was overcome with horror at the prospect of even two nights under that chilly roof. So, as the train steamed into Leeds station, he climbed up onto the luggage rack, and being small and slight, managed to become invisible under his coat until the train had steamed out again.

Except for the rare stays with families who had boys of his own age, only with his Aunt Meg and Uncle Cam and their children did he enjoy his holidays with relatives. His uncle was the Medical Officer of Health for North Yorkshire. He was the picture of a kindly uncle – tall and broad shouldered, always wearing a thick Harris tweed jacket and smoking a pipe. Meg and Cam had three children, two girls and a boy, and in the holidays David was joined by his sister, Mamie, three years older than himself who was now at Hunmanby Hall School, and occasionally by Margaret who had begun nursing in Birmingham. They had fun and they felt loved and wanted.

Although not a trained teacher, Aunt Meg ran her small school very successfully, and the Beaty children had the security, albeit briefly, of feeling they belonged to a large extended family. There was a big garden to play in and the Yorkshire Moors to explore.

Uncle Cam gave David his first taste of the thrills of flight. When the Alan Cobham Flying Circus came up to Yorkshire, Uncle Cam paid seven and sixpence for David to have a twenty-minute flip in the open cockpit of a Tiger Moth. David was not conscious of it lighting any determination to fly and yet the air was to be his medium and his destiny.

Sometimes in the summer, the family joined with Aunt Meg and Uncle Cam and their family to rent accommodation in one of David's favourite places, Cleeve Prior, in the Vale of Evesham. Aunt Meg's family had rooms at a guesthouse but the Beatys stayed with a kindly couple, the Adams, in a small stone cottage surrounded by orchards. They usually coincided their visit with the ripening of the plums, which

The cottage at Cleeve Prior where the family stayed.

David and Mamie helped Mr Adams to pick and which Mrs Adams made into the most divine plum pies ever tasted.

The cottage was near the river and they hired a punt. The highlight of one punting expedition was when the authoritative Aunt Meg, she who must always be obeyed, over-balanced while giving orders and fell with an enormous splash (she was a big woman) into the river. Most inconveniently she had only brought one pair of corsets with her and she was confined indoors while the heavy, thickly-boned garment hung on the line to dry.

All his life, Uncle Cam was a keen bridge player, and later taught David to play bridge and chess. Cam had a little group of like-minded enthusiasts, who were always served with coffee and biscuits and whisky. The children used to wait until the bridge players had gone home and then steal down to eat the remaining biscuits, drain the coffee cups and even the whisky glasses. One of the bridge players was a charismatic man who spoke English with a Russian accent. He was never formally introduced to the family, but Uncle Cam told David his name was Kerensky, that he had been at the centre of Russia's October Revolution. Elected at the age of thirty-one to the Fourth duma, Kerensky became Minister of Justice, then War Minister, until in July, in the midst of revolutionary chaos, he was made Prime Minister of the Second Provisional Government. But he was caught between the forces of military action on the one hand, and the

Bolshevik revolution on the other. He was overthrown by the Soviet of Peoples' Commissars, of which Lenin was President, Trotsky the Commissar of Foreign Affairs, and Stalin the Commissar of Nationalities. Faced with that formidable combination, Kerensky fled in disguise through Finland to Paris and England. He was, Uncle Cam said, the one hope that 'there might have been of a moderate Soviet government'.

The outside world and its political upheavals impinged on Kingswood itself. This was a time when British public opinion favoured the Germans rather than the French, with whom, it was said, the British had little in common. Helped by popular newspapers such as the *Daily Mail*, great supporters of the Blackshirts and Oswald Moseley, the British people were encouraged to be friendlier with our German cousins. Partly perhaps with this in mind, and partly perhaps because the founder John Wesley had been influenced by the ideas of the great German school at Jena, Mr Sackett and the Governors decided that exchanges should be effected between the boys of Kingswood School and a similar one in Germany. However their choice was strange. They chose Ilfeld, a military academy for the sons of officers.

The young Germans who arrived were brawny, healthy looking, vigorous and unacademic. When they arrived, David was immersed in study. A few years earlier, lacking the guidance of a parent, he had opted for Classics for his Higher School Certificate, mostly because the master who taught Classics was so desperately short of pupils and David felt sorry for him.

Almost too late, David realised he wasn't sufficiently interested in Classics, wasn't very good at them and wanted to study History. With difficulty, he managed to convince his teachers that he could still cover the History syllabus in one year, and so he did.

He was also able to look up from his books and study Kingswood's German guests. He said that having done so, when the war did come, despite their obvious efficiency, he felt more rather than less confident of the final outcome.

Instant obedience to authority, physical exercises, cold showers, route marches and heel clicking were the order of the Germans' day.

Unlike their British counterparts, who got up at the last minute, they leapt out of bed smartly at the first rising bell. They walked as if on a parade ground, holding themselves very erect in contrast to the well-known Kingswood Slouch. Their manners were faultless, their discipline excellent. The only point at which the Kingswood boys felt they could feel superior and snigger, was when the Germans prepared themselves for bed.

Then, freshly showered, they attired themselves not in striped pyjamas but in voluminous white cotton nightshirts daintily embroidered at the neck, which every red-blooded British boy reckoned were fit only for baby girls.

The senior German boys, among them *Herr* von Ribbentrop's son, shared the prefects' study. David was by this time a prefect and Head of his house. It was the custom at the end of the school day for the prefects to sit round the pot-bellied stove in the study and toast bread and crumpets. In order to maximise the heat from the stove, the prefects removed their trousers and warmed their thighs at the same time. The Germans regarded this with horror.

The prefects were thus engaged on the afternoon following the broadcast news that Hitler had invaded Sudetenland. The head boy at Kingswood was a tough rugby-playing boy called Tom Lund, who subsequently, on 611 Squadron, became one of the heroes of the Battle of Britain. As he sat comfortably in his underpants, he took it upon himself to announce slowly and very censoriously between toasting a crumpet and scratching his thighs, 'We were very shocked indeed when *Herr* Hitler invaded Sudetenland.'

The German boys leapt to their feet, clicked their heels and marched out. The British boys felt they had struck a blow.

Politics were forbidden and the subject was never mentioned again. David was quite sure that young Ribbentrop had formed the opinion, which he no doubt passed on to his father, who in turn advised Hitler on the British attitude, that the youth of Britain was lazy, effete and undisciplined and no match for the German youth and the fast expanding German war machine.

Ribbentrop was at that time a favourite with Hitler. He had delighted his *Führer* by brokering the Anglo-German Naval Agreement, whereby Britain allowed Germany a larger Navy than the Versailles Treaty had laid down. But now he had become unpopular in Britain. It was said that he had bought his name, married his money and swindled his way into office. More heinous still, the English aristocracy dubbed him 'no gentleman' and he had committed the gaffe of giving the Nazi salute to King George VI.

With their noses to the scholastic grindstone, the Kingswood boys knew little of this. The Higher School Certificate examination results were very good. David not only achieved excellent marks in his subjects but he also won an Open Scholarship to Merton College, Oxford, as well as county scholarships.

Although their futures were uncertain, the senior boys began to consider what they would do after university, always supposing they were lucky enough to live that long, which was very doubtful. Nevertheless the future had to be thought about. Both Dick Posnett and David with his Ceylonese background were attracted to the Colonial Service and duly applied.

Then before he went up to Oxford, with war looming, David scraped enough money together to book a trip to Ceylon. He was eager to see the land of his birth again and he had never forgotten the excitement and warmth of a long voyage east. Besides, not only were his parents out there again, but also his eldest sister Kathleen who had married Max after a five-year courtship by letter. True to his promise Max had become a missionary in Ceylon and they had set up house in Martara. David's next sister, Margaret, was nursing in Colombo, and his youngest sister Mamie had come out as a Guide Commissioner. So it was a last gathering of the family before war broke.

After Kingswood, the SS *Arora*, on which David embarked at Liverpool, seemed luxury itself. The food was excellent and plentiful, the Goanese stewards deft and smiling, the passengers mostly colonial servants or tea planters bent on enjoying themselves. There was dancing on the deck and in the lounge, fancy dress parties, deck sports, swimming galas and shipboard romances. It was a dazzling scenario for David, after the no drinking, no women, and very little play of the Kingswood regime.

In the teak-panelled dining room, David, who had now grown into a slim, good looking young man, was seated at a table with a middle-aged colonel, his rather daunting wife, and a very pretty woman of thirty-five, Mrs Grey, going out to join her marine biologist husband.

She was elegant and sophisticated, wore lovely clothes and expensive perfume and danced beautifully. She taught David the Charleston and the Black Bottom and the Tango, as well as the more conventional dances like the Waltz, the Foxtrot and the Quick Step. She taught him well. He was always a very good dancer and he was enchanted by her during the voyage.

But he said goodbye to her on the quay at Colombo and was immediately absorbed in his homecoming to Ceylon. He smelled again the beguiling fragrance of the Temple flowers and the datuna, and the mixture of rich spices that he remembered from childhood. He went up country to Hatton, and climbed Adam's Peak, the mountain crowned by the Buddha Guatama's footprint, which had so dominated his childhood.

He stayed with his parents and at Martara on the south coast of the island with his eldest sister Kathleen, and her blonde, good looking husband Max. This was the first time David had met him and their two young children, Gillian and John. Max, an ex-pupil of Kingswood School, turned out to be a great cricketing enthusiast who taught David how to improve his game. Cricket had taken a firm hold on Ceylon. It was played everywhere, especially along Galle Face, an open stretch of grassy land between the sea at Colombo and the lake. There they watched naked boys playing cricket with a stick and a bundle of coconut fibre for a ball, and the thick end of a coconut branch for a wicket, calling 'Leg before!' and 'Out!' and 'How's that?' even though they spoke no other English.

David also met again many of the Methodist community that had remained and was welcomed by members of his father's vast and wide-spread congregation. The Reverend Small looked even frailer and more emaciated than David remembered. He gave him news of Edgar, now about to leave school in Germany. He said that Edgar was very well and from his photograph had developed into a strong muscular young man. He had become very keen on physical fitness and had joined something like the Boy Scouts, called the Hitler Youth Movement, in which he was distinguishing himself.

CHAPTER THREE

THE DREAMING SPIRES

David returned to England to take up his scholarship at Merton. It was the autumn of 1938, shortly after Neville Chamberlain had flown back waving his piece of paper and declaring 'Peace with Honour'.

Europe was in an uneasy and molten state. People in Britain were uncomfortably aware that we had betrayed Czechoslovakia but at the same time thankful that we were not going to war. Yet the Spanish Civil War rumbled on. In its early stages it had been marked on both sides by a ruthlessness that had astounded Europe – mass executions, the murder of thousands of priests and civilians, the burning of churches. The shape, although we didn't know it then, of things to come. Several students had left Oxford to fight in that war, although foreign combatants were supposedly made illegal in February 1937.

Yet Oxford was a magic place to be in during those unreal times. There was a whiff of the last dance before Waterloo. Oxford was the stamping ground for rich young men and women with a leaven of bright youths from poorer families. Money for those poorer students was a problem. The Reverend Beaty's salary as a minister was small. He made his son an allowance of £60 per year which was very generous of him. For the rest, David had to rely on his scholarship.

Early on, the less well off students discovered a temporary solution to their financial difficulties. They opened an account at Blackwell's, bought books on credit, then sold them straight away second hand.

David was fortunate in his accommodation. He was allotted the small hexagonal pair of rooms at the top of Merton tower from where he had views of the quads, a sliver of the formal gardens and the river, and where he could hear the chime of all the bells.

Politically and academically Oxford was a melting pot for the awakening youth of changing Britain. A number looked to the Soviet Union for inspiration, some sympathising with the hunger marchers, others from families that helped to break the general strike. Amongst most of the students, patriotism was not the order of the day, memories of the slaughter in the trenches of World War One still lingered.

The Abdication and Edward VIII's affair with Mrs Wallis Simpson had tarnished the concept of monarchy. Earlier on, the students had passed a resolution that under no circumstances would they fight for King or Country.

There was vigorous political debate. Oxford was awash with talent. Aware of the storms brewing in Europe, there was a sense that life as they knew it was vanishing and they had to lay hold on what they could of it. One of the most vigorous laying hold on life was Leonard Cheshire. He was well known for the wildness of his parties and his challenge of authority.

David was wakened one night to the sound of loud crashings and smashings. Going out onto the landing to investigate, he saw Leonard Cheshire perched on the roof with a pile of chamber pots stacked perilously beside him, and these he was hurling onto the street below.

David had further experience of Cheshire's wildness a few days later when the Freshers' Blind was held to introduce the new students to Oxford's social life. Sandwiches and sausages were laid on, and free beer. Behind the bar, a smiling Leonard Cheshire was making sure that the beer flowed. But unknown to the naive freshers, Cheshire was liberally lacing the beer with gin and vodka.

David, brought up in a temperance household and having attended a school where alcohol was forbidden (a pupil was expelled for having drunk a glass of cider), was a lamb to the slaughter. He drank one glassful of the powerful beverage and had the distinction of being the first freshman to fall flat on his face and be carried out unconscious, to the cheers of the Cheshire contingent.

As well as the drink, the food at Merton was superb. Merton was one of the richest colleges and it was possessed of the best chef in Oxford. Undergraduates could enjoy a four course dinner in Hall for less than £1, but many of them, David included, could rarely afford this privilege.

Literary-wise, however, David flourished. He wrote short stories. He became editor of the *Cherwell* and, later, Keith Douglas joined him as co-editor. David introduced me to Keith's poetry when David and I first met at RAF Oakington, maintaining that Keith Douglas was the first genius he had ever met, and decades before Keith's talent was recognised by the literati, David talked and wrote about him.

He found Keith Douglas a complex, unpredictable character – a mixture of the artist and the militarist, wanting to be alone, and yet at times afraid to be alone; falling in and out of love, despising the rich young rulers and yet desperately wanting to be one of them. Douglas joined the mounted section of the University OTC to get free riding

Left: David and his mother on holiday at Cleeve.

Below: David on his mountaineering scholarship.

Below David at Oxford. Photo taken by Keith Douglas.

and he went around dressed in jodhpurs and hacking jacket. Like David he was attracted to an exquisitely beautiful Chinese girl, Yingcheng, whom David and the others always called Betty Zee. She had been a pupil at Cheltenham Ladies' College, and it was the tradition there to give Chinese girls the most English sounding names.

The *Cherwell* flourished. Later-to-be-distinguished figures like Denis Healey contributed articles. Iris Murdoch, known as Irish, regularly wrote stories and poetry. She once confided to David that she had to do so. That she wrote 'out of biological necessity'.

David loved Oxford. He revelled in its beauty and intellectual opportunity. He read. He wrote constantly. He conceived an admiration for Max Beerbohm and founded the Max Beerbohm Society. He went to concerts. He made several close friends; Raymond Pennock, destined to become Chairman of the CBI with a seat in the House of Lords, then a handsome Rugby playing Yorkshireman; Drake Brockman who was persuaded to go climbing with David; Philip Schapiro, black-haired and pale faced, with a precise, pedantic manner; Abu Taylor, a Nigerian law student; Hamo Sassoon, nephew of Siegfried whom David greatly admired; Derek Peyton Smith, kindly and good-humoured but with an acerbic wit; and Hugh Latimer, an accomplished debater.

Besides editing the *Cherwell*, David was now having success with his short stories and articles which he submitted to national magazines. But war loomed. Preparations were all about. Sandbags appeared outside strategically important buildings. Windows were criss-crossed with tape to minimise flying glass. And amongst the youth of the country, the dread word 'Conscription' was breathed. And how to get out of it. For the youth of World War Two did not go to their deaths as to a party.

They had read and heard from their parents about the useless slaughter of a generation. The very arbitrariness of conscription was offensive. So was their country's treatment of its heroes. They had seen for themselves the fate of the survivors of the Somme and Passchendaele, seen the unemployment and despair, seen how society itself had suffered because of the loss of what was truly their country's flower. They were reluctant to trust authority and to be another lost generation.

Besides, many of them sincerely believed that war was evil, that the only solution for mankind was in strengthening the tottering League of Nations. David, enjoying the freedom and intellectual stimulation of Oxford and having been brought up as a Methodist with their strong pacifist leanings, was as reluctant as any. He believed, like

Saint-Exupéry, that we are 'all inhabitants of the same planet, passengers on the same ship'.

He was approaching the age of conscription when he could be directed into any service that the Conscription Board decided upon. In the spring of 1939, David gave himself a diversion from study and the threat of war and conscription. Merton offered a scholarship of £50 to any student who wanted to climb a mountain. It was offered in memory of that great climber Irvine who, with Mallory, had perished on Everest.

David applied. He nominated Chamonix, Le Brévent and Mont Blanc, gave a reasonable appraisal of how the expedition could be accomplished and was given the £50. His friend Drake Brockman, who had sufficient funds of his own so long as the expedition was frugal, accompanied him.

The purchase of even cheap climbing boots and equipment dug into the £50. But they each possessed a bicycle and once they had crossed the Channel, food and accommodation were cheap. They stayed at youth hostels, where the strictly segregated boys and girls were locked in every night to make sure they didn't wander. They cycled down through a politically troubled France. Franco had defeated the elected Socialist government of Spain. Britain and France had recognised his government. But few people in France talked about the implications, though they were uncomfortably aware of them. The weather was fine, the roads good and arriving at Kisere, without any preparation, they began to climb.

David found his new cheap boots excruciatingly painful and a third of the way up he took them off, left them under a tree, promising himself he would return and collect them. He then changed into a pair of sandshoes which he had prudently brought with him.

The sandshoes were totally inadequate, the climb a floundering disaster through ever deepening snow. Finally when it was up to their chins and the weather was deteriorating, they called a halt, slithered back to civilisation without stopping to find the boots. But they continued on to St Gervais, tackled Le Brévent and the Mer de Glace before, at the end of the fortnight, cycling back through France to the Channel. And although it wasn't a climbing success, at least the expedition produced a short story for the *Cherwell*, 'In the Footsteps of James', which David began writing on the ferry home.

They learned on their return to Oxford that Hitler had denounced the Anglo-German Naval Treaty and the Polish Non-Aggression Pact. Hitler had his greedy eyes on Danzig and Poland, but Britain had guaranteed the integrity of Poland. The feeling was that Britain could not dishonour another pact. War moved ever closer. Discussion of conscription became more urgent.

Two of David's Kingswood friends, who were at another Oxford College, advised him that the best way to avoid conscription was to follow their example and join the University Air Squadron. Thus, when the time came they would have entry into the Royal Air Force, which was the most dashing and colourful of the three services.

The idea appealed. Until then, David had regarded flying as a desirable aesthetic experience. He had read Antoine de Saint-Exupéry, France's pilot/poet and thrilled to his descriptions. In boring lessons at school he, like his friend Alec Atkinson, had made paper darts and used a ruler lodged under the flap of his desk to perform aerobatics. But his sole experience of the air had been Uncle Cam's gift of the seven-and-sixpenny flip.

Yet undaunted by his inexperience, indeed unaware that any aerial experience would be required of him, David applied for membership of the University Squadron and was duly requested to appear for interview.

David was very much into his literary persona at the time and, never one for appearances, turned up in an old crumpled shirt, an incongruous cream silk tie he had been given years before with a large bobble at the end of it, shabby flannels, dirty socks and scuffed leather sandals.

However, the smiling, fair-haired flight lieutenant who conducted the interview was relaxed and friendly. He offered a cigarette, lit one for each of them and sat back comfortably in his chair to conduct what seemed more like a chat than an interview.

Except that after a while the flight lieutenant began to ask questions. The first, somewhat surprisingly was, 'What do the initials DR stand for?'

That was an easy one. 'Doctor,' David replied promptly.

But that was not the required answer. In aeronautical terms DR stands for Dead Reckoning, the slightly less smiling flight lieutenant pointed out, but of course, yes, Doctor is perhaps the one the non-flying public would plump for.

The next question was on the internal combustion engine. Would David like to explain its workings?

He would have dearly liked to of course. But he could not; except in general. He knew it was something to do with the cylinders going up and down and the firing thereto.

So, how many hours flying had he?

David trotted out his twenty minutes with the Alan Cobham Flying Circus.

'Actually flying an aircraft,' the flight lieutenant asked, getting a little irascible.

The answer was of course none. But the flight lieutenant's disappointment and disdain quickly vanished and he was smiling and friendly again by the time he showed David to the door.

It was therefore with acute disappointment that a week later, just when David was beginning to visualise himself as a dashing RAF pilot, he received a terse letter informing him that he was not considered suitable for membership of the University Air Squadron.

Shortly afterwards came the conscription papers. Still with the RAF beguilingly in mind, David opted for the RAF aircrew or ground staff.

He was turned down there too.

David had ruled out the Navy as he was always seasick. Now clearly the Army beckoned. Making the best of a bad job, he decided to join the University OTC, and here he was welcomed with open arms.

Better still, he was drafted to tanks and armoured cars, exciting and impressively noisy to handle. Round Oxford he thundered, driving his lethal vehicles to the admiration of the girls.

His euphoria was dispelled by the tough ex-regular army sergeant who was in charge. He warned his pupils that if war came, on no account were they to join the Armoured Cars as the British tanks and armoured cars were rotten. He showed the boys for themselves, made them examine the vehicles underneath. He pointed out that there was insufficient armour plate on their floors and that they could be blown up by something as small as a hand grenade tossed into the road.

On 24 August the world was shocked by the Non-Aggression Pact between Germany and the Soviet Union, which appeared to give Hitler a free hand in Europe, and on 1 September German forces invaded Poland.

Two days later, at 11.15 on 3 September 1939, Neville Chamberlain became the first British Prime Minister to announce over the radio that Britain was at war with Germany. More sandbags were piled in the streets. Barrage balloons floated in the sky. Everyone waited for the air raids that didn't come. Meanwhile Anderson shelters – little galvanised metal igloos – were being issued to households. Now that war had actually come, there was talk among the students that maybe it was best to volunteer rather than wait to be conscripted.

But the Oxford dons had already decided that they were going to get in on the act. A letter was circulated telling the students that under no circumstances were they to volunteer. The University was going to have its own recruiting board to which students would be summoned. The Chairman of the Board was to be Lindsay, the famous Master of Balliol.

David received his summons in October. He was told to report to the Bodleian Library and here he was given yet another form to fill in.

Since the RAF had turned him down and having ruled out the Navy, he had no choice but to opt for the Army. An usher took his effort to the chairman, to be put in his file with the other papers.

Eventually his name was called and in he went.

Ahead of him was a long table, with the chairman at its centre. It was full of dons with the recruiting officers from the three services seated at the far end.

The line of dons stared at David, scrutinising his suitability for war, while the Master of Balliol studied his papers, taking an inordinately long time so to do.

Finally he looked up and said, 'I see you applied for the RAF, Mr Beaty?'

'Yes, I did.'

'But here you have put down for the Army.' He held up the offending form.

'The RAF turned me down.'

'Turned you down?' The chairman's eyes opened disbelievingly wide and swung right to the far end of the hall where sat the recruiting officers of the three services. They focused on the nice fair-haired flight lieutenant. 'Why did you turn down Mr Beaty for the RAF?'

'Well, sir . . . Mr Beaty has no flying experience. He has no mechanical knowledge whatever.' Then he brought out what he thought was his trump card. 'He is an Arts man and . . .'

'An Arts man. An Arts man.' The great Arts man Lindsay's voice thundered down the full length of the hall. 'Mr Beaty is an Oxford man. And an Oxford man can do anything!'

Minutes later, out went David into the pale autumn sunshine, clutching a note which read, 'Highly recommended for a commission in the RAF as a pilot.'

CHAPTER FOUR

THE FLEDGLING PILOT

For a while David heard nothing. In common with other students and elderly dons, he was recruited into the LDV, the Local Defence Volunteers, later to be known as the Home Guard. Armed with garden rakes and scythes and broom handles, they patrolled the outer peripheries of the Colleges keeping a sharp look-out for fifth columnists and German parachutists.

Then a few weeks later he received a railway warrant and a summons to attend RAF Padgate in Lancashire. There he was attested, but because of the shortage of instructors and aircraft, put on deferred service awaiting a flying course.

He returned to Merton and sat the BA examination in History. He produced a special edition of the *Cherwell*, called 'The Decline of Oxford' number and invited Keith Douglas to design a new cover for it, a pale brown with an idealised male and female portrait centre. Shortly afterwards Keith joined David as co-editor.

It was a strange period of time, half in and half out of war. The prosecution of the war had advanced from the phony period wherein the few bombers of the RAF merely dropped leaflets and in any action took care lest German industry be damaged. Poland had been eliminated by a new style of warfare, the *Blitzkrieg*, a crushing combination of armoured onslaught and intense dive-bombing.

In April 1940, Denmark was overrun and Norway invaded. On 10 May, at dawn, the Wehrmacht turned its huge force against France. The French Air Force was in decline. The majority of its fighters were underpowered Moranes and there were insufficient of the faster Dewoitine 520 and the Bloch 152C which were the only fighters comparable to the Messerschmitts.

Little thought had been given to planning the battle or to co-operation between the aircraft and the troops on the ground. Thus the RAF, it has been said, were faced with paying the price of other people's mistakes.

47

The British Army had dragged its feet over the Continental commitment. But in May it roused itself. Roads and railway stations were filled with soldiers on the move, as the thirty-two divisions of the BEF began to depart for France.

Before David left Oxford, for the last issue of the *Cherwell* which they co-edited, he and Keith Douglas produced a special poetry number with the new redesigned cover. Keith Douglas contributed six of his own poems, two of those under his pseudonym, Peter Hatred. David wrote two short stories, 'Pot-eyed in Port Said' and 'Oxford Obstacle'.

The atmosphere at Oxford had now changed. Keith Douglas described it at that time as bordering on the hysterical. A number of students committed suicide; there was a shooting incident at University College when a pacifist stole a sniper's rifle from the armoury, lay in wait for a colleague at the top of the tower and shot him repeatedly in the stomach till he fell dead on the path.

Keith Douglas was convinced he would die in this war. He frequently prophesised that his name would be on the Merton memorial. He touched the inlaid plaque on the wall and said solemnly to David, 'My name will be here.' He was almost right. In fact there were so many names that another plaque was dedicated on the opposite wall, and there was his name.

Just before David was finally told to report to the RAF Receiving Wing at Babbacombe, he received a letter from the Colonial Office telling him that his application had been successful and offering him an immediate job in the Colonial Service. His friend Dick Posnett was also offered a job which he decided to accept and in which he did brilliantly, becoming Governor of Belize and then Bermuda, and receiving a knighthood.

But the Battle of France was still raging, and David was now determined to fly. He therefore declined the Colonial Office appointment and proceeded to the Receiving Wing.

Close by the Receiving Wing at Babbacombe was the Pilots' Initial Training Wing at Paignton. The U/T (under training) aircrew were lodged in the comfortable Palace Hotel on the sea front. Proudly wearing the white flash of aircrew under training in their forage caps, watched by little boys and teenage girls, they were drilled by a regular air force warrant officer, who did his best to knock them into some sort of marching shape.

There were lectures in the public rooms of the hotel – Navigation, Aircraft and Ship Recognition, Morse Signalling, Elementary Mechanics. With the summer sun glittering on the sea, Paignton

A de Havilland Tiger Moth, David's first trainer.

seemed a long way from the war, from the evacuation of Dunkirk and the Battle of Britain that was about to intensify.

Confident of victory (Göring had forecast that the defence of southern England would last only four days), the *Luftwaffe* had already begun its attacks on Britain when David was posted from Paignton to Prestwick to begin Elementary Flying Training.

The training was on Tiger Moths. David found himself depressingly slow to learn the skill of flying. He felt clumsy. He had difficulty in telling left from right. In the course of time he was to recognise this laterality problem, as one of the basic human factors into which he initiated the first study. And in common with a number of other U/T pilots, he found the innocuous-looking Tiger Moth hard to handle.

But early in September he flew solo, completed the course satisfactorily and was sent to the Flying Training School at South Cerney near Cirencester to learn to fly twin-engined Oxfords.

These he found very wayward and difficult. Evidence that other trainee pilots had also found them to be so was evinced by a large photograph of the men on a previous course which was pinned up on the noticeboard. A discouragingly large proportion of these had inked in over their heads either a halo or a bowler hat. With this photograph at the forefront of their minds, they began their flying over Cirencester and its environs.

Cirencester, as David wrote in his novel *The Wind off the Sea*, was, 'on the edge of the Cotswolds and only woke up on Mondays when they sold sheep. There's a cinema and a few good pubs and a YMCA where you can get a salmon roll and a cup of tea for fourpence.'

There was no great need to buy tea and salmon rolls, however, because RAF Cirencester was a peacetime station and the trainee pilots were housed in the Officers' Mess. David reckoned he had never been so comfortable. 'Thick carpets, two ante-rooms, and the food is out of this world,' he enthused in his diary.

The trainees were a mixed bunch, mostly twenty-year-olds, but a few that were older. One was Geoffrey Lane who survived the war and later became Lord Chief Justice. He was in the same hut as David. He was, apparently, a very good pilot, a good companion and a good raconteur of racy but unrepeatable stories.

It was impressed on the trainees that they must work hard on the ground syllabus. The instructors were mostly, as David wrote, 'schoolmasters dipped in blue uniform.'

> 'Bomb aiming consists of lying prone behind a contraption of wheels and wire, watching a roll of photographed landscape go by six feet below, and pressing the buttons like you'd throw a dart. Skeletons of

David (2nd left rear) and the rest of the course at South Cerney in September 1940.

50

Neolithic aeroplanes attended by an ancient museum curator – that's Airframes and everybody goes to sleep.'

They were all agog however for their first take-off and landing on twins. They had to kick their heels for hours before the programme even started. The sky was overcast, the wind cold and an intermittent rain had begun to fall when David was called out for his instruction at half past noon. He tightened the harness of his parachute and with it thudding like a satchel around his back went waddling first across the tarmac, then across the grass to the waiting Oxford.

The instructor first of all pointed out the 'knobs and tits', and then he took her off as sweetly as a bird. Once airborne, he handed over to his pupil. The twin-engined Oxford was vastly heavier than the Tiger Moth and had very delicately balanced controls which highlighted any mistake. It appeared, too, to have a mind and a will of its own, swinging, ground looping, ballooning and wing-dropping. David was not alone in experiencing considerable difficulty in mastering it. But when he did, he wrote that he, 'glimpsed the sheer aesthetic beauty of flight. It was an odd sensation, physical and sensual as well as emotional, piercing the body like a spasm of desire.' The beauty of flight was something which all his life he tried to express. Professor Forsberg, in her book *The World of David Beaty*, brackets him with Saint-Exupéry in the quality and evocation of his descriptions of flight.

Meanwhile, in the sky above the trainee pilots, there were signs that the Battle of Britain was still being fiercely fought – dog-fights, vapour trails, aircraft spinning in, the desynchronised throb of enemy bombers.

By the time the Battle of Britain was over, the course had all gone solo. Flying alone above the Cotswold countryside, David wrote in that year's diary that he experienced thirty of the loneliest yet happiest moments of his life.

But twelve hours daytime flying was followed by the dread night flying, which took place on the dispersed site at Bibury. This, rumour said, was where they were really sorted out. The average casualties per course were two pupils killed and one seriously injured. There was a grave always ready-dug in South Cerney churchyard.

The weather deteriorated. The Cotswold fields were covered with snow. Fog hung in the valleys causing the flying schedule to be postponed. But eventually the skies cleared. After half an hour's dual with the instructor, one after another, the trainees were airborne.

Even the sounds of the *Luftwaffe* droning over to attack Birmingham could not diminish their triumph.

But David never forgot Bibury. Professor Forsberg recalls that he told her:

> 'I remember when I was learning to nightfly at Bibury, a training aircraft lost an engine taking off on a pitch dark night. Unable to rise, it flew a few inches above the ground, till the inevitable Cotswold stone wall loomed up ahead. Just before they crashed, the warrant officer instructor turned to his pupil, and said, "Brace yourself. Brace yourself, boy!" That in his difficulties he should still find time to think of the other human being in the aircraft touched me – and long afterwards I made them George Gort's words in *Cone of Silence.*'

Before they left for the next stage of their training, the Navigation School at Blackpool, the trainees were required to fill in forms stating the type of aircraft they would prefer to operate. There was little chance, they were told, of getting onto Spitfires or Hurricanes and David disliked the idea of bombing cities, expressing a preference which in retrospect seems to belong to a long ago, much more chivalrous era, to fight against uniformed men. He chose Sunderlands, partly because he had conceived a great mistrust of the Blenheims, Battles and Hampdens. In fact he had spent quite a time trying to convince some of his friends at South Cerney not to opt for them.

From Blackpool, the pilots flew Bothas on cross-countries, practising their navigation. But so unreliable were the old Bothas that several were lost in the narrow strip between Blackpool and the Isle of Man,

The Botha at its base. It was flown on navigation exercises from Blackpool.
(Photo courtesy Imperial War Museum)

Above: David with his parents shortly after getting his wings and becoming a Pilot Officer.

Below: Alec Atkinson who wrote the foreword of this book, photographed during the Battle of Britain.

Above: Wings! At the end of the training course.

Below: Edgar Small when the pilot of a Heinkel He 111 in the *Luftwaffe*.

and once David got mixed up with a whole flight of Hurricanes, to their dismay and his.

On this course, while flying one of the Bothas, the instructor cut the port engine. David writes in his diary, 'I put on full port rudder, causing the aircraft to make a mad whirl to the left. My instructor and I put that down to no more than sheer finger trouble.' But in retrospect, he realised that this was another clue to the human factor of left/right confusion.

Having passed out in Navigation, David was posted first onto a brief Conversion Course at Silloth, at an airfield close to where his parents used to go for holidays, and then to 221 Squadron of Coastal Command at Limavady in Northern Ireland on Wellingtons.

He loved the countryside and the people of Northern Ireland. The food was excellent – juicy steaks and the Guinness 'flowing like mountain streams'. He loved the Irish attitude to life. One night, having bought a broken down car for five pounds he had taken some friends out for a pub-crawl. They were driving back, somewhat erratically, to the airfield through the town when ahead, they saw a swinging bull's eye lantern and out stepped a policeman, urgently waving them to stop. Mindful that he had no licence for himself, no tax for the car, that the car had no lights, hardly any brakes and only minimal steering, David was counting up the likely charges at a court martial. When he at last managed to stop the car, the policeman put his head through the open window, and sighed reproachfully, 'D'you know you're coming up a one-way street?'

To balance the advantages, the weather for flying was rough – fierce gales and sudden headwinds, sometimes so strong against aircraft battling home that they ran out of fuel. Another hazard was that to the east of Limavady was the mountain Bienvagh, nicknamed by the crews 'Ben Twitch' for its effect on pilots returning in low cloud.

The aircraft themselves were not easy. To begin with they were clapped-out rejects from Bomber Command. But the instruction was good. The instructors communicated well with their pupils. One of the instructors taught his pupils a mnemonic which David never forgot, to help them remember the vital before-take-off checklist. The Gloucester Police Fined Me Three Groats.

Gloucester – gills fully closed: Police – Pitch fully fine: Me – mixture rich: Three – throttle nut tight: Groats – gyro uncaged.

Onto these old Wellingtons had been festooned aerials of the first airborne radar – ASV, Anti-Surface Vessel. The acquisition of these reduced the Wellington's speed to just over 100 mph and made it impossible to maintain height on one engine. The Pegasus engines, being air-cooled, were slightly more reliable than those of the Whitleys, but if one engine failed then that was it. Several of David's South Cerney friends who had been posted to Whitleys were lost at this time because the liquid cooled Merlin engines were unsuitable for low level work and simply packed up miles out over the Atlantic as they tried to hunt the U-boats.

On the last day of July, having done numerous sweeps to the Spanish coast, David saw his first action during a cross-over sweep in the Bay of Biscay. Operating as second pilot to Flying Officer Watson, a regular RAF officer, in Wellington Z8706 they sighted a submarine on the surface. Immediately they made a direct attack, diving to mast height. As the submarine tried to submerge they dropped three 450 lbs depth charges. Damaged, the submarine disappeared. The Wellington patrolled low on the water. They saw an oil slick and bubbles, but these the pilots pronounced inconclusive.

The following month, they were on more Bay of Biscay cross-over patrols, escorting large convoys and flying on Atlantic sweeps. This was the time of the Battle of the Atlantic. Many experts now reckon it to be the most vital of the war. Three years before war was declared the *Kriegsmarine* had been decoding much of the Royal Navy's anti-quated coding system and could send course, speed and escort details to Admiral Dönitz's U-boat headquarters in Wilhelmshaven. Germany had anticipated the declaration of war and a week before had positioned two pocket battleships and fourteen U-boats in the Atlantic. Thus on the night of 3 September 1939 at 9.00 pm the liner *Athenia*, outward bound across the North Atlantic, had been torpedoed by a German submarine with the loss of one hundred and twelve lives, including twenty-eight American citizens.

Churchill was to say later, 'The Battle of the Atlantic was the dominating factor all through the war. Never could we forget for one moment that everything happening elsewhere on land, sea or in the air depended ultimately on its outcome.'

Unfortunately, armament-wise Germany was prepared. Britain was way behind, especially in her ability to maintain the Atlantic life-line. Defence cuts, ignorance and an Admiralty belief that U-boats could not operate at night had led to the abandonment of naval escort building.

In 1940 had begun what the German U-boat aces Schepke, Kretchmer and Prien called 'the happy time'. Operating with only a handful of U-boats in the Atlantic they sank 435 Allied and neutral ships. Dönitz remarked scornfully that 'the aircraft can no more eliminate a U-boat than a crow can fight a mole.'

Of that time, David wrote:

'The Battle of the Atlantic had developed into a huge and dangerous game of scientific chess. Top British scientists had been called up. Professor Blackett had established the Operational Research Unit manned by brilliant men. Britain already led the world in radar that had helped win the Battle of Britain. Now it was Coastal's turn to benefit from the dedication and ingenuity of the boffins. Bletchley Park had begun breaking the German codes and reading the wireless traffic of U-boats in home waters through the settings of the German Enigma code. On 8 May the navy had a lucky break. U110, captained by the man who sank the *Athenia*, was attacked and blown to the surface. Surrounded by warships, the crew abandoned the vessel after setting the detonator on the secret equipment, but this failed and as a result, Bletchley Park received a full set of U-boat ciphers and current U-boat settings.'

Now the Germans were placing great importance on the Atlantic battle, rapidly increasing their U-boat fleet and building massive concrete pens to house them along the French Atlantic coast. From the middle of 1941, the building of surface ships was to cease and all energies transferred to the construction of U-boats and aircraft. By late 1941, twenty new U-boats a month were being turned out.

To be closer to the Battle zone (their aircraft had a range of only three hundred miles), David and his crew were sent briefly on detachment to RAF St Eval, to find and attack U-boats in the Bay of Biscay.

But in September 1941, a more distant theatre of war requested aircraft and trained crews urgently. So three Wellingtons of 221 Squadron were posted away from U-boat hunting in the Atlantic for a special mission to the tiny island of Malta in the Mediterranean.

Of the Wing Commander's pep talk before they left St Eval, David wrote, 'He didn't actually say, "Sooner you than me." What he did say was, "Wish I was going with you." Which in the language of the Squadron meant precisely the same.'

CHAPTER FIVE

MALTA, GEORGE CROSS

Mussolini, eager to share the spoils of his apparently victorious friend Hitler, had declared war on the Allies the previous year and had immediately bombed Malta. The British government had hoped to bribe him to keep out of the war by offering him Malta together with other French and British territories, but by the narrow margin of three to two the War Cabinet had voted against such a craven surrender. Lord Halifax and Chamberlain had been all for it, but Churchill, Attlee and Greenwood won the vote.

Malta had no official air defences and few guns. Her total muster of aircraft comprised five Swordfish used by the Fleet Air Arm for target towing, one Queen Bee pilotless drone and eight boxed Sea Gladiators destined for HMS *Glorious*. But as *Glorious* had been sunk, Admiral Cunningham allowed the RAF to open the crates and assemble the biplanes, and thus the famous Faith, Hope and Charity saw the light of day.

The collapse of France shortly after Italy's entry into the war robbed the Allies of the powerful French Navy in the Mediterranean which, it had always been understood, would deal with its Italian counterpart, the *Regia Aeronautica*. It also meant that with the French coast hostile or occupied, Hurricanes destined for Malta could not be flown in stages from the UK, so they were delivered aboard the ancient carrier HMS *Argus* and flown from her decks off Malta.

A small band of Hurricanes put up a brave fight against the *Regia Aeronautica* with their Stuka dive-bombers. But early in 1941, the German High Command resolved that Malta must be given the *coup de grâce*.

Luftflotte 11 had been moved back from the sector round Moscow and returned to the Mediterranean with a vengeance, re-occupying their bases in Sicily, just a few minutes flight away. Malta buzzed with rumours of invasion.

Totally surrounded by the enemy, a thousand miles from the nearest friendly base and only fifty miles from Sicily, Malta lay at the crossroads of the Mediterranean shipping lanes and on the direct route from Italy to Tripoli, the capital and chief port of Italy's North African Empire. The German generals were pressing for Malta to be obliterated (Hitler had refused a request to invade but agreed that Malta should instead be sunk by bombs) and an end to the attacks on his supply line by Malta-based flotillas.

The historian John Tremaine wrote, 'Thanks to them, and to the RAF and the Fleet Air Arm based on the island, Rommel fought most of the Desert War with a ball and chain at his ankle.'

Malta bound on 1 October 1941, Flying Officer Watson, David and their crew were accompanied by two other Wellingtons and their crews, Pilot Officer Spooner's and Sergeant Reason's. They were to become the Special Duties Flight and were the first radar-equipped aircraft in the Mediterranean.

The normal Wellingtons were already operating above their designed maximum all-up weight – 29,000 lbs against a designed maximum AUW of 26,000 lbs. With the extra aerials needed for the early airborne radar, the Wellington VIIIs could not sustain flight on one engine. Furthermore, the extra aerials had a dangerous propensity to pick up ice in the cold, moist, night air.

Describing that Mark VIII Wellington David wrote, 'Aerials and masts and antennae stuck out from her like the banderillas in a Spanish bull one second before the *coup de grâce*.'

They flew for nine and a half hours uneventfully across the Bay of Biscay, keeping a sharp look-out for enemy aircraft and shipping, and landed at Gibraltar for refuelling. There they were told that a preceding Wellington had turned right instead of left after reaching the southern coast of Spain and had disappeared over the Atlantic on a westerly course. David writes that at the time, 'I regarded this as yet another compass red-on-blue silly mistake of which there had been several.' But thinking about it later, he saw it as another example of left/right – port, starboard – confusion.

At Gibraltar, David also received dire reports from the ground crew about conditions in Malta. The island, they were told, was being bombed and starved into submission. A whole squadron of Blenheims had been wiped out the previous week, the previous delivery aircraft shot down. Surrender was imminent.

Rumour was not altogether wide of the mark. With the French Navy surrendered and insufficient Royal Navy vessels able to be spared, supplies and shipping were at the mercy of the powerful Italian Navy commanded by Admiral Angelo Iachino. Malta was being bombed by the much more experienced and ruthless *Luftwaffe*. With Greece and

Tony Spooner who commanded the Special Flight at Luqa and author of several books on Malta.

Yugoslavia overrun and Crete fallen, she was even more vulnerable. The Italians were confident they could overwhelm Malta within a few months. But regardless of all these circumstances, Churchill and Cunningham believed the island had to be defended at all costs.

Famously, Churchill said at that time, 'The eyes of all Britain and indeed the whole British Empire are watching Malta.'

The Gibraltar airmen who refuelled the Wellingtons expressed doubts that they would ever get to Malta. The Mediterranean was patrolled by Me 109s. Just beyond the wire that separated Gibraltar from Franco Spain, the RAF was even now being watched by Axis spies. The Gibraltar runway was short, had been made from a racetrack 'and the betting was 5-1 against their radar clobbered aircraft ever getting off'.

But keeping a sharp lookout for the *Luftwaffe*, the Wellingtons took off into an evening sky dotted with nothing more threatening than banks of cumulus. The sea below was calm. Behind the pilot, the navigator studied the ASV or airborne radar. This had a fuzzy green time-base measured off in miles, out of which would shoot echoes or blips like needles of light. Liners would show up at thirty miles, destroyers at twenty, submarines at eight. A big green scribble would announce land at a range of eighty miles or more.

A hundred miles into the Mediterranean two Me 109s appeared from the west, heading for them, forcing them to corkscrew then climb into the shelter of the nearest bank of cumulus. It was an uncomfortable shelter. The seemingly friendly white clouds were full of vicious upcurrents and downdrafts.

But when they emerged the Me 109s had disappeared. All was smooth flying for another half-hour. Then there was a sudden spurty sound, a shower of sparks and the screen went blank. The navigator swore, 'Blast . . . that's the ASV packed in!'

Down below a strong swell was running, and the wind had freshened and changed. The sun was setting. They knew that it was too dangerous in Malta for them to light a flarepath. So there would only be glidepath indicators to guide them in.

But they managed to find the island. David wrote that peering out, 'between the dark cloud and the dark sea, ahead now was a thin space a shade less black like the filling of a sandwich.'

Nearer, it was so small he thought at first it was just a bank of low stratus cloud on the sea. Then he caught sight of six tiny glimmering lights in a row with a glidepath indicator at one end.

They were there.

The Wellingtons, bristling with their cumbersome antennae, were the first radar-equipped Wellingtons that Malta had seen and were the objects of some amusement. Although the squadron had called them 'Sticklebacks', they were immediately christened 'Goofingtons'.

As the crews made for Operations, deep in the rock and approached by a winding staircase, another air raid began. All around echoed to the stutter of Bofors guns and the boom boom of sticks of bombs. Before these Wellington crews left Malta, they were to endure over 1,400 air raids.

Combined Headquarters was in the Baracca, its entrance dug in what looked like a giant molehill beside the Auberge de Castille where the Spanish Knights of the Cross used to live. Here, David learned that his job on the Special Duties Flight would be to co-operate with the Royal Navy in an attempt to sever Rommel's supply line to North Africa.

Swiftly after they arrived, Tony Spooner, in collaboration with the Navy, worked out a strategy for the Special Duties Flight (of which he was immediately put in charge) to co-operate with Force K.

Force K consisted of two 6 in. gun cruisers, *Aurora* and *Penelope*, both of 5,299 tons and two destroyers, *Lance* and *Lively*. Spooner arranged

Goofington – a Vickers Wellington with ASV antennae flying close to the Suez Canal.

for an ASV beacon, locally made and devised by F/O Glazer, the flight's technical wizard, to be rigged up on *Aurora*'s masthead. The device was nicknamed 'Rooster'. The blip that this produced would appear as a special shape in the Wellingtons and it could be picked up at an enormously enhanced range. Captain Agnew, his signals officer and Tony Spooner invented their own private wireless code, reducing all signals to seven messages for speed of communication.

A typical sortie would start when the Navy received an intelligence report from one of their 'men on the pier' that a supply convoy was due to pass through the Straits of Messina or was to leave Naples or Palermo on a certain tide. Naval navigators would work out where the enemy was likely to be at various times during their passage to North Africa, thus working out where Force K could attack at night.

Left: Captain W.G. 'Bill' Agnew CVO, DSO – the Captain of HMS *Aurora* and in command of Force K.

Below: The cruiser HMS *Aurora.*

One hour before dusk Force K would leave Grand Harbour, Valetta, and in their line astern formation would head towards where they hoped the enemy would be, while Wellingtons of the Special Duties Flight would head towards the area of probable interception. They would be loaded with fuel and flares. Tony Spooner writes:

'Sometimes as night fell, we would pass over Force K. It was a thrilling sight to see our ships in a long straight line of foaming wake heading at speed away from the island.

'We were their aircraft, they were our ships.'

The dangers were not only from the enemy. With winter approaching, airframe and engine ice menaced them whenever they had to fly in cloud. Sometimes the enemy was not there. Sometimes it took hours to find them. Having found them, the aircraft made one low-level run over the ships to ascertain numbers and size and passed that information to Captain Agnew. The Wellingtons would then shadow by ASV keeping out of sight and beyond earshot so as not to alert the ships below.

Next, they turned back towards Malta, plotting their time, course and speed until the special blip from *Aurora*'s masthead ASV beacon showed up on their ASV screen and vital information about Captain Agnew's distance and direction relative to the enemy could be passed to him.

Backwards and forwards they flew between the convoy and Force K, sending information to enable Captain Agnew to work Force K into the best position to launch his attack, silhouetting the enemy ships against the moonlight while he remained hidden in the darker segment of the sky.

If there were no moon, the Wellingtons would be tasked to drop parachute flares. Each flare, weighing about twenty-five pounds, had to be hand launched through a small chute in a draughty part of the fuselage and considerable skill and judgement were required to make them drift slowly down two or three miles from the enemy, illuminating the enemy but keeping Force K hidden.

Within days of its formation, the Special Duties Flight was out searching for enemy shipping, encountering heavy flak off the west coast of Sicily. On 11 October, F/O Watson and David in Wellington Z8703 sighted a convoy off Lampedusa Island and guided the Navy, two waves of Swordfish and one wave of Wellington bombers to the attack. The convoy was broken up, several large merchant ships sunk, their five escorting destroyers sent 'milling around in all directions.' The action headlined in the *Times of Malta*, as, 'One more Convoy crippled in Seven Hour Attack by FAA and RAF.'

Shortly after arriving in Malta, David had been made up to aircraft captain after a brief proficiency test with Tony Spooner who now, with similar speed, had been made up to Acting Flight Lieutenant. Malta was now not just defending its right to exist, but carrying out a powerful and vital offensive role against the enemy.

David took part in the location and sinking of a troopship carrying a panzer division heading for North Africa and located a convoy of which Force K sank ten merchant ships laden with supplies and three destroyers.

On 8 November, David, in Wellington 8717, with his crew and carrying Lt Paine of the Fleet Air Arm found and duly reported the convoy carrying vital supplies for Rommel's Afrika Corps from Brindisi to Benghazi, which was now in Axis hands. The carbon pile regulator aboard his aircraft became unserviceable, forcing his return, but according to his log book, '*Aurora* found convoy and sank the lot.'

By the end of November 1941, to the consternation and fury of the Axis powers, sixty-three per cent of the supplies for Libya failed to arrive due to the activities of Malta-based aircraft. Rommel was becoming so desperately short of oil that they were sending it on warships from Italy.

Force K, in a matter of weeks virtually stopped all supplies going to the Afrika Corps.

In the words of the German Vice-Admiral Weichold, speaking of the German's appalling November shipping losses:

> '26,000 tons were sunk and 21,000 tons damaged. This was seventy-seven per cent – the highest tonnage lost and also the remaining 8,400 tons was the lowest monthly delivery . . . the battle for Cyrenaica [Western Desert] was not decided during a month of actual land fighting, but rather by these external factors. The battle had already been lost by the Axis months previously through the British mastery of sea and air.'

*   *   *

As the North African see-saw went up and down, as the Axis commanders discussed the invasion of Malta, south of Sicily David and his crew intercepted two heavy cruisers that had left Palermo stuffed with oil barrels. As soon as the captain of the cruiser realised they had been spotted by the Wellington, he changed course to 315° and charged off at full speed to get as far away as possible from Malta, putting himself too far away to be attacked by Force K or the Fleet Air Arm Swordfish and getting as close as possible to Corsica as the crew of the Wellington watched helplessly.

David wrote, 'Having no bombs, we dropped flares and lemonade bottles which were purported to make a nasty whistling sound as they descended and watched them take violent evasive action. They eventually turned and went back to Palermo.'

Not long afterwards, David and his crew spotted two light Italian cruisers also carrying cased oil on their decks bound for Tripoli from Palermo. Realising they had been seen, they returned to Palermo. On this occasion, Force K had remained in port to conserve fuel, now desperately short on the island. But on receiving David's information, a torpedo-carrying strike of Swordfish was laid on.

A 'box barrage' of anti-aircraft fire over Grand Harbour. Enemy pilots respected Malta's air defences as 'More deadly than anywhere else'.

Before it could take place, by coincidence, a division of four Royal Navy destroyers was *en route* from Gibraltar to Alexandria under the command of Commander Stokes aboard the destroyer *Sikh.* He decided to attack. Reducing speed to cut phosphorescence, and invisible against the high ground of the Tunisian coast, he engaged them. Both Italian cruisers were hit by torpedoes, but it was the effect of close-range gunfire on their cargo that was devastating. Both destroyers were set ablaze.

The Swordfish crews felt cheated. Commander Stokes received the following cryptic signal: 'St John, Chapter ten, Verse one.'

On consulting their Bible, the text proved to be, 'He that enterest not by the door into the sheepfold, but climbeth up some other way, the same is a thief and a robber.'

In November, another flight of Hurricanes was flown off *Ark Royal* and *Argus,* but of the twelve Hurricanes that left *Argus* eight failed to arrive in Malta due, it was said, to 'navigational error.'

Too many events were taking place in Malta for that navigational error to be investigated or even discussed, but when he thought about that event, it reinforced David's determination to research the human factors that caused such fatal errors.

At the time he had other more immediate preoccupations. Returning to Gibraltar from the aircraft ferrying trip, the ships encountered a

U-boat pack led by Reschke's U205. Thirty miles from Gibraltar, *Ark Royal* was hit by a torpedo from U81. Later HMS *Barham* was hit by a salvo of three torpedoes from U331 and blew up in a cloud of smoke.

In December, the Italian Battle Fleet made a sortie out of Taranto. A reinforced Force K and practically all the warships in Alexandria set sail to engage. It was a daunting sight. The weather was appalling. David wrote:

> 'Gale force winds and turbulent seas. We were out for thirteen hours trying to distinguish which ships were ours and which were theirs. The cruiser *Neptune* ran into a minefield and sank. The cruiser *Kandahar* steamed in to pick up survivors, and hit another mine and was crippled. Senior Officer Force K had to forbid any further attempt at rescue.'

There were only two survivors from *Neptune*. Her loss was particularly poignant as the ship had been transferred to the NZ Navy and a New Zealand crew had been sent to take her to New Zealand.

Poignant, too, was the message David intercepted from *Kandahar* to *Neptune*, when *Kandahar*, herself in trouble, had been forbidden to attempt further rescue, 'I clearly cannot help you. God be with you.'

The captain's lifelong friend was on board the stricken ship.

David patrolled the battle scene to the limit of his fuel, then south of Crete, he headed for home and into the wind. A few minutes later, the starboard engine began to fail. The rpm indicator was going up and

A radar-equipped Wellington after a crash-landing at Luqa.

down like a jack-in-the-box, the speed was dropping off, the engine was clattering and they were struggling against severe gales.

As he well knew, the Mark VIII Wellington, encumbered by its aerials, could not maintain height on one engine. Reluctantly David sent an SOS though there was little anyone could do to help them.

Then just before they ran out of fuel, suddenly through the rain and the storm he saw the cone searchlights in Malta and landed safely.

The following day one of the other three radar-equipped Wellingtons located *Kandahar* and homed Air Sea Rescue launches on her, so all on board were saved.

After that incident he pondered the unpredictability of aircraft and how some are more trustworthy than others, and in fact develop a character of their own. A few weeks later, just before Christmas, he was detailed to fly a Wellington which immediately struck him as having a strange ominous aura round it. In the event, the schedule was cancelled, so he didn't fly it. But on its next flight, it disappeared without trace and without any message from the pilot.

The Axis powers were now smarting under the blows to their shipping. In retaliation, they subjected Valetta to intense and relentless aerial bombardment. Early in December Hitler issued a War Directive. In it he appoints Field Marshal Kesselring 'to secure mastery of the sea and air between southern Italy and North Africa, in order to secure communications with Libya and Cyrenaica, and in particular to keep Malta in subjection.'

Despite Hitler's directive, despite bad weather, despite the storms and the howling winds in January, the Wellingtons were airborne searching for the enemy. On 23 January, the ASV failed on board David's aircraft, but they kept on with the search, until, flying low on the water, they visually sighted a very impressive convoy consisting of a large liner and four freighters with an escort of one battleship, four cruisers and fifteen destroyers. The liner was the *Victoria*, a ship described by Count Ciano, the Italian Foreign Minister, as 'the pearl of the Italian merchant Fleet'.

On her trials her four 8-cylinder Sulzer engines drove her at over twenty-three knots, which made her the fastest motor liner in the world at the time, as well as one of the earliest quadruple-screw motor ships. When operating on the Trieste to Bombay route her superior speed, accommodation and cuisine had captured passengers from P and O's *Empress of India*. Now with her glamorous paintwork covered by war camouflage, she was carrying a panzer division to Rommel. The freighters were carrying tanks.

David circled, dropping flares and alerting the Navy, despite constant

Above: Sailors and soldiers re-arm a Spitfire in its anti-blast pen in Malta.

Left: Bomb damage in Malta. Over 30,000 buildings were hit on this island which is smaller than the Isle of Wight.

attack from escorting Ju 88s, remaining until the torpedo-carrying Albacores he had been waiting for arrived and immediately began their onslaught.

The first hit was from Lieutenant Ginger Ellis of 826 Squadron. His torpedo struck her under her forward funnel, but as he went in to attack his own aircraft was hit by flak from a destroyer. Pursued by Ju 88s, Ellis had to leave the scene. The fight was carried on by two other Albacores, one commanded by Sub-Lieutenant J M Brown, the other by Lieutenant-Commander Corbett. Within half an hour the *Victoria* sank. A battleship and motor vessel were badly damaged. Of the 1,455 men on board, 1,064 were rescued by an escort vessel.

On 22 February, again patrolling in atrocious weather in Wellington 28725, to David's frustration the oil pressure began to drop to 120 lbs. Again in the starboard engine.

He returned to Luqa, but immediately took off again on patrol and located a Littorio class battleship, three cruisers and five DRS. They were separated by twenty miles from a convoy of six large M/Vs. He circled, dropping flares and alerting the Navy. The Navy moved in swiftly and claimed three hits on the MVs.

In David's log book, he has written that this incident with the failing starboard engine inspired his first novel, which was originally called *The Starboard Engine*, but which was published in Great Britain

Rubble-strewn Malta.

under the title of *The Take-Off* and in America as *The Donnington Legend.*

In one brief off-duty period, to the usual convulsions and cacophony of an air raid outside, David was drinking gassy Maltese beer and chatting to a quiet, good-humoured intelligence officer, Flight Lieutenant John Green. Diffidently, John Green told him that in peacetime he had been a literary agent with a firm called Curtis Brown and diffidently David told him that he hoped to be a writer. The name Curtis Brown meant nothing to David. But he pocketed the card which Green handed him and, years later, remembered it.

The spring of 1942 saw the heaviest offensive ever mounted by the *Luftwaffe* against Malta. In a five-week period there were over 2,000 air raids. Aircraft were destroyed on the ground and severe damage was done to the airfields, particularly Luqa. Ground crew, for whom David conceived tremendous admiration, worked gallantly to service aircraft under heavy attack. Luqa was often out of use due to cratering of the runways. There was no electric flare path, no bad weather landing aids, only a few gooseneck flares which were put out during periods of 'All Clear'. Billets and barrack blocks had been demolished, the Poor House cum Leper Colony where the sergeants were accommodated had been hit and the men had to sleep in slit trenches until makeshift beds, made of steel tubes earmarked for airfield construction, were erected. The village of Luqa was a shambles, with only the dome of the church standing. So great was the agony of the Maltese people that despite their devout Catholicism, BOMB ROME was chalked up on the church's ruined walls.

For beside the bombing there was the threat of invasion and starvation. Bread was rationed. The staple diet was of ground-up and boiled hard tack 'biscuits', which it was rumoured had been left over from previous wars, probably the Boer War. The ground-up hard tack was flavoured with whatever was to hand, chopped fig fragments or the juice from a pilchard tin, then wrapped in copies of the *Times of Malta*, (cloth could not be spared) and boiled into a sort of 'duff'. The Maltese had produced a meat called shote which was supposed to be the result of the mating of a sheep and a goat, but now all the goats appeared to have been eaten.

Clothing couldn't be replaced. And there was no soap to wash it in. One Spitfire pilot, hastily scrambled as yet another air raid began, took off wearing a tie but no shirt.

The island had few natural crops and had relied heavily on imports. With storage tanks approaching empty, all fuel, especially aviation fuel, had to be carefully conserved. Force K had on occasion to stay in port and not engage the enemy for that reason.

Mending the craters on the runways was carried on even while the ferocious bomb and machine-gun attacks were still continuing. So unpopular and dangerous was airfield maintenance that offenders up on a charge were given it as a punishment instead of 'jankers'.

More unpopular still was burial duty. Not only because of its frequency but because the cemetery was unhealthily close to the dock-yard which was regularly bombed. Halfway through one funeral, German dive-bombers began screaming down. The officers, a flight sergeant, two corporals and the padre of the funeral party all took one aghast look at the screaming bombers above them and leapt as one man into the open grave, while the firing party blazed away at the dive bombers with the rifles intended for the farewell salute.

Despite the enemy bombers, convoys carrying supplies struggled to get through. The Navy gallantly tried to deliver more much-needed fighter aircraft which were flown off their decks. But landing condi-tions at Luqa were terrible, without tractors, without hangars, without refuelling bowsers, aircraft having to be refuelled by hand from four-gallon cans. Two supply ships at that time virtually kept the population alive – the *Welshman*, a fast minelayer carrying deck cargo and the *Breconshire*, a Navy freighter-cum-tanker.

In February 1942, a convoy bringing vital supplies to Malta was beaten back. Force K's HMS *Penelope* was severely damaged in action and became known as HMS Pepperpot.

The last Italian convoy David sighted was on the 24 February. It was just off Pantelleria. The Wellington was fired on by the coastal anti-aircraft there and the accompanying destroyers. They dropped flares, but Force K was so severely damaged that it was unable to put to sea again.

During the last week of March, Admiral Vian tried to force help through to Malta. Accompanying a slow convoy with six destroyers, one of which was *Lively* from Force K, and five light cruisers, he was spotted by the Italian Navy. In the Gulf of Sirte, he manoeuvred his force between the convoy and the Italian fleet, beating off a relentless attack by six heavy cruisers, a battleship and several destroyers. The weight of Italian broadsides was 24,000 lbs against Vian's 5,900 lbs. Dive-bombed by *Luftwaffe* aircraft, the *Clan Campbell* was sunk. *Cleopatra*, Admiral Vian's flagship was hit, killing twenty seamen. Nevertheless the admiral, the captain and the gunnery officer were on deck ordering her towards the enemy in battle formation.

Finally, though the skirmishing continued, Admiral Vian was able to signal the C-in-C Alexandria, 'Enemy driven off.'

The convoy was split into groups of four ships, each with the pro-tection of a Hunt class destroyer to make their own way to Malta.

71

Insofar as any battle could be over near Malta, the Battle of Sirte, or what came to be known as the Battle of Passion Sunday, was over. Heartbreakingly close to Grand Harbour, Malta's good friend the *Breconshire* was badly hit and set on fire. Going to her assistance, the Hunt class destroyer *Southwold* struck a mine.

Despite the *Luftwaffe* attacks, *Breconshire* was towed into Kalafrana Bay, where she burned and sank. Nevertheless, men went to work on what remained of her, salvaging anything they could of her cargo and oil.

The *Pampas* and the *Talabot* struggled in. Immediately every movable gun was assembled to ring the harbour and protect their precious cargoes from *Luftwaffe* attack.

Mercifully, the weather grew worse, grounding the *Luftwaffe*. Every single man on the island prepared to unload the ships, waiting for the unloading order to come.

None came.

To quote Captain Tony Spooner, 'It was a blunder of the first magnitude.'

A number of RAF personnel of all ranks anticipated the order and desperately began to unload the vital spares and engines.

Rumour was that the powers-that-be had not ordered the unloading because it was Passion Sunday and these were Holy Days.

The next day the weather cleared and Ju 87 dive bombers and the Ju 88s screeched down. More bombs dropped round Grand Harbour that day than had fallen on Coventry. *Talabot*, *Pampas* and the damaged cruisers which had limped to their berths were shattered.

That afternoon, the Special Duties Flight Wellington crews were told that their replacements had arrived and they would be leaving Malta. It was not before time. Since their unit had been formed in Malta they had seen No. 38 Squadron depart, No. 104 Squadron arrive and depart, No. 40 Squadron arrive and depart. They had completed six months of long nighttime operations under peculiarly difficult circumstances, twice as many operational hours as the other squadrons.

They were given a short valedictory talk by the GOC, who mindful, perhaps, that they were about to be catapulted from the deprivations of Malta to the jazzy temptations of Cairo, warned them not about the enemy's armoury or strategy but about sexual relationships.

Then they took off from an embattled Luqa.

David wrote in his diary, 'The night was without moon, not very clear or starry. My last air raid in Malta was in progress.'

John Tremaine in *The Right of the Line*, writes of Malta, 'In the early months of 1942 the ordeal reached its height, and brought the threat not merely of fierce bombardment, but of invasion and capture. And 1942 was when the intimate connection between Malta and the Desert campaign was heavily underlined.'

He goes on to point out that in November 1941 Malta actually caused a weakening of German forces on the Russian Front by 'the movement of *Luftflotte* 2 from the sector before Moscow to Sicily' and he goes on to cite the orders Kesselring was given to suppress Malta.

'Kesselring,' John Tremaine writes, 'embarked upon this task with habitual energy: some two hundred aircraft attacked the island, making the Royal Air Force their chief objective.'

So immense and so courageous had been the RAF contribution that in a then secret cypher to Air Ministry that great wartime leader, who became Marshal of the Royal Air Force Lord Tedder, passed on a suggestion from the indomitable Air Vice-Marshal Hugh Pughe-Lloyd that the RAF in Malta be authorised to wear the 'ribbon of the George Cross superimposed by the Maltese Cross on the right shoulder of the tunic.'

Tedder strongly endorsed this recommendation. But apparently, the same Authority who had not allowed the vital ships to be unloaded on Passion Sunday, would not agree to that suggestion either.

For David, Malta had been a fiery crucible. In it his future had begun to form. The novel he must write, and later, his study of human error as it affected pilots. The card from the intelligence officer/literary agent was still in his pocket.

But that night, all the aircrew were too tired to think. David didn't think about his future or even if he had one. He didn't glance back for a last look at Kalafrano Bay, at the flarepath or at Malta. All he could think of was sleep.

In another part of his diary he writes:

> 'I left Malta on the Feast of our Lady of Sorrows when all the remaining cinemas were closed, and reached Cairo on Mahomet's Birthday, and the only drink they'd sell us was lemon water.
>
> Symbolic perhaps, especially as the 28th was my birthday.'

His twenty-third.

CHAPTER SIX

TEST PILOT

Landing at Faijoum, a small airfield in the desert twenty miles south of Cairo, they discovered that after leave in Alexandria they would be returning to England via the Cape, it being too dangerous to cross the Mediterranean and the Bay of Biscay.

After six months of constant bombing and long hours of night flying, of poor food, bad water, of bouts of Malta Dog (a form of dysentery) the crew were exhausted and suffered from a variety of skin diseases exacerbated by the lack of soap and disinfectant.

Expectations were high. There were cheering rumours that they were going to be accommodated in one of Farouk's palaces, a luxury hotel or a houseboat on the Nile. But in fact they were driven down a long tarry road to a vast tented transit camp with primitive washing arrangements and wickerwork toilets without partitions or doors, but with a huge notice in lurid crayon, 'Shut the lids. Don't give the flies a meal.'

The transit camp was full of men from the three services – sailors who had lost their ships, soldiers posted to new regiments, shot-down airmen, all tossed this way and that by the see-saw of the Middle East war.

For David, it was an unexpected re-union with people from the past. He met a pilot from South Cerney days who gave him news of others, most of them now dead; a naval lieutenant, who had been at Oxford, now an MTB commander.

The Wellington crews escaped from the camp to Alexandria to spend their six nights' leave at the Junior Officers' Club, and to eat bacon and eggs while their money lasted. David, with his friend and navigator Foxy, caught the Metro to Cairo for the price of one and a half ackers. Then going into the Sporting Club:

> '. . . there suddenly was Philip Schapiro in ill-fitting hospital kit. In the Intelligence now, a second lieutenant. He was living at the Continental. I asked about Hans, and Keith, are they here?
>
> '"But of course", he replied in his precise way. He wanted me to go to an Oxford and Cambridge dinner – but I didn't go.'

So David never saw Keith Douglas again. Keith, stationed then with the Sherwood Rangers in Palestine, had made friends with a transport pilot who frequently gave him lifts into Cairo where he stayed at the flat of an Oxford friend, David Hicks. Apparently a circle of literati, including Olivia Manning, George Seferis and Robert Liddell, trapped by the war, flourished at that time in Cairo – even producing a poetry magazine – as the Middle East campaign surged this way and that around them, and as Arab shop keepers painted signs in German for the conquerors-to-be.

Keith Douglas was at that time champing at the bit to get into the action after a spell in hospital. He saw that action eventually in tanks and his premonition that he would not survive the war was fulfilled. He was killed shortly after D-Day. Having fought courageously in the landings, he had climbed out of his Sherman tank to make an intelligence report when he was hit by a stray splinter from a mortar exploding in a tree above his head. He had once written, 'I move towards my end as a mosquito moves towards her shadow.'

In the early hours of the next morning, the Special Duties Flight Wellington crews left by train for Suez. The harbour was crowded with ships of all sizes. The crews embarked onto a packet steamer which ferried them to a large grey liner with black funnels 'adequately armed, at least at the rear.' *The Isle de France.*

There were already three hundred troops and hundreds of German prisoners-of-war on board. The crews were allocated cabins, four to a double one. Fresh water was available only between 06.30 and 07.30 a.m. The weather was very hot and a sirocco was blowing. The portholes had to be kept closed, there were no fans and it was stifling. The entertainment was sparse, the passengers quarrelsome, the staple drink Van der Hom diluted with ginger ale. There was a good deal of sickness and on the way down the Red Sea, a young sailor, having survived a torpedoing, died of some unknown infection.

He was buried with honours, the three services assembling on the decks, the Poles leading the hymn singing. It was a ceremony which, inured as they were to death and destruction, the men found very moving. The mood on the *Isle de France* became more restless and irritable.

Arriving in Durban, eager for a decent drink and entertainment, the British forces were given a frosty welcome. They asked a man on the quayside about the cinemas and were told, 'This is Sunday. We are not heathens.'

They then discovered there was a clamp-down on alcohol. No drink was to be served after eight in the evening. This because an Australian convoy had preceded them in. Some of the troops had been lying drunk in the streets, had overturned trams, had commandeered milk drays and been careering around in them; the pavements had been thick with broken glass and worst of all a woman making a telephone call in a booth had been set upon and raped.

They also heard the news that the Germans were now bombing smaller British towns, including Bath.

After a brief stay in Durban, the Wellington crews embarked on the *Empress of Russia*, a 'dirty old coal burner built in 1913'.

Before he went on board, David sent a cable to his parents, now in Leamington, 'Expect me when you see me.'

At Capetown, the *Empress of Russia* embarked the survivors of the cruisers *Cornwall* and *Dorsetshire*, which, as the Japanese war machine advanced, had been sunk by Japanese aircraft three hundred miles south-west of Ceylon.

Shortly after embarking them, the *Empress of Russia* slipped out of Capetown accompanied by the cruiser *Colombo* and sailed north-west, calling at the small port Pointe Noire in Free French Equatorial Africa for the cruiser to take on more oil and later stopping further up the African coast to coal in Freetown. Passengers watched, fascinated, as the *Yorktown*, a coaler from Toronto, came alongside, her bunkers full of coal, preceding a string of laden barges. *Yorktown*'s decks were thronged with Nubians, making the scene, as David wrote in his diary, 'like a coal black Breughel.' The coaling teams toiled right into the night, 'their bodies rippling and glistening under the arc lights' to get the troop-ship quickly underway again before a large eastbound convoy came in.

Impatient now to get back on duty, the crews heard more about the Japanese advance, about the bombardment of Colombo and Trincomalee by Japanese aircraft protected by the newest and very effective Japanese fighter, the Zero.

From bases in England, RAF Bomber Command had bombed Essen, and the *Luftwaffe* were bombing historic British cities in reprisal. In the desert the battle of Gazala was about to begin.

After leaving port, there was a minor excitement as the *Colombo* fired at some invisible enemy. A Sunderland and Skuas appeared and flew low overhead. The fore and aft guns on the *Empress* swung round but didn't fire.

David spent his time reading, turning over the plot of his novel, playing deck chess and drinking the same unpalatable concoction of Van der Hom and ginger ale or Tom Collins if they were lucky.

Boredom, frustration at their own inactivity in the face of the advancing enemy, skin disease, drinking, tension and the stifling conditions produced fights. David spent the best part of one night chasing a drunken room-mate running amok, stark naked, waving his revolver intent on killing a former friend who had used the drinking water to wash in.

Tension increased as they left the African coast. The sea began fading from a bright, sequinned blue, to a more familiar shade. They were approaching the real U-boat hunting waters. All on board were given a lecture on U-boats by a Commander Jonas and gun practice was initiated. When the Azores materialised out of the mist on their port bow, the cruiser left them to refuel at Ponte del Gardo, while the *Empress of Russia* circled round with its corvette, keeping a sharp look-out for U-boats. There was news that the RAF were mounting a thousand bomber raid and there was speculation among the Wellington crews that Coastal Command would once more be nudged aside and deprived of its aircraft by the demands of Bomber Command.

Gradually the blue of the sea lost its last brilliance, the waves became a dirty Atlantic grey. The *Colombo* left them. A Sunderland and a Hudson flew over them for a while. There were two destroyers on the horizon, presumably the remains of their escort. The submarine-hunting Wellington crews were uneasily aware that these were favourable U-boat attack conditions, good visibility, high layered cloud and that this was one of the U-boat's favourite hunting areas.

Then, going up on deck early one cold morning, they saw Tory island and the mountains of Donegal, purple in the mist. After that they were sluicing through calm waters to moor at dusk in the Mersey.

Because of her mixed load of passengers, everyone on board was put through extra medical checks, so disembarkation procedures took two days. Finally they were on shore, given three weeks leave (an extra week for having been in Malta), food coupons and clothing coupons and a railway warrant home.

The door at the Beaty home in Leamington was flung open ecstatically by David's young nephew and niece, John and Gillian. When war broke out, the family had returned in a crowded blacked-out ship from Ceylon. Max, Kathleen's missionary husband, had volunteered as a naval padre and was aboard HMS *Illustrious*. Kathleen was pregnant again and she and the children were staying with David's parents. The Reverend Beaty, now the incumbent at Leamington Methodist Church, showed David a letter he had received from the Reverend Small telling him that Edgar, too, was a pilot and serving with the *Luftwaffe*, but he did not know in which theatre of the war he was serving and he was very worried because he had not heard from Edgar recently and feared he might have been killed.

Meanwhile, six-year-old John was an aircraft enthusiast and he and

Coastal Command Development Unit. David is fourth from the right in the front row.

his sister were eager for their uncle to provide entertainment. But David, like many of those who had served under the awful conditions in Malta had felt ill for most of the journey home and was in acute pain, having developed a large abscess in his groin.

Rather than make a fuss or spoil the homecoming by asking to see a doctor, he lanced it himself with a razor blade dipped in Milton. Then, in worse pain than before, he tottered around the toy shops with the children, escorted his mother to the cinema to see Rosalind Russell and Clark Gable in 'They met in Bombay', and then took himself up to Edinburgh to see his youngest sister Mamie.

She herself was about to embark for the Middle East as a Queen Alexandra Nursing sister. David's middle sister Margaret was already serving in the Princess Margaret's RAF Nursing Service.

After 'a wad of National Bread and a cup of tea' at the station David met Mamie in her grey-and-red uniform. They dined at the Caledonian. To his horror, the meal set David back thirty shillings for soup, stringy pheasant and an ice 'which I swear was iced porridge – you could even get the oats out of it'.

But Edinburgh catering was redeemed by McVitie's who next day provided a traditional Scottish tea of sandwiches, scones and cakes. They stayed at the chilly Tontine hotel – no fire because of fuel shortage – and then they took a train to visit his uncle and aunt, where they were warmly welcomed. David was given the bedroom he had stayed in as a child. His uncle, still wearing his old Harris tweed jacket and smoking his pipe, expressed great astonishment that David was a pilot at all, let alone the captain of a bomber.

His father had already expressed sympathy at the responsibility David must feel at having the lives of all his crew in his hands. But as David wrote in his diary, it was not just the lives of his crew for whom he felt responsible, it was their wives, their children, their mums and dads, and their girl friends, and their grannies and grandpas who all seemed to clamber on board the aircraft with them every trip.

Soon the sober leave was over, with none of the temptations the GOC Malta had warned them of and David found himself posted to Tain to test fly in the Coastal Command Development Unit there.

Here lay a new challenge. With detachments to Thornaby and Boscombe Down and Ford, he and the eight other crews flew every type of aircraft in Coastal Command – Whitleys, Wellingtons, Ansons, Oxfords, Proctors, Beauforts, Blenheims, Fortresses, Hudsons, Catalinas, Halifaxes, Hampdens. He tested the engines and ASV bomb sights, completing 'pilot dropping by eye' tests, doing low-level attacks on HMS *Glasgow* and the trawler *Kuvira* in the Irish Sea and on HMS *Howe*, HMS *Abdiel*, HMS *Ajax* in the Pentland Firth. He tested new radar and other anti-submarine devices, doing what were known as Vixen and Jellyfish testing.

The Vixens were Most Secret devices for use with Mark 2 ASV. The Germans had found a way of counteracting the ASV and the Vixens were meant to counteract the Germans' counteraction and leave the ASV unimpaired. After meticulous testing, David strongly recommended that Vixen should be installed in the Wellingtons.

Flying 5661 – one of the many times on a GSR trial.

HMS Glasgow, one of several ships used for practising low-level attacks. Note the interrupted camouflage. (IWM Photo)

On Boxing Day 1942, David flew in a Whitley to East Fortune, an RAF airfield at the mouth of the Forth. There he converted to Blenheims. With him was a Polish pilot, Flight Lieutenant Moscowski, whose whole family had been murdered by the Nazis. He was obsessively dedicated to his task of killing as many Germans as possible before he himself was killed. He viewed the organisation of the RAF and the casual behaviour of its aircrew and their lack of hatred with sad amazement. His stock comment was, 'One day I write a book about the RAF. A fonny book.'

After conversion to Blenheims, the pilots converted to Beaufighters, which had the reputation of being difficult to handle.

That the Beaufighter had a fearsome reputation, I knew from when I was stationed at a Northumbrian airfield, the home of a Beaufighter squadron. The pilots found them so difficult to fly and there were so many fatal accidents in them that airfield maintenance had to make a temporary morgue for the pilots' bodies because the permanent morgue was full.

David continued on Beaufighters and was detached to Ford. He actually enjoyed flying them and developed fighting tactics on them which were to stand him in good stead. And once, finding himself late for a very important engagement, flew a Beaufighter to be the best man at his school-friend, Charlie Wildblood's wedding. The wedding was to take place at a village between Bristol and Weston-Super-Mare, and the families were assembled punctually in the bride's parents house at 10 a.m. before departing for the church.

But there was no sign of David. Charlie Wildblood was pacing up and down anxiously. The minutes ticked by. Suddenly there was a tremendous roar. A Beaufighter streaked low over the house, then turned and flew even lower over a field beyond the end of their garden. Charlie swears that it twisted, then flew upside down. Whatever it did, out of the aircraft dropped an object, which when retrieved was found

An Armstrong
Whitworth
Whitley – one of
many types David
flew on tests.

to be an old sock, weighted with a spanner round which was wrapped a scribbled note, 'Landing at Weston. See you in twenty minutes.'

This David did and the wedding proceeded on time.

Still on Beaufighters, in April 1943, with Peter Laird and Foxy as his crew David flew Beaufighter JL729 on the Docker Finish Speed trials, reaching 305 mph at full bore. He enjoyed all-out flying. He often said that he never needed to buy fast cars because he had satisfied his taste for the thrills of speed early on.

Always flying different aircraft on different assignments, there were various minor happenings – the escape hatch flew off Wellington 5661 over the North Sea. His navigator, Foxy, wrenched his shoulder out of its socket trying to grasp it. A few days later David and his crew in Wellington 5672 were practising low level bombing over the trawler *Kuvira*; another armed trawler in the vicinity mistook them for the *Luftwaffe* and rushed to *Kuvira*'s defence, firing all guns at the low-flying Wellington. They were pretty good shots. On landing, David's crew found three .303 bullet holes through their tail.

A little later, on a windy afternoon in May, David was flying Whitley BD 570, on an AML test-sweep over a choppy Irish Sea with only the device designer, Dr Pickard, a highly intellectual, vague and very boffin-like gentleman on board, when the starboard engine coughed, smoked and suddenly cut out altogether. They were at three hundred feet. In his log book, David decides it was a glycol leak and probably cracked cylinder block. Unable to maintain height, he sent out a Mayday and ditched six miles north of Strumble Head.

Dr Pickard and he scrambled out onto the sinking fuselage. Neither Dr Pickard nor David was familiar with that particular aircraft. Neither had any idea where the dinghy was, or indeed if there was one at all, because few aircraft on test carried dinghies. As BD 570 sank

David flew this
Consolidated PBY
Catalina Mk IV B in
May 1943. He was
testing an American
ASV (Air-to-Surface
Vessel) Radar that
can be seen above
the cockpit.

Bristol Beaufighter Mk VI,
V8526. David flew this
aircraft on flight-tests in
January 1943.

lower in the water, Dr Pickard said he thought if there was a dinghy it
might be behind a plywood panel three-quarters of the way down the
fuselage. David therefore lowered himself back inside and dog paddled
through the flooded fuselage till he found a panel and broke it loose.
To his relief, he saw a glimmer of orange. There was the dinghy, which
he dragged out and hauled up to the surface through the rising water
in the fuselage and inflated. In they scrambled, just in time as the
Whitley sank to the bottom of the sea. And as the wind rose, they swung
up and down on ever bigger waves, hopefully awaiting rescue.

Dusk was falling when rescue came, first in the shape of their old
friend, the *Kuvira*, and then HMD *Glen Heather* of Air Sea Rescue
which brought them safely into Fishguard.

They learned later that the dinghy had only been put in the night
before. BD 570 until then did not carry one. They owed their lives to
an unknown maintenance man who had decided on the spur of the
moment to put one in.

The incident formed the basis of a prize winning short story which
David wrote and made him even more determined to persist with his
novel, *The Starboard Engine*.

By the time he had completed his CCDU tour, his flying assessment
was Exceptional. This, after he had been judged at Oxford as not the
flying type, and after he had judged himself to be very clumsy and slow
to learn in his initial pilot training.

82

CHAPTER SEVEN

FLYING THE HEAVIES

In September 1943, David, now a flight lieutenant, was posted to the Fortress conversion course at COTU Thornaby. Here he met his new second pilot, Jim Glazebrook, and the rest of his ten-man crew. They were to be with him in some very tight and dangerous corners.

Jim had returned from the Bahamas where he had finished his OTU and been in command of a B25 (Mitchell). After a period of dual, and practising emergency systems and dinghy drills in a swimming pool, they were sent to Longtown, north of Carlisle, and the original home of David's Beaty forebears. Here he met Squadron Leader John C Graham, a charismatic, softly spoken Canadian of Scottish descent, always known as JC, who became a staunch and trusted friend. There they completed fighter affiliation exercises, and here David's experience on Beaufighter tactics came into its own.

Jim Glazebrook remembers to this day David showing his crew how he could turn a Fortress inside a Beaufighter and therefore inside an enemy fighter or an enemy submarine. 'So that he couldn't line up his guns on us.' This skill was to prove vital some months later.

After the Fortress conversion course David and his crew were posted to 206 Squadron. There, something was afoot. At the end of the summer, the squadron had been taken 'out of line' to prepare for movement to an overseas destination. On 1 October, the main party sailed for an unknown destination. Two days later they were told that the destination was an airfield in the Azores and that they were to set up a mid-Atlantic base there.

An Air Ministry hand-out stated, 'The vast wastes of the Central North Atlantic, so long out of reach of patrolling aircraft, were soon to come under the watchful eye of Coastal Command.'

The Azores occupy a lonely, but in wartime a strategically important, site in the Atlantic. The archipelago lies between 36° 55' and 39° 55' N and between 25° and 31° 16' W. The nearest continental land is 800 miles away, Cape da Roco in Portugal, so the Azores are further from

Left: Fortress R flying out over the Atlantic.

Below: The Fortress and crew after an Atlantic patrol from the Azores.

the mainland than any group of Atlantic islands and an ideal base for U-boat hunting.

On 8 October, the 206 Squadron seaborne convoy arrived off the Port of Angro do Heroismo, capital of Terceira, the second largest island in the Azores. Disembarkation began immediately. Equipment and personnel were brought ashore by lighters, then transported by road the eighteen miles to the airfield. This turned out to be in a narrow valley, four miles long and varying in width from a few hundred yards

Building the runway
at Lagens.

to two miles. The airfield itself was little more than two thousand yards long and about fifteen hundred yards across at its widest point. It was bounded on the west by the lower slopes of a mountain which rose to a peak more than nine thousand feet high and separated from the sea on the east by a ridge four miles long and varying from two to four hundred feet in height.

The landscape is dramatic and beautiful. Mountains rise directly from scree-lined shores, well-known for shipwrecks, the channels being difficult to navigate because of the constant west and south-west winds.

The airfield surface was grass covered but flat and firm enough for landings in dry weather, although this had yet to be proved. Meanwhile, work was commenced without delay on the building of a two thousand feet long single metal strip runway down the length of the field. All available personnel, both aircrew and ground staff, worked hard and long to complete it in the shortest possible time.

Jim Glazebrook who wrote the War History of Number 206 Squadron quotes the following article:

'Landing of British Forces in the Azores.
'Lagens Airfield, 18 October, 1943.

'The gradually closing net in the Central North Atlantic to U-boats operating against Allied shipping was tightened today when two of the first detail of Fortress aircraft, which are to be used in this battle against the U-boats, arrived at Terceira, in the Azores, after a 1,300 miles non-stop flight from St Eval, England.
'The landing was a thrilling and historic one – the culmination of much intricate planning by Coastal Command, to say nothing of the

diplomatic negotiations which it has entailed between the British and Portuguese Governments.'

In November came the wet season and soon the red volcanic topsoil was churned into thick mud. Cloud descended on the mountain tops and even the ridge was shrouded. With few radio aids, bad weather was particularly dangerous. The island was 'a small pinprick of land in a vast ocean', the nearest diversion base Gibraltar, over a thousand miles away.

Although the Portuguese, our oldest ally, had granted the use of Terceira to the British Forces, Portugal was still neutral so they insisted on the neutrality of the other islands in the group and the RAF were forbidden to fly within three miles of them. More than once an aircraft returning in the darkness from a patrol was shot at by the over-zealous anti-aircraft gunners of San Miguel, which maintained a German presence, nominally diplomatic. This was the biggest island in the Azores and here was a small airfield. It could be used for landings in emergency only, provided permission had previously been obtained from the Portuguese Military Governor.

But this was a contradiction in terms, because if an aircraft were in dire necessity to divert the captain would have neither the time nor the opportunity to get permission from the Military Governor.

On 14 January 1944, David flew Fortress FA 699 to Lagens with his new crew and Squadron Leader Graham. JC was to take over as Flight Commander. His predecessor, Squadron Leader 'Pop' Pinhorn, a very skilled and experienced pilot, had been shot down only a short time before by the guns and cannon of a U-boat.

David wrote in his diary:

> 'Terceira was covered in cloud when we first spotted it. Pat had the beacon to port for some considerable time (fifty-five miles) and we saw it, the eastern corner pushing out of an oyster coloured cumulus. I took a look at the white houses and the white Forts – as Pat remarked, it was the perfect camouflage – the small abrupt square fields and stone walls, rather like a greener Malta.'

Workers were still humping the PSP (pierced steel planks hooked together with interlocking lugs) that formed the artificial runway, which as David remarked, 'Apart from a certain springing effect as though on a roller-coaster, and the fact that it always made a clanking noise when you landed, wasn't a bad runway.'

Landing and taxiing to Dispersal, J C introduced David to 'a stocky Wingco with a red face, and the DSO, DFC, Wing Commander

The Officers' Mess at Lagens in the Azores.

Right top and bottom: The airfield and village of Lagens.

Thomson and a Canadian Squadron Leader "Butch" Patrick.' They then began helping the ground staff to unload the cases and the beer and heave them onto a big three tonner which they then climbed aboard. At Operations, there was some excitement because George Hart had just attacked a U-boat.

206 Squadron Headquarters was set up in an old winery, which all members of the squadron took their part in converting to flight offices, crew rooms, and facilities for training.

Personnel were accommodated in small tents and the messes were marquees, apart from the Officers' Mess which was a whitewashed building with orange tiles and a beamed ceiling. There were no modern conveniences. Water pipes were still being laid, wash houses built and latrines dug.

Frank MacManus, David's radio operator/air gunner wrote:

> 'After breakfast we tended to gather at the latrines near the Squadron Headquarters. These were in an open-ended structure about sixteen feet long and eight feet wide. The seats were egg-box style in two facing banks with half-a-dozen-or-so holes on each side. We would sit here reading or discussing the day's programme, and every day one or more of the local Portuguese women would peer in and ask unconcernedly "Roupa?" (Portuguese for clothing) meaning had we any clothing for washing. Our laundry was always immaculately presented, and these ladies charged a pittance for their service.
>
> 'The locals' lifestyle was very basic and we soon found out that they showed great interest in our rubbish. Empty cans were much in demand and were taken to a tinsmith in a nearby village who converted them into a wide range of containers and utensils. For a small baked beans tin, we would be offered two eggs.'

But though the accommodation was primitive it was set near banana and eucalyptus trees and orange groves. David christened the latrines, 'Banana Grove's sack-clothed pits'. He managed to get hold of a single tent which he pitched in splendid isolation. His kindly Portuguese batman, Danny, brought him tea each morning, and he was adopted by a stray hen from a nearby farm which nested by the flap of the tent and laid him a fresh egg every day. And from his tent he could admire the American Skymaster pilots 'fly their great loads slap on the deck without bouncing an inch.'

Almost immediately the Fortresses were on patrol in five-hundred mile sweeps searching for U-boats north and east of the Azores, practising high and low-level bombing, doing ASV training. Those searches were usually of eleven to twelve hours duration. But with

David and the crew of
206R after the successful
attack on U575.

Left to right: Jimmy
Cunningham, Frank
MacManus, John Johnston,
Norman Draper, Jim
Glazebrook, David Beaty,
and Leo Meaker.

their bomb bays full of extra fuel, the patrols could be extended to
thirteen and a half hours. The Fortresses carried up to six depth charges
mounted externally under the wings. And for these long hauls, besides
the packed meal of sandwiches, fruit, flasks of tea and coffee, the crews
were also offered 'wakey-wakey' pills of Benzedrine amphetamine.

Soon after their arrival in the Azores, bearing in mind the possibility
of needing to divert, Jim Glazebrook suggested to David that they seek
permission to have a look at the little airfield of Santa Anna in order
to familiarise themselves in good weather with the landing ground they
might one day have to use in bad. Permission was granted.

David, his crew and a party of pilots and navigators flew to
Santa Anna accompanied by another Fortress similarly laden. The
other Fortress became bogged down in the soft ground beside the
runway.

While David returned to base, the crew and passengers of the other
Fortress had to remain overnight. It was no hardship. As there was no
accommodation on the spot, they were driven across the hills to Ponta
Delgada, where they dined with the British Ambassador and slept in
the best hotel in comfortable beds. But the next morning, the Fortress
was extricated and back they flew to grim reality.

That winter, when Gibraltar like Lagens was closed by fog, a
206 Fortress arrived back from convoy escort, very low on fuel. Unable
to land anywhere, it crashed at Carnero Point. There were no
survivors. In February, David and his crew were out searching for a
lost Wellington crew. A wing was sighted but again there was no sign
of any survivors.

David and the crew in the Azores. *Left to right:* Norman Draper, John Johnston, David Beaty, Jim Glazebrook, Frank MacManus, Leo Meaker and Jimmy Cunningham

*   *   *

On 13 March came the opportunity for David to use the skill he had learned in turning and corkscrewing the Fortress.

At 01.51 on that morning a Leigh light Wellington had sighted and attacked a U-boat, the VHF class U575, five hundred miles north of the Azores. The U-boat was waiting in the direct path of a large convoy ON 227. The U-boat submerged. After radioing its position, the Wellington left the area on reaching its 'prudent limit of endurance' (PLE).

Immediately the attack signal was received at Lagens, David's crew was called and briefed for a sortie. Airborne in Fortress 206R FA700, he set course for the position indicated, a course worked out with his navigator, Johnny Johnston.

Cloud was covering the moon and visual sighting was difficult. In the words of Jim Glazebrook:

> 'We had been flying for about three hours and the navigator was in the act of saying, "I think we should be about there, Skipper," when I saw the Wellington's flame floats.
>
> 'It was not quite light and David had turned the controls over to me to circle while he crawled forward to the nose to work out a search pattern with the navigator. It was getting light and there were great

Above: The airfield at
Lagens showing 206's
tents.

Right: The airmen's mess.
Cooking in the open and
eating on the hill-side.

patches of water that were absolutely glass-like – as still as an inland
pond. I actually had my eye on one patch and was marvelling at such
a sight in the middle of the ocean, when, right in the spot I was gazing
at, the bow of the U-boat broke surface.

'I sounded the alarm bell and commenced a deep diving turn, while
David scrambled back to his seat, but we were too high and too close
to get into an attacking position before the U-boat was fully surfaced
and manning its guns. Having lost the element of surprise, David
decided we should try to get a signal to base before we attacked, but we
were too far and too low to make contact, and we dared not climb for
fear the U-boat would dive.'

The periscope of U575 is just visible at the top of the photo.

Of this David wrote, 'So I was faced with the dilemma, do I attack without reporting my position, or do I wait till I do get through before going in? The suspense of risking U575 diving was too much, so in the end we did attack.'

But first he asked the crew if they were game. As an illustration of David's concern for his crew, Jim Glazebrook writes:

'We were all conscious of the fact that Squadron Leader Pinhorn had been shot down presumably by a U-boat a few weeks before and that was why David wanted to get a signal away before we attacked. Without that, we would not have been missed for ten hours or more if we'd been shot down and ended up in a dinghy. But as it was, we were too far away – and too low – for the wireless operator to be able to make contact with the Azores, the UK or Gibraltar (he tried all three) and we dared not

92

J of 220 Squadron
attacking U575.

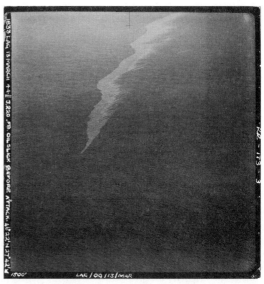

The oil slick from U575 which David
attacked and the Navy finished off.

The oil slick eventually blitzed
by the Navy.

The last round of the battle.

climb in case the U-boat dived when we were too high to attack. In the event, David would not take an arbitrary decision (though as Captain he was entitled to do so) but sought and received the agreement of all the crew before attacking.'

The navigator came forward and manned the front gun. David continues, 'The front gunner and the mid-upper fired as we went in. The flak was heavy, but we weren't hit. I made a diving turn to port, at fifty feet attacking thirty degrees to port of line astern.'

The four depth charges slung externally – all that could be carried on the Fortresses so that range could be increased – fell one on one side of the U-boat and three on the other. After the explosions, the submarine appeared stationary on the surface, then it submerged, stern first, with the bows at a steep angle, and with two larger oil patches beginning to spread on the surface.

They then climbed, radioed their position and circled for five hours, homing on Fortress J/220 Squadron and the Naval Task Group.

The severely damaged U575, a Type V11c, with five torpedo tubes, was armed with 88 and 20 mm guns and strengthened AA armament, twin 2.5 low velocity guns mounted on platforms (one platform directly by the conning tower). It was only the second U-boat to be fitted with the new Schnorkel breathing device, and was the first Schnorkel-equipped boat to be sunk by the Allies. It was further attacked by Fortress J of 220 Squadron and finished off by the Navy.

Commanded by Wolfgang Boehmer, based in Western France, the U575 had been hunting successfully without returning to base since the beginning of January. It had a fearsome record, having destroyed eleven ships, including HMS *Asphodel*. There were twenty-three survivors, including the captain.

Jim Glazebrook ascribed the success of the attack to David's cork-screwing dive which saved them from being shot down by the submarine's guns, as happened to Squadron Leader Pinhorn and to Wing Commander Ronnie Thomson, who after his shoot-down, had to ditch in a minefield.

David was awarded the DFC, as was the pilot of the 220 Squadron Fortress, Pip Travell, and John Patrick Finnessy, who had first spotted U575, also received the DFC.

David's superb crew were Jim Glazebrook, Frank MacManus, John Johnston, Norman Draper, Jimmy Cunningham and Leo Meaker (RAAF). The following day a signal was received from the Commander-in-Chief Western Approaches sending his warmest congratulations.

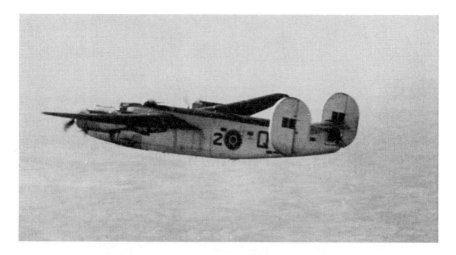

Converted to Liberators.

Jim Glazebrook wrote recently:

> 'One thing I would underline is David's superb skill in taking the evasive action during his attack on U575 that resulted in not a single bullet or shell from the U-boat's cannons hitting us, when so many other aircraft in similar circumstances had been shot down or at least severely damaged ... I would want to see something said about how well David treated his crew, and the tremendous loyalty that we all felt towards him.'

Within a week of that episode, news came that the squadron was once more to be taken 'out of line' and was to prepare for a move to the UK.

Rumours were rife. The one that proved to be true was that they had flown their last Fortress operation. Another important theatre of the war beckoned. Their work in the Azores was to be carried on by 220 Squadron, while they were to take part in the great invasion of Europe. This time on Liberators.

David was posted to 1674 Heavy Conversion Unit at Aldergrove for conversion to Liberators. The snub-nosed B24 Consolidated Liberator has been described as possessing 'modest aesthetic qualities'. It has also been described as 'a hard to handle over-rated, under-powered flying bomb'.

However, the new B24H was an improvement. It had uprated engines and the nose was replaced by a Bendix gun turret with twin .5 inch Browning heavy machine-guns. It had a radar with a rotating scanner aerial which provided more accurate bearings. It also carried sonar buoys.

206 Squadron – David in the centre of the front row. Taken in the Azores just before they left.

206 Squadron Liberators.

The Liberator was to be an aircraft with which David would become familiar for a number of years. And with the conversion course completed, David was posted with the rest of the squadron to St Eval, where they continued their anti-submarine sweeps across the Bay of Biscay and down the Spanish coast. Meanwhile St Eval was becoming more and more crowded, with four squadrons stationed there. In the words of Frank MacManus, 'We knew that something big was brewing.'

On 6 June the Second Front, the reason for their return to a UK base, was opened up. What has been described as 'the greatest amphibious operation in history' was launched. The wind was strong, the sea rough and pitching, but it was an interlude between the squally weather of a few days before and an approaching cold front.

The Liberators were assigned to doing what were called 'Stopper patrols'. Nicknamed Operation *Cork*, they stretched along the Western Approaches, south-west of Ushant and the Scillies, then up close to the U-boat pens. These patrols were designed to guard the Allied armada and keep the U-boats at bay.

Three of the patrol belts were laid across the western end of the English Channel; two between the coasts of Cornwall and Brittany and a third from the west of the Scillies to Ushant. The Liberators carried twelve 250 lbs depth charges and one five-hundred-pounder.

From D-Day onwards, for a period of six weeks, twenty-four hours a day, Liberators patrolled these belts on the 'endless chain' principle. They were so spaced that a watcher on either shore opposite a point on

David at the controls of a Liberator.

the end of one of the patrols would see an aircraft pass every half an hour. During the day, 206 and 547 Squadrons operated the patrols: after dark the Leigh-light carrying Liberators of 53 and 224 Squadrons took over. Twenty-five sorties a day were flown from St Eval. The aircraft watched over the destroyers shelling the batteries on the French coast, the operating of the Mulberry Harbours and the troops landing.

In fact, the Mulberry Harbours had been largely designed at David's old school, Kingswood, then commandeered by the Department of the Civil Engineer-in-Chief. The Chief Engineer's office looked out over the school mulberry tree and it is believed that the code-name 'Mulberry' was suggested by it. Unaware of this connection, in his diary David described his feelings on the first of those Cork patrols.

> 'Woke very early thinking of what we would be expected to do, and wondering how dangerous it would be – remembering the Wingco's words, "I'm expecting losses, you know." but I was too tired to figure it out, so I went to sleep again.
>
> 'I saw M had written a letter "to be sent off in case I am killed or missing" and wondered if I should do the same, but decided against it . . . so went back to sleep.
>
> 'We were off at half past twelve in O for Orange on I patrol down to the Sept Isles. This was to be done seven times. We could hear "France and Islands thirty miles" on the radar, gradually creeping down until we saw the lighthouses stuck on crags of rock with Lammon and the mainland behind.

'The weather was blue-skied at the French side with a warm front creeping in on the English side, so I went down to fifty feet past the French lighthouses, then with them behind me I would slowly climb to 1,000 feet and then down again.'

Meanwhile the weather was rapidly deteriorating at the English end. The aircraft were recalled to Dunkerswell in Devon.

On another patrol, enemy aircraft blips followed them, but they avoided their pursuers, and on 15 June David took off in aircraft G:

'this time on a patrol down to Ushant. We got nearer the French coast than we'd bargained for and roared over some fields at nought feet. Some French fishermen in a rowing boat got up and cheered wildly, standing on their seats, and it gave me a great sense of pride to show them at such close quarters my red, white and blue roundel on its huge white background.

'At about 12.00 hrs, MacManus on the starboard beam saw a column of smoke going up to 1,000 feet. We went over towards it and there were three frigates deep depth-charging. A thick black scum of oil spread raggedly over the calm sea. Yellow dinghies and men bobbed around in it – about forty to fifty. We circled. A Sunderland and a Lib came up – the Sunderland tried to land but had to take off again. We tried to flash to the ships, but they would take no notice of us, continuing on, not troubling to pick up any of the survivors. So continued to circle and sent off a signal to base.'

These Liberator operations were a hundred per cent successful. They completely stopped the U-boats' penetration. Not a single U-boat was able to break through and attack the invasion shipping off the beach heads. Although, as has now been discovered, the Germans were aware that a second front was about to open and ahead of D-Day proposed to use their U-boat fleet as their big weapon to stop the Allies gaining a foothold on the European mainland. But the aircraft patrols foiled that plan.

On 9 June when the invasion was well under way, the *Daily Mail* commented , 'There is a big story still to be told about the fighting off of a determined bid by U-boats to reach the invasion lanes across the English Channel. Coastal Command of the RAF helped by aircraft from the US Navy have maintained an elaborate pattern of patrols between all U-boat bases and the Channel.'

Some time later, a *Croix de Guerre* was conferred on 206 Squadron for 'Gallantry in the Liberation of France'. Flight Lieutenant Banks, the enthusiastic and daring senior navigator on the squadron, was chosen to wear it.

CHAPTER EIGHT

'U-BOATS' BACKYARD BOMBED'

In July 1944, 206 Squadron arrived at Leuchars and their anti-submarine patrols now took them up to the most northerly part of the Atlantic and into the Arctic Ocean.

In August, the squadron began to receive a later version of the Liberator, the Mark VI equipped with Leigh lights; these were enormously powerful lights, designed by Squadron Leader de Verde Leigh which were fitted under the starboard wing. They were meant to help the crews see enemy shipping by night. By the same token they allowed the enemy an illuminated picture of the attacking aircraft from which to get their range and were therefore dangerous to carry. Also, their light came from a carbon arc, which continued to glow after the current was switched off. Training on the use of these lights took place in August.

Halfway through the month, Jim Glazebrook, David's second pilot, was given a command of his own. It was well deserved and David was delighted, but at the same time sorry to lose such an excellent pilot with whom he had established great rapport. His new second pilot, Len Cogan, was a conscientious pilot, a dapper and clever young man, and the crew morale stayed high. Subsequently he was succeeded by Gerry Clements, fair-haired and shy, looking even younger than his twenty years, but who being both conscientious and courageous became a very good operational pilot.

Fitted with the Leigh light, 206 Squadron continued its searches for enemy craft off the coasts of Norway and the Faeroes, and in November the crew went on No. 39 joint RAF/RN anti-submarine course at Maydown near Londonderry. The Liberators were temporarily based at RAF Ballykelly and the flying exercises took place from there, and associated with the course were two RN submarines. The exercises required the RAF to locate the submarines off the coast of Northern Ireland while the submarines had to try to

The Crew at Leuchars.

An airman cleaning the Leigh light
on the Liberator's wing.

escape detection. On some of those exercises the aircraft carried RN
personnel and the aircrew went down in the submarines.

Neither enjoyed the others' environment. David and his crew found
the submarines claustrophobic. The submariners thought the aircrew
were mad to fly hundreds of miles out to sea in such fragile land planes.
But all found the exercises very valuable.

After the course, David and his crew began Arctic patrols associated
with the Russian convoys, north of Trondheim. Some of the patrols
lasted eleven hours. The weather was atrocious, with snow falling from
the Arctic to the Mull of Kintyre. The aircraft were freezing cold and
although aircrew were provided with specially warm boots and jackets
and gloves and linings they were clumsy and not enough.

Their crew complement was now made up to eleven men. Frank
MacManus, Jim Julian DFM, Pat Philip, Johnny Baugh, Norman
Draper, Gerry Clements, Johnny Johnston, Leo Meaker, Peter Laird,

David in a submarine when roles were exchanged. The aircrew submerged on an exercise while the submariners flew in Liberators.

The crew. Back row – left to right. Frank MacManus, Leo Meaker, Jimmy Cunningham, Norman Draper and Pat Philip. Front row – Johnny Johnston, Len Cogan, David Beaty, Peter Laird and Johnny Baugh.

Jimmy Cunningham, the additional navigator, WOP/AG and gunner introduced at the time of Liberator conversion being very welcome on the long patrols.

Frank MacManus writes:

'The nose turret proved to be a mixed blessing for the navigators. There was a pair of sliding doors in the turret itself and a hinged, windproof door between the turret and the navigator's compartment at the front of the aircraft. When the door was swung open to permit a change of gunners, a howling gale blew charts, pencils and instruments all round the aircraft. The navigator tried to hold everything down but was seldom 100% successful. To minimise this disturbance the gunners had to endure a two-hour stint in the nose turret.

'It was an odd experience to sit in those turrets since one seemed to be floating alone. Only by swinging the turret to the limit of its rotation could one see the wingtips and outer engines. Another nasty thought was that the gunner couldn't get out until someone opened the inner door, so if there was a serious aircraft problem he was in trouble. If the rear gunner could squeeze his parachute pack into the turret, he could swing his turret to one side, open the turret doors and bale out backwards, but if the nose gunner were to try this he would drop straight into the airscrews of the inner engines.'

And now as winter tightened its grip on the Atlantic the U-boat war was changing. More U-boats had been fitted with the Schnorkel device by means of which they were able to use their diesel motors while remaining almost completely submerged, and practically invisible to searching aircraft, for indefinite periods. It also meant that when an attack seemed imminent they could descend in a few seconds out of range of any aircraft's shallow-set depth charges. At the same time, the U-boat crews were becoming more desperate and even more dangerous.

Increasingly, as the U-boats developed the strategy of lying in wait for large convoys, the Liberators would search the areas ahead of the convoy to prevent an ambush. In February, when the weather was so severe that it was doubtful if even the submarines would be operating, David and his crew were directed up to 66°50' North to escort a Russian convoy. They refuelled up at Tain to increase their range, took off into a wind of eighty-two knots and headed north. Their instructions were to make contact with the Russian convoy escort's senior officer, who was aboard a light aircraft carrier.

The convoy was up beyond the Arctic circle, the strength of the headwind was increasing and the Liberator's speed was reduced to a crawl. After more than eight hours they reached the estimated position of the convoy but the visibility was so low, the sea so turbulent, that even with the radar they had difficulty in finding it and by this time, fuel-wise, the Liberator was reaching the end of its endurance.

Frank MacManus writes:

> 'After much searching, we found the carrier and exchanged messages with a signal lamp (radio silence to avoid giving away the convoy position). The sea was absolutely frightful with waves breaking right over the flight deck of the carrier, which pitched forward, bringing its propellers clear of the surface. We had taken so long to reach the area and to locate the SNO (Senior Naval Officer) that our message simply said "Sorry. We must go. Good luck."'

On the way back to Scotland they passed a northbound Catalina. So strong was the wind that they swear the Catalina, at the best of times a slow aircraft, was flying backwards.

Soon there began the last all-out offensive against the U-boats. Until then, attacks were usually made by lone aircraft. But on the night of 2 February 1945 a mass attack was scheduled for the whole squadron; their target, Germany's innermost U-boat sanctuary in the Baltic Sea. Guarded by fighter airfields in Norway and Denmark, the *Kriegsmarine* had built huge U-boat pens. The comparatively slow and unmanoeuvrable Liberators had not previously run the gauntlet of the Skagerrak and the Kattegat.

The plan was that the aircraft would form into two waves, flying parallel paths two miles apart, make the passage through the Skagerrak and Kattegat, cross the southern tip of Sweden into the Baltic, and surprise the unsuspecting U-boats anchored overnight in the training area off Bornholm.

That night, in a blinding snowstorm, all fourteen Liberators of 206 and 547 Squadrons took off from Leuchars within a few minutes of each other. One unfortunate Liberator had a fire on take-off and had to divert to Wick. Casualties for this operation were expected to be high.

Frank MacManus writes:

> 'As a senior crew we were to be in the second wave . . . We cut across neutral Sweden, illegally of course, and the Swedes duly banged off their anti-aircraft guns at us; but not very accurately, possibly because by this date Sweden was neutral on the side of the Allies, whereas in the years before they were quite definitely neutral on the side of Germany.'

Then they swept up the Skagerrak in darkness, keeping semi-distant between the coasts and down to less than two hundred feet above the water to avoid the enemy's radar detectors. The first wave had found numerous contacts on their radar, had switched on their Leigh lights to expose resting U-boats, and made attacks.

Having penetrated deep into the Skagerrak, near the island of Bornholm, David and his crew flying in Liberator 206E got a radar contact and, switching on the Leigh light, spotted a heavily armed destroyer, five U-boats and a merchantman, in convoy. He went straight in to attack the destroyer, and in Frank MacManus' words, 'All hell broke loose.'

The *Sheffield Telegraph* of 4 February headlined the attack with 'U-boats' backyard bombed', and goes on to report:

> 'Searchlight carrying Liberators of RAF Coastal Command penetrated to the Baltic in the early hours of yesterday to take the U-boat war into the backyard of the enemy . . . The raid involved a round trip covering approximately 1,000 miles flown at extremely low altitude and most of the way in darkness. Heavy flak was encountered from shore batteries and surface vessels and opposition also came from enemy fighters.'

The newspaper report continues:

> 'As Beaty flew into the flak to drop his depth charges, the destroyer opened up with heavy and light guns. The crew could feel the flak hitting the sides of the aircraft but escaped injury.
>
> 'For a few seconds the Liberator went out of control as pieces of flak had severed the cables of rudder and rudder trimmer. Another piece hit the bomb bay, knocking both doors open. At one time the failure of the DR compass sent them flying round in circles, in face of the fire from the destroyer.'

The fire from the destroyer and the shore batteries had been so severe and so precise because, unbeknown to David and his crew, that same convoy had just been attacked by Flight Lieutenant Jim Glazebrook, his former second pilot. Jim Glazebrook had had to break off the engagement because of an electrical failure, but not before the destroyer was alerted to the presence of Liberators. When David illuminated the destroyer in his Leigh light, the destroyer's crew thought it was Glazebrook returning and were prepared to throw everything at him. Thus, though David yelled to the navigator to put out the Leigh light, 206E 'received the full weight of the anti-aircraft barrage'.

In fact, the actual damage to 206E was far worse than that described in the newspaper. In addition to the damage which the newspaper listed, an engine had been hit and rendered unserviceable. Two other engines had been damaged and a large hole blown in the fuselage near the beam gun position.

David in the cockpit with the crew on the fuselage of their Liberator at Leuchars.

With an immense effort, David managed to regain control of the aircraft, and ordered the jettisoning of all heavy equipment. One of the crew who prided himself on his handsome appearance, tried to hang on to his expensive fitted toilet case, but David insisted it be thrown out. Then, with their weight slightly decreased, David was able to haul the aircraft slowly up to four thousand feet.

He sent his engineer, Jimmy Cunningham, aft to assess damage. When he returned his assessment was brief and to the point, 'We've had it, Skipper! We've had it!'

That was also David's conclusion. Because a cannon shell had nearly demolished the port engine and two others were damaged, he had very little power, and because of the severing of the cables, no rudder control. The ailerons were damaged. The fuselage had taken so much flak that it was virtually un-airworthy and the whole aircraft was almost unflyable.

David therefore decided they should struggle over the coast and bale out over neutral Sweden, so a course was set for Sweden and the order given to the crew to prepare to bale out.

His decision to do this was not only because the aircraft was virtually unflyable but also because David knew they would be totally unable to take evasive action and would be 'easy meat' if attacked by enemy fighters over the North Sea.

However, in the difficulty of buckling on parachutes in the darkness, one crew member caught hold of the rip cord instead of

The damaged Liberator brought back from the Baltic. Over 600 holes were found in it.

the carrying handle of his parachute and the silk billowed out into the aircraft.

The crew member in question offered to jump with his parachute tucked under his arm, someone else offered to share his parachute, two of them hopefully descending clasped together. But mindful of the danger of the parachute tangling round the tail-plane, David refused to countenance either scheme.

Jim Glazebrook comments: 'So [once again putting the interests of the crew first] David decided to take a chance on getting home without being attacked by fighters.'

Frank MacManus writes:

> 'The night fighters were often fitted with guns which fired vertically upwards. They were guided to their target by ground radar, then they would get beneath the aircraft by visual detection – very difficult on a dark night – and blast the target from below. We kept as low down as possible in the hope of avoiding the ground radar and the fighters.'

As they skimmed the wave tops, no fighter spotted them. And when they reached the normal limit of fighter cover, they further reduced their weight by throwing out the free mounted guns and all the ammunition.

Frank goes on:

> 'We flew with one wing low in a sort of permanent turn to counter the asymmetric engine power with no rudder control. This meant that the two pilots had to apply their full strength to maintain this condition and by the time we reached Scotland they were both exhausted. I stayed on the wireless throughout, since I had established a good rapport with the operator at the MF direction-finding station. I had cancelled the SOS

and kept asking for steering information. This was obtained by two or three MF D/F stations hooking on to my transmission to obtain a bearing. The two (or three) bearings were then plotted on a chart at the main station to fix our position and they then gave me a heading-to-steer to reach a suitable destination. In fact they guided us to Banff on the Moray Firth which had a long runway in an east-west direction.'

David said afterwards that he bounced the aircraft rather than flew it, and somehow, ably helped by his co-pilot Gerry Clements, the two pilots managed to hold the aircraft in the air.

On the approach, Peter Laird, who had stayed up front with the pilots, took over the wireless and dealt with the final approach details.

'David Beaty made a smooth landing without further damage. It looked as if all personnel on Banff had turned out to watch us land.'

Frank MacManus goes on:

'They were probably expecting a spectacular crash. The fire and ambulance crews who chased us along the runway probably felt a bit let down.

'We climbed out of our Liberator and left it where it had come to rest at the end of the runway. The second engine had packed up before we reached Banff so the aircraft would not have stayed airborne for much longer.

'We walked round the plane and were staggered by the amount of damage.'

Peter Laird told his wife that forever etched on his memory was the sight of David grimly struggling with every ounce of his strength every second of that flight to hold the aircraft in the air.

Watchers on the ground saw the moonlight shining through the shell holes in the aircraft. When she flopped down, they counted hundreds of holes. Yet no one was injured.

The entry for all that in David's log reads: 'Baltic strike. Illuminated Narvik destroyer, Damaged by flak, Landed Banff.'

David received a Bar to his DFC and to David's great satisfaction, Jim Glazebrook received the DFC. The following day, the crew returned to Leuchars and were back on escort duty over another Arctic convoy.

Early in March, the squadron was withdrawn from the line to re-arm with Mark VIII Liberators, fitted with Mark X radar and Low Attack Bombing (LAB) equipment – a blind bomb-sight used in conjunction with the radar equipment and designed for low-altitude night operation against U-boats and surface vessels. 206 Squadron was the only RAF squadron to be thus equipped. LAB involved close co-operation between navigator and pilot – control of the ailerons and rudders being taken over by the navigator (i.e. Direction), the elevators and throttles remaining with the pilot (i.e. airspeed and rate of descent). A period of intense training began. David was airborne every day practising with LAB. And in April, the squadron was undertaking regular night patrols as well as the Baltic raids.

On the night of the third of May, David in Liberator 206C and Flying Officer Glazebrook in 206E were detailed for what had now become the usual patrol in the Kattegat. On arriving at the eastern end of the Skagerrak, they saw an astonishing sight. The entire area between the Danish and Swedish coasts was a mass of shipping. All the vessels in this armada carried riding lights and were steaming northwards in orderly rows.

The great mass evacuation from Denmark to Norway had begun.

But the ships were not unprotected. They were escorted by *Luftwaffe* fighters, several of which shadowed the Liberators until they left the area.

Next morning, the remaining German forces in Denmark and North West Germany capitulated.

But the Allies were still mindful of the strength of the German forces in Norway, the grim determination of the large U-boat fleet, and they had no idea of their intention. On 5 May a personal signal was sent out to all Coastal Command stations from the Air-Officer Commanding in Chief Coastal Command.

'In spite of the surrender of German forces on the Continent, there is as yet no indication that they contemplate surrender in Norway. We may therefore expect the continuance of intensive U-boat operation from Norwegian bases.

'All ranks must realise that for Coastal Command the war goes on as before. We started first; we finish last. I call upon all squadrons for a great final effort against our old enemy. It falls to Coastal Command to strike the final blow against the enemy's one remaining weapon.'

On 7 May 1945 David and his crew patrolled in the Skagerrak, bombing a suspicious foam patch that indicated a lurking U-boat. Shortly afterwards they heard Admiral Dönitz calling on all U-boats to surrender. Dönitz told the U-boat captains he recognised that surrender called for great forbearance on their part, but that he expected absolute obedience to his order, since failure to comply would bring severe consequences and suffering to the German people.

It was a bitter blow to the U-boat captains and crews, many of whom were still hyped up for the battle and who desperately wanted to fight on. They signalled back to Admiral Dönitz that it went against the grain to surrender their boats and it was only in loyalty to Dönitz that they so did. Therefore, in compliance, most of the U-boats duly surfaced and, flying the black flag, proceeded to their allotted surrender points.

It was a moment for the Coastal Command crews to remember.

The following days they were airborne between the Shetlands and the Faeroes and along the Norwegian coast, acting as the Navy's sheepdogs, rounding up U-boats and shepherding them into British ports.

Flying Officer Glazebrook accepted the first surrender of a U-boat to the Squadron on 10 May when he located and photographed U552 west of the Shetlands. He sighted his next U-boat, U1231 three days later off the North coast of Scotland. It was not intent on surrender but, contrary to orders had not surfaced and only its periscope was visible. He therefore dived to attack and, as he made his run, bomb doors open, the U-boat crew hastily surfaced. Some of the officers appeared on the conning tower and gave the Nazi salute. But they hoisted the black flag and surrendered. Mindful of that Nazi salute, Flying Officer Glazebrook stayed overhead until a ship came to escort the U-boat into port.

Flying Officer Frost found one of the new 250-ton pre-fabricated U-boats in the North Sea heading for Denmark. They stopped when called upon to do so, but pretended not to understand the instructions being given them to alter course for Scotland. However they understood when Flying Officer Frost dropped a depth charge in front of them. They turned round smartly and were escorted into Dundee harbour by relays of aircraft. And there the Liberator crews were able to see their former adversary and his ship at close quarters. Subsequently the crew expressed their gratitude that they had not been sunk, sending a note thanking 'Mr Frost that he dropped it far enough away to not do any harm.'

Throughout those weeks, flying low on a clear day over the Norwegian coast, they saw people waving joyfully, and over Denmark and the Netherlands, flags and bunting and cheering crowds. The population of Northern Europe was close to starvation. So, descending over the streets, the crews dropped their sweet and chocolate rations. It was little enough, but now at least something was being organised for the starving of the Occupied countries. Lancaster bombers had been modified to carry panniers and in Operation *Manna* were flying in over the Low Countries at almost hedge-top height to drop food to them.

On the way back to base, David and his crew saw a memorable and historic sight – the washes of German ships steaming to surrender.

CHAPTER NINE

A FATEFUL LANDING

After VE (Victory in Europe) Day, plans were afoot for a new peace-time use for the Liberators. The war against Japan still continued and there were troops to be ferried out to the Far East theatre of war and to Palestine where the British mandate sat uneasily; and on the return journeys, troops and liberated prisoners of war to be brought home.

In June 1945, 206 Squadron was transferred to 301 Wing, Transport Command. It was re-organised on a basis of forty-eight crews of five members each – two pilots, navigator, wireless operator and flight engineer. The Liberators were flown to Gatwick, at that time merely a small airfield with only grass runways, for conversion to troop carriers. The armament was taken out, the bomb bays were sealed. Eight seats were put into the bomb bay and eighteen in the main part of the fuselage. Extra crews were posted in to the squadron. Some of them had flown Coastal Command Halifaxes, so a conversion course to Liberators was set up. David was promoted to Squadron Leader and made Flight Captain B Flight and put in charge of training.

He flew a Liberator out to Lydda, refuelling at Shaiba to assess the route, and on 30 July, the Squadron was posted to RAF Oakington, near Cambridge, until then the home of 7 Squadron of the Pathfinder Force, Bomber Command.

The weather forecast given to him at Leuchars before he took off for the flight to Oakington was of low cloud and mist. Sure enough, flying down the coast he encountered very bad weather over Flamborough Head and had to come down low. A small unimportant incident which had a disproportionate effect on his subsequent career decisions.

He arrived in the circuit at Oakington and, while looking down on the airfield in its tranquil Fenland setting, he experienced an overwhelming feeling of *déjà vu*, a certainty that Oakington would become tremendously important to him, and that down below him there lay his fate.

He had sometimes experienced sudden insights, but none so strong and certain as this. However, it was a transitory feeling and he dismissed it. He made a copybook landing, reported in at Flying Control where he met Squadron Leader John Martin, his opposite number commanding the other 206 Flight (A Flight). John was a handsome, urbane and erudite son of the manor house, who had flown Hudsons in the anti-U-boat campaign, followed by a tour of duty in Nassau in charge of aircrew training. While there his striking looks and charming manner had caught the predatory eye of the Duchess of Windsor who had repeatedly selected him as her dancing partner. The Duke had not been amused.

Together John Martin and David strolled up to the Officers' Mess.

It was a fine peacetime neo-Georgian brick building and they were well pleased with it. They pushed open the glass swing doors. They saw the curved, polished oak bar, the mirrored shelves behind glittering with bottles and glasses, and standing there two people, the Station Medical Officer, recognisable by the caduceus on his lapels and a young WAAF Section Officer, me, then the junior equipment officer.

Again he felt that sudden insight. Both he and I recognised it for the fraction of a second as a fateful time-stopping moment without realising why. Then, like a film that has momentarily stopped and suddenly restarted, everything continued as before. Nobody exchanged greetings. Neither the Station MO nor I stepped forward to welcome the newcomers or greeted them at all. David and Johnny Martin walked through to the Mess office to be allotted their room. The MO and I continued our conversation. Both David and I dismissed the strange feeling and forgot it.

But somewhere that moment must have buried itself in my subconscious for at tea time in the Mess three days later, sitting with two other WAAF officers who were discussing the merits and de-merits of the new squadron, David walked in. As he passed us and took his seat at the senior officers' table the WAAF signals officer asked me, 'Do you like Squadron Leader Beaty?'

I had had a busy day catching up with the paperwork on the departure of 7 Squadron. I had missed lunch. I was hungry and busily spreading jam on my bread and butter, not taking much part in the conversation, and anyway, it was an unanswerable question because I had never met David, never spoken to him, never exchanged a smile or even a nod. So, without thinking I replied, 'No. But I shall marry him.'

Immediately I came to, as if out of a dream. I shook my head to clear it. 'That was a silly thing to say,' I told them. 'I don't know why I said it. I've certainly never thought it.'

The next day, David went on leave. When he returned, he found himself Duty Station Commander. On that same night, I was WAAF Orderly Officer. One of the duties for each of us was to pay a short visit to any party that was being held in any of the Messes – that night there was a party in the Sergeants' Mess, and it seemed logical for David to suggest we went together.

Even on the short walk there, we found an immediate and astonishing empathy, an ability to talk to each other, a delight in the other's company. It was like opening a window on a vista you didn't even know existed.

The party was in full swing when we arrived. A loud band was thumping away vigorously. The air, as usual at all Mess parties, was thick with cigarette smoke and the floor awash with beer.

We were greeted by the Mess President and drinks thrust into our hands. Before David had time to drink his, a very attractive blonde teetered over. Unlike we WAAF, dressed in unyielding blue serge uniforms, blue shirt, starched collar, thick grey lisle stockings, heavy black lace-up shoes, she was poured into a slinky low-cut number in emerald green silk. It was dangerously becoming. So was her hair. All WAAF hair had to be plain and one inch above our collars. Hers was a blonde and shiny chignon. Her make-up was lavish and flattering, her perfume expensive. She was the guest of the equipment flight sergeant, my right-hand man in Stores. But as fast as she could on her high-heeled silver sandals, she was ditching him. A hand through David's arm and she was pulling him onto the floor, the chignoned head resting on his shoulder, for that entire dance and for all the next.

As I was swung around in the disgruntled arms of my flight sergeant, we both watched them suspiciously over each other's shoulders. That tiny moment was suddenly important to both of us. I could only guess what the flight sergeant thought. But I was thinking if David is the person I believe he is, he'll be back. But if he isn't, then that empathy, that delight, were just part of an illusion and would be best forgotten.

But they weren't an illusion. As politely as he could, David freed himself and returned. We danced one slow waltz. Then, renewing that feeling of communication and empathy, we walked back to the Officers' Mess together as, from then on, though there were many separations, we walked through life.

We made a date for dinner in Cambridge, the first of many. We explored the fens by bus. We cycled (with difficulty as I, to David's disgust, was an uncoordinated cyclist) to a pub – the Pike and Eel at Needingworth. Only a couple of miles from Oakington, it could be reached quite easily by bike. Then the bikes could be propped against an ancient willow while the Pike and Eel's customer rang a bell for the ferry. Over came a battered boat, hand-hauled along a chain that spanned the river Ouse by an even more ancient boatman.

The Pike and Eel squatted low in a garden that ended in the river.

Victory on the North Atlantic. Coastal Command Liberators escort the German cruiser *Nürnberg* to surrender after the armistice.

Built of crumbling stone with oak-beamed ceilings, diamond paned windows, worn red-patterned carpet (that carpet is still there today), a big open log fire, good food and a warm welcome, it became one of our favourite haunts.

We looked up two of David's school friends who had returned from the army to complete their studies at Cambridge, Freddy Beales, a gentle courteous academic and Monkey Wright, who was a Rugby blue and played for England.

We drank brown ale in an old-fashioned unspoiled pub called The Volunteer, and there David didn't indulge in anything as romantic as a proposal but simply said, as someone dispassionately stating the obvious, that come what may our future was together.

Occasionally we walked down from the airfield on a Sunday evening for Evensong at Longstanton church. Early on in our walks round Oakington and Longstanton, David had told me his aim in life was to be a writer and he already had in his mind the plot of his first novel, based on his own experiences with the starboard engine. Neither of us had any doubt that a writer was what he would become. Nor did I doubt then or since that he was a genius.

Meanwhile, the flying training programme for the India run was under way. The crews were issued with tropical kit – khaki uniform and shorts. They looked very attractive in them apart from the fact that they had to take mepacrine to guard against malaria and with some of

A Liberator converted for troop carrying.

them it produced the unfortunate reaction of turning their faces a dandelion yellow.

One small irritant at that time was a signal from Air Ministry. On David's flight down from Leuchars to Oakington, two SPs (Service Police) had seen him flying necessarily low over Flamborough Head. This they had reported as flying unnecessarily low and as a danger to the public. The report had gone through to Air Ministry, together with a weather report, not from Flamborough Head, which had been swathed in mist, but from thirty miles inland where the weather was clear. Air Ministry was threatening action, even mentioning a court martial.

David was incensed. He tried telephoning Air Ministry. They refused to budge. Finally, to convince them, he took a Liberator up to Leuchars and obtained a copy of the original weather forecast. As soon as Air Ministry received that, the matter was of course dropped. But the sheer waste of time and money and effort angered David and it had an effect on his decision taking later on.

Meanwhile, David, a conscientious training captain, was busy with organising schedules and pioneering the route, reading all he could

David and his crew in tropical kit on the way to India via Shaibah.

115

David and the crew at
Oakington. Back row – Peter
Laird and Jim Cunningham.
Front row – Johnny Baugh,
David and Gerry Clements.

about it and preparing the crews for their change of role. And as
Oakington and the squadron had changed their roles a new station commander had taken over. He had very little wartime flying experience,
having spent a considerable amount of the war in Washington and other
corridors of power, but he was vigorous and good at getting things done.

The crews had mixed feelings towards the India run. Obviously it
was a welcome change not to be shot at by enemy submarines, battleships and aircraft. Their passengers, at least the ones homebound, were
delighted to be on board, despite their cramped conditions. But the
sandstorms of the desert, the monsoon weather and the heat of India
were a different challenge. David carefully studied the met reports
about monsoon flying, reports from pilots, and a Transport Command
publication on 'Lessons of Monsoon Accidents'.

In the met reports, cloud tops of over 16,000 feet were cited, and
conditions so bumpy that the pilots had no control, and a sudden dive
at 4,000 feet per minute was not uncommon. Pilots were warned of
huge and powerful clouds, called 'Dowagers.' One report is headed,
'Thou shalt respect my domain, Mighty are the powers within.'

So mighty that aircraft could break up in the buffetting of the clouds.
Struggling through a huge thundercloud the port outer mainplane on a
Dakota broke off four feet from the root ends. The mainplane was swung
back, tearing off the port tail plane and completely severing the tail unit.
The starboard main plane also broke off just outboard of the nacelle. The
port main plane was split in half as if it had broken when it was swept
back on the tail unit. The aircraft crashed into the ground upside down.

One report also described how the leader of a formation of sixteen aircraft led them into a heavy monsoon cloud. After barely three seconds within the cloud, the aircraft lost contact with each other, were flung about by the violence of the up and down currents. Their instruments were useless. Eight of them crashed. As a result, instructions were issued that any captain who suspected he was approaching a monsoon thundercloud should avoid it, or turn back to his last stopping place.

David was well aware of these hazards. But there were others. He was also concerned that, mainly for political reasons, the route was being hurried into use before it had been thoroughly investigated. He was particularly worried about the length of the runways and voiced his opinion that the one at Melsbroek in Belgium, being only 1,850 yards in length, was too short for Liberators. He was overruled.

Flying Officer Jim Glazebrook landed at Melsbroek from Oakington in the B24 J modified Liberator KK375, having flown from Oakington that morning. At Melsbroek he took on board a group of soldiers, recently stationed in Germany. They were being rushed to Palestine to strengthen the security there as Zionists and Arabs clashed with British forces. The soldiers carried heavy baggage and equipment and bulky souvenirs from their service in Europe.

Jim Glazebrook was told that he would be leaving an hour after sunset. Mindful that the Liberator frequently had a reluctance to rise off the ground, he asked if he could leave in daylight, as he was worried about taking off after sunset with so much weight on board, and so short a runway. He was told that this would not fit in with the schedule to get the soldiers to Egypt and then on to Palestine. He was further worried that no check seemed to be made of the amount of baggage that these soldiers were carrying on board.

He had evolved his own individual method for lifting off the Liberator by getting its nose in just the right position, but he could not judge this in darkness. He discussed his concern with his engineer, Frank Angel, who suggested that instead of the forty-eight inches of manifold pressure on the engines, he would try to produce fifty-two, which would give Jim that extra power on take-off. This the engineer succeeded in doing.

It was a damp evening with a low cloud base, but Flight Lieutenant Glazebrook managed to take off. Even so, he reckons that he took up every inch of the runway and some of the perimeter track so to do.

They reached Benghazi, landed there and the aircraft was taken on by the slip crew, while Jim Glazebrook and his crew awaited the next Liberator in, which was captained by Flying Officer Peter Green. It never came, having crashed on take-off at Melsbroek killing all the crew and the twenty-six soldiers on board.

CHAPTER TEN

THE SCHEDULE TO INDIA

David felt the loss of those lives keenly, especially as it was another occasion when he had pointed out a danger and been overruled. David argued for weight restrictions, especially as the Liberators, like many of the wartime aircraft, were already operating above the maker's maximum weight specifications. After the Melsbroek crash, weight restrictions were immediately brought in, but the Melsbroek disaster deepened David's determination to find out more about accident prevention.

Of that trooping, Squadron Leader Martin wrote at the time:

> 'We are off this afternoon to Brussels/Melsbroek to collect a batch of twenty-five troops destined for India. We shall feed the poor wretches into the converted bomb bay of our Liberator where they will sit in semi-darkness facing each other with their knees interlocked on two wooden benches running the length of each side of the aircraft. The one very basic loo is aft in the tail, and should any of us on the flight deck need to use it they have to pass us back and forth like parcels across their inter-twined knees. They will have some heating, but unlike us, no oxygen, and the longest leg of the trip, from Cairo to Karachi could take some twelve hours or more . . . Melsbroek is just tents and caravans as far as our trooping operation goes. Tea and sandwiches in a marquee, very cold, which makes the tea go through you like pouring it down a copper pipe, delay upon delay . . . depressing but determinedly discarded rumi-nations on the coming take-off with over 60,000 lbs up and only 1,850 yards of runway into a night like the inside of an especially opaque cow . . . an airman fitter in search of whom I had to walk a mile and pull off the wing of a Stirling, looked at our aircraft in the light of the floods and said, "Yes, you still have four engines. I'll sign them up as O.K."
> 'Such was Melsbroek.'

Also on that route, like many of the crews, David found the poverty and disease in India so much worse than even the Middle East. He often deprecated the fact that when his health card listed potentially

118

Left: Professor Ian Donald when 206 Squadron's Medical Officer. He later developed the technology used in U-boat hunting sonar for use in pregnancy scanning.

Right: Squadron Leader John Martin, A Flight Squadron Commander.

fatal diseases like cholera, enteric fever, smallpox and tuberculosis as widely prevalent then in Karachi, it also had a big stamp on it which read, 'The state of health in Karachi is satisfactory.'

Then too, the terrain they were flying over had its own peculiar dangers and difficulties. The crews were exchanging the wastes of the Atlantic for the wastes of the desert, and a forced landing on the desert had other perils besides heat and thirst. The tribes, enthusiasts in cutting the oil pipelines, were also enthusiastic severers of vital bodily parts and were so hostile to the West that the crews carried silk 'goolie' chits printed in various languages, bidding the finder of the hapless airmen to treat him well and a reward would be given. Bearing in mind that most of the tribes were illiterate, the goolie chits weren't of much use. A failing engine spelled a painful disaster and in the Mess at night the crews sang rudely and lustily about the Sheikh of Baghdad's friends and what they did with their pruning knives.

But the India run had its better side. The warmth of the sun was welcome after so long operating over the bitter cold of the Atlantic. Tripoli was an attractive airfield then, vivid with scented flowers, while Karachi was a happy shopping ground; beautiful silks, delicate silver-work and jewellery, and carpets were to be had at very attractive prices. Rarely did a Liberator return without its load of Indian carpets and rugs. David's parents, who had moved into The White House at

Dear Friend,

I am an Allied fighter. I did not come here to do any harm to you who are my friends. I only want to do harm to the Japanese and chase them away from this country as quickly as possible.

If you will assist me, my Government will sufficiently reward you when the Japanese are driven away.

FRENCH

Cher Ami,

Je suis un combattant allié. Je ne suis pas venu pour vous nuire à vous qui êtes mes amis. Je veux seulement nuire aux Japonais et les chasser de ce pays le plus vite possible.

Si vous voulez m'aider, mon Gouvernement vous récompensera généreusement quand les Japonais seront vaincus.

ANNAMITE

Cùng anh em Việt Nam yêu dấu,

Tôi là một quân đội Đồng-Minh. Tôi tới đây không có mục đích gì để phá hại đến chúng Annam là con thân của tôi. Tôi chỉ muốn phá hại và quất Nhật và đuổi chúng nó ra khỏi nước—Đường cho đặng mau chóng. Nếu các anh có thể dàn được cho tôi đỡ một gần tôi trợ binh của Đồng-Minh ; thì Chánh-Phủ của có sẽ ban thưởng cho các anh một cách rất xung đáng

HAKA

Ka Ko',

Kei-a ne Mirang ralkap ka si. Mi-hin nangua sifak pek awk ka ra o. Ka hoi-kom nang shi, Japan ra' tuk awk ka ra. Japan mi nang khwa ram in zok zok rawel ka du.

Zangfai on. n-ng-a Mirang in Amerikan ralkap ; um 'rak lam nai by k a nang ka kalpi a rhun, ka sao-za-ea laksawng a cam-pi pek lai

KACHIN

Khau Du n',

Ngai gaw Ingalit hypenma ral nga ai. Ashte gaw ma-hka hpe aru na jaw na matu sa n rai. Ahkwa Japani hpe Myar-mung kaw na shachynt kau na matu sa ni ai.

Khauni anhou Khau hpyenmasi dap de gadum ai lam kaw ra shargun dot yang, gumhpraw sungut awyani law law jaw na ra ai.

LAIZO

Ka Rual,

Keimai in Mirang ralkap kasi. Hinak nanmah tonca. peek dingah ka ra o. Ruala tha nan si. Japon ral ih, ronasi pezii ih, nar khau ram in zamcang tan dawi bia na duh.

Kanmah Mirang le Amerikan ralkap pawl um nak a rai bik ah zanglah ten in feh pi le, ka bawi pawl in laksawng tha a lo pe ding.

KAREN

[Karen script text]

BURMESE

[Burmese script text]

MALAY

Kawan,

Saya inkar pelak berikan saya tida datang sini besat bekin maana maana kita orang. Orang Sumatra (Malay) saya pasta kawat saya mow bekin soera gara orang djepen salja sesir de-ah dari negri lekas kalow kita taolong saya, saya pinta kompeni kawat perasa sama tuai, belah orang djepan sudh di-osar.

SUMATRA

Kepada tuean Jang terima.

Saja sold adoe Inggeris. Datang sini, tidak saja maoe menjoeakkan ta'abat saja orang Sumatra. Dengan orang Djepoen sadjaca, a berpersai sahingga di-dorair dar negeri Melaoe ini, Kalau tolong saja, kerajaan saja tentu memhalas hard. toean cenger djoekoep ia-doe tila orang Djepoen t-a haa, a di-halau.

TAMIL

[Tamil script text]

CHINESE

[Chinese characters in vertical columns]

JAWI

[Jawi/Arabic script text]

THAI

[Thai script text]

W. SHAN

[Shan script text]

E. SHAN AND N. THAI

[Shan/Lanna script text]

BENGALI

[Bengali script text]

Selly Oak Colleges where his father had been appointed Warden, were the recipients of a lovely pale-green Indian carpet for their sitting room and a white one for their hall. Some of the crews bought carpets for resale, making handsome profits. One crew member, subsequently a millionaire, is reputed to have founded his fortune on flying in carpets which he flogged in London.

206 was lucky in its squadron doctor, Ian Donald, who took a keen interest in the well-being of everyone in it. He insisted on flying the route to assess its effect on the health of the crews. He subsequently became Professor of Gynaecology at Glasgow University, and adapted what he had learned on the squadron about ASDIC, the sonar device for locating submarines, to invent the scan that is now so widely used on pregnant mothers. A few years ago, a Royal Mail stamp was issued to commemorate his work.

After several trips to India, David was asked to fly the station commander on a familiarisation flight to Karachi and to Colombo. The prospect of it delighted David because of the opportunity to visit Ceylon again.

The day they were to leave, in came a signal from Bomber Command to Oakington posting me to Headquarters Maintenance Command at Andover. Postings were always liable to happen. More so with the

Opposite: The 'goolie' chit carried by the crews promising a reward to tribesmen for an airman's safe return.

Right: David at Oakington.

121

advent of peace, the changing roles of stations and squadrons, and the general shifting around of personnel. But David and I were dismayed.

The Station Commander indicated that the posting should be cancelled. So the Station Administrative Officer, in charge when the Station Commander was away, immediately signalled Air Ministry requesting the cancellation. Sometimes Air Ministry would oblige, or allow a postponement. But mostly, they disliked their postings being questioned and this time they refused, sending a signal back that I was to proceed to Andover immediately.

Next day I was in the Station Adjutant's office collecting my railway warrant when I overheard something more worrying than a posting. A group of pilots were talking about a met forecast of appalling weather over India and Ceylon, and the weather lay more or less in the path of the Station Commander's Liberator.

He was not the most popular of Station Commanders and one of the pilots said cheerfully and hopefully, 'We might get rid of him yet!'

'Who's the pilot?' asked another.

'Beaty.'

They all groaned. 'Then we won't get rid of him. He'll be all right with Beaty.'

And so it was. After a very bumpy trip they landed safely in a tropical storm at Ratmalana near Colombo. Meanwhile off I went clutching my railway warrant without even the opportunity to say goodbye to David.

On the face of it, a posting to any Command Headquarters was a very desirable, plushy job, and would mean promotion, in my case from Section Officer to Flight Officer.

Headquarters Maintenance Command was in a grand country mansion close to Andover surrounded by stately, well-maintained grounds. The interior of the mansion had been made very comfortable – anterooms with deep armchairs, a plentiful supply of RAF issue rugs over the polished floors, and a general aura of good living.

The dining room was large and impressive. And on warm evenings, the doors were thrown open to the stone balustraded terrace and the formal gardens. White-coated batmen hovered around bringing the officers pre-dinner drinks on silver salvers. The terrace was usually full of the grey hair and gold braid of high ranking officers, all very kind and gracious to a new junior WAAF officer, but I straight away asked to be posted back to Oakington.

In charge of my department at Andover was a most kindly white-haired Air Commodore who, he told me, had four daughters of his own and had bitter painful experience of what his daughters were like when separated from their men. He sympathised with me entirely and therefore struck a bargain. If I would work really hard to get the particular assignment of the moment done – an assignment which involved helping evaluate redundant airfields and deciding which should be closed down – he would ensure I was posted back to Oakington.

We both kept our bargains. The job was finished in a month and back to Oakington I was posted.

Here a pressing difficulty had presented itself. The Liberator was an American aircraft. It required American spares. But with the surrender of Japan, on 21 August, less than a week after V-J Day, President Truman had announced the cancellation of all contracts under Roosevelt's Lend-Lease-Act, which had been until then a lifeline. The India route, with its variations of temperature and weather, the clouds and the sandstorms, was a particularly punishing one and there was a constant need to renew aircraft parts. For quite a while the stock of spares lasted. But just as they were running out, round came a stern directive to all station equipment officers forbidding them to indent for Liberator spares. Once their stocks were finished that was it. *Catch-22* had not yet been written, but it was a Catch-22 situation.

The Senior Equipment Officer at Oakington was a very laid-back and charming Irishman. He had a proposal to make. Namely that it might be worth approaching the Yanks at nearby Alconbury to suggest that as the RAF couldn't *buy* Liberator spares, would they consider actually *giving* us some of theirs.

Americans seem to like giving. They obliged, in the first instance, with some oil filters.

After the oil filters, we acquired from them a few airspeed indicators, oil pressure gauges, two wing tips and some navigation lights and antennae. Then, just as we were beginning to establish a fairly constant, albeit small, supply, we had a considerable set-back.

The Irishman was suddenly posted to another station. His replacement was a tall, studious ex-schoolmaster, Flight Lieutenant Dickinson, a highly intellectual but extremely cautious man who immediately announced that he was a 'by the book' officer. Rules were rules and not meant to be bent or broken. He was scandalized by this unorthodox method of obtaining spares. He feared that its unorthodoxy bordered on the illegal and it must cease.

However, he had his Achilles heel. It also turned out that he was a loyal Oxford man, indeed a Merton man, and when David dropped into the section, as he frequently did, for a cup of tea, Flight Lieutenant Dickinson chatted to him nostalgically about Oxford and fell under his spell. David always possessed the quality of inspiring enthusiasm.

Flight Lieutenant Dickinson gradually became as enthusiastic as David to maintain the squadron's schedule to India. However, that being said, he baulked at having to do any of the suspect negotiations himself.

Meantime the situation had become dire. Oakington was having to put aircraft on the Q form (a disgrace to any equipment officer) which meant the aircraft were unserviceable for no other reason than that they were short of the necessary spare. Reluctantly therefore, with much head shaking and many worries as to the deterioration of his own integrity, Flight Lieutenant Dickinson allowed me to take a van and driver to Alconbury with a view to scrounging whatever free spares the maintenance officers felt inclined to give.

We returned with a full van, and an invitation to repeat the process.

A basically very kindly man, Flight Lieutenant Dickinson wrung his hands and said he felt like an improvident father sending out his child to steal.

But it wasn't stealing. It was a gift from our Ally. The Yanks were generous and lavish, and they always had far more equipment than they needed. The fact that our government did not have the dollars at that moment to pay for the spares was a technicality. They wanted the men flown home from India. They wanted troops flown out to the Middle East. The aircraft could not fly if they were unserviceable for lack of spares. And the spares were close at hand and being generously offered.

Better still, many of the Yanks were about to go home, so the American stations were beginning to close down. Situated as we were close to other American stations dotted throughout the flat lands of East Anglia, we spread our net beyond Alconbury. Most of the hangars and huts and shelves and cupboards of these redundant stations were still full, and they couldn't take their spares with them.

In fact a massive house clearance was beginning on East Anglian airfields. Orders were given from the USAAF Command that stations were to deposit all unused spares on tips and then bulldoze them into the ground.

The idea of bulldozing precious spares was horrifying. So we contacted the stations pleading with them not to bulldoze, but to let us know when they had built their tips and we would come and collect whatever we could scavenge. All stations, including Alconbury agreed.

So for the next few weeks, suddenly there would be a phone call to say that if a large truck were to go to say, Number 2 hangar on such and such an airfield, they might find a tip containing something to their advantage.

Often, so great was the waiting pile that more than a single truck was needed. Alconbury at one time requested a Queen Mary (a long low-loader capable of carrying an aircraft fuselage) and several trucks, and on that occasion a whole caravan of vehicles trundled from Alconbury to Oakington laden with spares.

In the course of time, other stations similarly short of spares discovered our plan and immediately followed suit. As the USAAF departed, there were dozens of tips over which blue uniformed figures were scavenging like ants. Even now in old age, I can hardly see a tip without wanting to climb over it and search for the gleam of a possible spare.

The Americans were also generous in other ways. Believing that British service men and women were underfed, they often provided a hot meal, and it was their pleasure to seat the drivers and equipment assistants in the big base canteen while the cooks and anyone with nothing better to do crowded around to watch the spectacle of the hungry being fed. Following the meal there would be fistfuls of chocolate bars and chewing gum and sometimes wedges of pie and muffins to take away.

As the old Liberators flew backwards and forwards to India the need for spares became more urgent and the East Anglian sources began to dry up. I explored further. I was allowed unlimited transport from the MT section, and as David was in charge of scheduling the 206 training flights on Liberators, these could sometimes be made to coincide with the hunt for spares or the collection of those already unearthed.

Early in December, there were spares to be had at Ballykelly in Northern Ireland. David put himself on the detail for that Liberator flight and off we went to collect them. By some strange coincidence, besides the spares there was a fine load of turkeys all ready dressed and packed in wooden crates ready for Oakington's Christmas and these we loaded too.

As heavy winter rain descended and the airfield ground became soft, the urgent need at Oakington was for artificial runway – perforated metal strips, as had formed the runway in the Azores – to use as hard standings for the aircraft. But many other transport stations were similarly suffering from the soggy ground and similarly searching the length and breadth of Britain.

Finally, the only airfield that could provide any was found to be Orly, near Paris.

It was not an unpleasant discovery. For although the facilities at Orly still suffered from the ravages of war, most people were eager to touch down in France and see Paris after Liberation.

On 17 December, a training flight was scheduled to collect the artificial runway, and again David put himself on the detail. The WAAF Signals Officer, an attractive blonde, Section Officer Diana Colbeck, asked if she could come along as a passenger, and this David allowed.

We flew in J-Jig, which was one of the older Liberators and had seen considerable service. Watching the engines being run up, watching the engine cowlings shiver and shake, Diana and I thought it looked as if it were about to fall apart.

But David seemed satisfied. We taxied to the head of the runway and climbed up into the grey sky, bumping a little in the cumulo-nimbus over the Channel and then to a smooth landing at Orly.

The airfield looked disappointingly ugly and unreal – grey and muddy, and full of American personnel in jeeps and armoured cars further churning up the grey ground.

The artificial runway was located and signed for and, while David elected to stay with the aircraft and oversee the correct loading of it, Diana and I asked if we might be allowed to pop into Paris for a quick look.

Reluctantly, suspiciously, clearly against his better judgement, David allowed us two and a half hours to do so and off we set to thumb a lift. It could not have been easier. In no time we were experiencing the tremendous thrill of being in the centre of an exciting liberated Paris.

Diana had been to Paris before, but I hadn't. Even with the marks of war, or perhaps in a way because of them, Paris was magic. It was an historic time too, to see it. The people in those beautiful streets were bemused but friendly. And despite the difficulties, the grief and anger and dark memories of humiliation underneath, still revelling in liber-ation, still walking around in a mild euphoria. Slowly, still smiling at everyone, we strolled down the Champs Elysées.

Before we left Oakington, we had taken the precaution of buying forty cigarettes each from the Officers' Mess Bar. Now we marched straight into the first perfumery we saw. We were greeted with curiosity and courtesy. In our schoolgirl French, we asked if they would ex-change English cigarettes for French perfume, at the rate of exchange of forty cigarettes per bottle.

There was no argument. They were as eager for our cigarettes as we were for their perfume. Out came a large bottle of Dior for each of us. Each bottle was carefully wrapped and popped into a little carrier bag. Cigarettes and perfume were duly exchanged. Then we were bowed out, with more than an hour and a half of our allotted time still to run.

Unfortunately, it was more difficult thumbing a lift back to Orly than it had been in the other direction. Vehicles going there were few and far between. The sky had become heavily overcast and it had begun to rain. But eventually a jeep stopped for us. We clambered aboard. We asked the driver to take us right round to J-Jig's hard standing and we arrived, clutching our perfume bags, only a few minutes late.

David was standing beside the aircraft, absolutely furious. He lectured us both in no uncertain terms. Which was understandable. He had just received a horrendously bad weather forecast and was anxious to be on his way before the thunderstorms rolled up the Channel.

It was too late. Almost immediately after take-off, we were in the midst of a ferocious storm that rocked the aircraft this way and that. Diana and I were both scared stiff. We sat in the fuselage watching the sky blaze with forked lightning, the rain stream down the wings and the plates almost falling apart, feeling guiltily that this was all our fault. Also we couldn't help noticing that there was what seemed to be an ominous fuel leak that spurted out of the filler cap on the starboard wing and made an ugly little channel on it every time the aircraft rolled. I had visions of it flowing off the edge and being ignited by the exhausts. I considered pointing it out, but in the end I didn't dare to.

Instead I kept my eyes on the back of David's head, as he tried to hold the aircraft steady, and found it immensely reassuring.

When we landed at Oakington, he disapprovingly told Diana and me to declare our ill-gotten perfume to the Customs Officer in the makeshift customs hut where returning crews were supposed to declare their loot. This we apologetically did. Luckily, the Customs officer took the view that we had gone without perfume for all the years of war, so now he would turn a blind eye to this indulgence. He sent us away and told us to enjoy it. So we did. And so did David, eventually.

CHAPTER ELEVEN

GALLANT YOUNG
GENTLEMEN INTO FUSSY
OLD WOMEN

Some time before this, David had been gazetted to a permanent commission, and he was giving the matter serious thought. He never wavered in his determination to be a writer, but he had also learned to love flying and he wanted to travel, to see the world and study the people in it.

He had also applied to British Overseas Airways Corporation (formerly and again later, British Airways) and to British South American Airways, the creation of Air Vice-Marshal D D Bennett, the hero of the Pathfinder Force, a great navigator and the author of a book on navigation which was almost a navigational Bible. David had been offered a job as second pilot with both these airlines.

In the end, he decided to turn down the permanent commission although that would have been the more comfortable job. Partly, he turned it down for that very reason. The nascent civil aviation would be more of a challenge, in which he wanted to take part. Also he hated war. He wanted to pursue his own thoughts and insights and he suspected he might find the peacetime RAF too rigid. This suspicion was reinforced by the low-flying over Flamborough Head incident and also by another.

There was some controversy in *The Times* about the RAF. David wrote a letter defending the RAF, but because he was a serving officer, he had to submit the letter for approval before he could send it in for publication. The approval was withheld; he was not allowed to publish.

So he reasoned, as we discussed the matter together, punting along the Backs in Cambridge, or sitting in the Volunteer, if the RAF wouldn't let him publish a letter that was defending them, how much less would they allow him to publish any that were critical of them?

And how could a writer thus compromise his freedom from the outset? We both felt his freedom to write as he wanted was more precious than a comfortable career.

Then too, in that spring of 1946, the RAF began to change back into its peacetime image. Gone was the carefree, iconoclastic spirit that had characterised it in wartime. There were to be dining-in nights, greater attention to dress, no scarves and sweaters underneath jackets, more parades, more formality between ranks; in short, more bull, and David could see his freedom of expression being confined.

His friend and fellow flight commander, John Martin, also turned down his permanent commission. The group captain was round-eyed when they told him. He was so relishing his own permanent commission and had so enjoyed the comfort of Washington that he could not believe his ears. And, as he had exclaimed, 'to take on the growing pains of civil aviation!'

So having chosen civil aviation, David, to my relief, went on to choose BOAC rather than BSAA. I had seen and admired the press-on spirit of 7 and other Pathfinder squadrons, and been part of big station parades when we were addressed on that theme by Air Vice-Marshal Bennett, whom the crews regarded as only one ring lower than God. The press-on-against-all-odds spirit was marvellous and necessary in wartime, but to re-affirm Henry V, peace required other qualities. I was afraid that the press-on spirit might imbue BSAA and compromise its safety.

BSAA had begun as British Latin American Airlines – BLAIR – but had changed its name to British South American Airlines in 1945.

Its first services were with Avro Yorks and Avro Lancastrians, but in 1947 it replaced them with Tudor 4 airliners. The airline had difficulties with the Tudor and lost two under very strange circumstances.

However, both the North Atlantic and the South Atlantic were challenging and difficult routes, immensely fatiguing for the crews, and the loss of those two Tudors have remained a mystery.

In April, David was demobilised. He left the RAF with a further assessment of Exceptional as a pilot, which particularly gratified him as he had originally been such a slow, even mildly dyslexic learner.

As he was entering civil aviation, he had to sit the examinations in London for his B licence and Second Class navigation ticket.

David wrote:

'Even though fifteen years had passed since First Officers were called Mates, airline captains were still called Masters and a strong mercantile flavour permeated the hall in which I was examined. Dully lit, inadequately heated, the place seemed to smell of rope, tar, coal, sea water and twist tobacco. A bearded retired Merchant Navy captain regarded me solemnly over his spectacles and began to ask me searching questions on the lights shown by moored flying boats, tides and the rules of the sea.'

Meanwhile at Oakington, 206, the squadron which David held in such high regard and affection, was about to disband, although as it turned out, only temporarily. I was posted up to the RAF Maintenance Unit at Heywood, near Rochdale in Lancashire, a vast sprawling and ugly township of hangars and warehouses. Here David spent most of his demobilisation leave. With the war over and the greater part of its work done, this vast maintenance unit was being run down. The Officers' Mess was enormous, so David had no difficulty in being accommodated there. Most of the other officers went home at the weekends, as did the batmen and the cooks, so we had the run of the Mess with its big kitchens where we cooked our meals in ovens meant for hundreds. We went for long walks on the Lancashire moors, discussing David's novel, going to the cinema, and we spent one evening at the famous greyhound racing track in Manchester where we placed our money on a dog called Kittypaw, who, reputedly lame, came in at twenty to one. Altogether it was a few weeks' idyll until it was time for David to report to BOAC.

He signed on as a fully qualified First Officer, after six years in the RAF mostly as a four-engined captain, at a starting salary of £375 per annum and was assigned to the prestigious North Atlantic route which was then considered so challenging and dangerous that the crews received extra pay for flying it.

Even Winston Churchill was in awe of the Atlantic. After the Bermuda Conference in 1942, before he embarked as a passenger in the Boeing 314 flying boat, Winston Churchill wrote:

'I must confess that I felt rather frightened. I thought of the ocean spaces, and that we should never be within a thousand miles of land until we approached the British Isles. I had always regarded an Atlantic flight with awe. But the die was cast. Still, I must admit that if at breakfast, or even before luncheon, they had come to me to report that the weather had changed and we must go by sea I should have easily reconciled myself to a voyage in the splendid ship which had come all this way to fetch us.'

On this Atlantic route David would be flying, not like Winston Churchill in the bridal suite of the Boeing flying boat, but in the right hand seat of the very old Liberators.

The BOAC transport office at Heathrow in 1946.

The North Atlantic crews were based at Dorval Airport near Montreal, and as well as North Atlantic pay, the crews received a cost of living increment. After a while, North Atlantic pay became a source of envy and then intense irritation to pilots on other routes.

Only a few decades before it had been thought impossible to fly the Atlantic without help such as a floating platform in the middle, rather like an oil rig. In 1933, America had made plans for such platforms which were to be 1,000 feet by 300 feet, raised 100 feet above the sea by buoyancy tanks; they were to have, besides a runway, refuelling facilities, a wireless station and repair shops, even a hotel. David remembered seeing an exciting film as a schoolboy called *FP1, Flying Platform One*, starring Conrad Veidt, about terrorists trying to take over such a mid-Atlantic platform. However, during the war the Return Ferry Service flew empty aircraft to Britain and showed that the Atlantic could be flown without such a platform, with refuelling stops at Gander or Keflavik.

On 5 July 1946 David reported to a very primitive Heathrow Airport. The buildings consisted of an ex-RAF caravan which served as the transport office and a marquee for the passengers; all arrangements, all rosters were presided over by an energetic birdy lady of indeterminate age and immense efficiency called Minnie Mann. She knew all her crews and took all of them under her wing. In her house she had a dormitory for some of the younger ones, the only rule being no girl friends and, for all of the crews, no argument.

At Heathrow, David boarded Liberator AL 522, Yoke Baker, as a passenger for Montreal. In wartime he had spent many hours patrolling the Atlantic. He writes that the Atlantic was still the same dirty grey prison-clothing colour, flecked with the white arrows of waves breaking in the direction of the wind, as in his RAF days.

'Round about seven o'clock we began flying over icebergs. We crossed the rocky coast of Labrador and Goose Bay at 8.30. The sky was a magnificent raspberry colour, the air was like ice cold water, and Goose Lake was as calm as glass. The Mealy Mountains to the south showed up pale and luminous against the dark background of the firtrees. We had had a quick flight of 11 hours and 24 minutes, but now we stayed on the ground in the olive-green modern reception buildings, drinking endless coffee for nine hours, delayed with an oil leak. Even so, it was still light when we were overhead Montreal. The evening sun slanted a sideways searchlight beam out of a still blue sky. Looking out of the window, I saw the cross on the top of Mount Royal, the wide curve of the St Lawrence spoked by bridges. Five minutes later, doing a straight-in approach onto runway 28 (that is facing magnetic direction of 280 degrees), we were down. The whole trip had taken 24 hours and 28 minutes, but I was much too excited to feel tired.

'Like the Baines sisters of *The Old Wives Tale* before me, I had no inkling of my own minute place in history. There were two things I had to do next day and these I did immediately after a quick breakfast.

'The first thing I had to do was to get digs for myself, which I did with the Donnellys in Westmount, who welcomed me warmly, as Dan had been a pilot in the RFC during World War One. The second was to go to Macy's and, fresh from six years wartime rationing, order a steak and a double cream sundae.'

*   *   *

David had been fortunate in arriving at the Donnelly household. As well as Dan senior being an ex-RFC pilot, he was also, though a semi-invalid, a man of kindliness and wit. Lil Donnelly was a vivacious woman in her early forties and Dan junior a lively intelligent young man newly demobbed from the Army and studying at McMaster University. David and he struck up a lifelong friendship.

The three of them were the unquarrellsome part of a quarrelsome extended family which ran a trucking business. David was entranced by the accounts of the family's machinations, both personal and

A BOAC Liberator approaching Montreal carrying VIPs in 1946.

business, and their conversations and intrigues were grist to his mill.

He began on the BOAC course in local training and radio instruction at Dorval. The flying training was run by a Canadian, Captain Charlie Pentland, with whom David developed a strong love/hate relationship. The first thing Captain Pentland said to his pupils, all of them ex-RAF, most of them having flown in command, was, 'My job is now to turn gallant young gentlemen into fussy old women.' And this he set about doing.

In between simulator sessions and lectures, David took himself to the Westmount Public Library and there continued writing the novel he had conceived in the RAF.

When it came to the practicalities of having an aircraft to finish their training, there were problems on serviceability. Impatiently, the crews kicked their heels. David's feelings were mixed. He was anxious to get on with his training, impatient with BOAC for 'finger trouble' and at the same time grateful for the time to write.

Finally, in August, David made his first trip as a First Officer to London via Gander and Shannon. Years later, he described that trip in his book, *The Water Jump.*

> 'The most nerve racking part was at the beginning when over the R/T I was given our airways clearance. This was a complicated route out,

133

with heights and positions called out at breakneck speed in a Canadian accent from the Tower. It was the first officer's duty to repeat this back word-perfect even faster than it was received.

'I found it almost impossible, as did most of my fellow first officers. It was too fast to write, too long to memorise. Unless you had a pretty good idea of what your clearance was, you were, at any rate at the beginning, likely to stumble or not understand it.

'That August morning was blazing hot and the flight deck smelled of that peculiar Liberator smell – metallic, oily, petrol-sweet. In addition there was the flowery scent of the Captain's hair cream, for he carried a bottle in his brief case and brushed his hair regularly with it at intervals throughout the trip.

'While taxiing sedately round the perimeter, the clearance came at me with the unexpectedness of an ambush by machine-gun. I asked for a repeat – apparently a heinous offence. When it came at the speed of light, I repeated it back wrongly – an even more heinous offence. The Tower corrected me and the Captain repeated it all back, immediately and word-perfect – the most heinous offence of all.

'All he said to me was, "Wait till you get to New York."

'We carried a load of 4,000 lbs of freight and mail, with sometimes a staff passenger, a steward or sometimes the new genus of British aircrew, a stewardess, bedding themselves down on top of the mailbags in the icy draughty fuselage. The only Liberator with seats was Yoke Baker, now the training aircraft.

'At the end of the runway, the inevitable check on each of the two magnetos on each engine for a drop to show on the revolution counter – in ninety per cent of delayed flights the reason for piston-engined aircraft returning to the ramp. Then the four throttles would be advanced to 46 in manifold pressure, the brakes released, and we would be off.

'A slow climb over a different coloured Canada – parched olive-green in summer, blazing maple-red in the fall, glittering white with the St Lawrence a vast frozen diamond vein in winter – up to cruising altitude usually of 9,000 feet. Any higher and we would have to put on our rubber masks and suck oxygen, which nobody wanted to do unless absolutely necessary. The engineer would set up the throttles, revolutions and mixture for the most economical cruise, and then (he also acted as steward) he would deal out the ham and cheese sandwiches and the Canadian applecake which were invariably our rations, to the two pilots, the radio officer, the navigator and himself. Then he would pour out the coffee from the king-size thermos jar into the little white cardboard cups called in Canada "buttercups".

'These buttercups had another purpose. After drinking, a small amount of coffee was left at the bottom. Smoking was prohibited and

Above: A BOAC Liberator leaving the ramp at Dorval bound for Prestwick.

Below: A BOAC Liberator at Iceland during a flight to Montreal in the winter of 1946. Note the protective blanket to keep ice from forming on the wings.

consequently there were no ashtrays. So these buttercups became the receptacle for cigarette ends after a surreptitious smoke. When full, they were slung out of the window and it was said that there was no need of navigation. All you had to do was to follow the trail of buttercups and you would never get lost. So the Liberator operation was called the Buttercup Route.'

Meanwhile, I had been demobilised and had left the maintenance unit at Heywood and David came to see me at my parents' home in

Bradford. He brought with him ham and butter (which was still rationed) for our families, nylon stockings (in very short supply) and the chapters he had written of the novel. He read them to me, sitting on the moors between Keighley and Haworth. I was immensely excited by what he read. He was a born storyteller and has always had a strong narrative style. The characters, observed with a touching insight, came over with great clarity. The novel was so constructed that each character in turn gave a different angle on the plot and the device worked beautifully. We walked down to Haworth village and the Parsonage. It had then not been gentrified and Laura Ashley-fied and was still very much as it was in the Bronte era. I was more used to its strange brooding atmosphere, its damp black flagstones, its soot dark-ened church, the deserted steep and twisting streets, because it was a favourite expedition from school, but David found the atmosphere intensely powerful, the moors behind vividly evocative of *Wuthering Heights* and Catherine and Heathcliffe, and he longed to get on with his own writing.

After his initial trip as first officer, David flew to London as often as he could get on the roster. The autumn weather was rough. David had great sympathy for his passengers. As he wrote in *The Water Jump*:

> 'Roller coasting their way blindly through heavy turbulence, passengers were as sick as dogs. Not only that, they were frightened. An Atlantic storm still carried the punch of several atom bombs. The aircraft used to heave and toss, soar one moment, dive the next, heel over, waggle its tail. Beyond the grey wet cotton wool that fuzzed the portholes, to the tune of bottles and crockery crashing in the galley, passengers could just see the navigation lights going up and down like red and green ping-pong balls in time to the frantic waggling of the wings.'

Meanwhile I studied the situations vacant column in *The Times*. I applied for one of the newly created jobs of stewardess with British European Airways, and also for what I considered my real job and for which I had been trained, that of hospital almoner at St Leonard's Hospital, Shoreditch.

BEA responded first.

After an interview in London I was offered a place on their Number One Stewardess Training Course at Northolt Airport. Because life in the services engenders a desire to roam, I accepted the place.

BEA had no hesitation in exploiting the eagerness of girls to fly. After all, thousands of girls wanted to fly as stewardesses, while not so many wanted to wash up in concrete-floored kitchens. So every morning on the course we would-be stewardesses had to wash up the crockery from the staff canteen, the passenger restaurant and from the aircraft. When crockery ran out we had to clean silver.

In the afternoon, we were given lessons on aircraft and the internal combustion engine, first aid, appearance and the hierarchy of BEA. We were also taught company discipline. The catering officers, bent on empire building, tried to borrow from the services and insist that we stewardesses saluted them every time we met. We were taught how to serve a full silver-service meal although the aircraft only offered passengers a cardboard lunch box, containing a small sausage roll, two sandwiches and an iced cake. But regardless of that, we were supposed to learn how to carve and serve with a white napkin over our arm, and the serving of our elders and betters in the staff canteen formed part of the final examination.

So did several written papers and appearance. Hair must be off the collar as in the services, but much more make-up was allowed, even encouraged. Nails were frequently and humiliatingly inspected. There was very little about safety except evacuating the cabin. This evacuation was practised in the training fuselage, a wingless tube that sat outside the hangar.

With the examination passed, we were given our tailored navy-blue uniform suits, red, white and blue blouses with scarf ties, and an ugly tricorn hat. We were then allowed to fly. The aircraft were old Dakotas that had been flying throughout the war.

When David flew in to Heathrow, I had lodgings near Ruislip with an eccentric couple, a massive blonde lady and her five-foot tall husband. They lived in a modern bungalow imitation of an olde worlde cottage with diamond paned windows and thatched roof, all surrounded by a pretty picture-book garden inhabited by a tribe of red and green gnomes.

Inside there were distressed beams, chintzes and an enormous inglenook fireplace flanked by capacious log boxes. But though the bungalow was perishingly cold, the fire was never lit, and the log boxes were filled with brown Bols gin bottles.

In fact the lady, who had been a barmaid, drank prodigiously and had strange fantasies, one of which was that Princess Louise was daily threatening to come to tea and so the house must be kept immaculate. My landlady invited David to stay, lecturing him on the perils of damp beds in hotels.

But when he got into his bed, he found it not just damp but wringing wet and so cold that he had to sleep in his uniform overcoat.

When he left, she held his hand and, gazing piercingly into his eyes, earnestly promised him she would keep the radio on all the time so that she and I could hear straight away if his aircraft crashed.

That idea had probably been put into her head by a number of accidents which had taken place that awful winter. In a much publicised disaster, a KLM Douglas DC-3 taking off from Kastrup airport near Copenhagen crashed, killing twenty-two people including Prince Gustav Adolf of Sweden. The familiarisation flight which I and the other students were waiting for one snowy afternoon was postponed because the previous aircraft to take off had crashed on the runway.

These were early days for commercial civil aviation. Dakotas seemed to be frequently dropping out of the sky, and the lady had a great taste for disasters and drama.

So great that I decided I must move. Another stewardess on the course, a sad-faced girl, who had been among the first relief contingent into Belsen, recommended a bed-sitter she was just leaving in Earls Court.

My strange blonde landlady would have enjoyed the drama when a few months later a bomb exploded on a BEA aircraft, blowing a hole in the fuselage near the galley. I think it was the first time a bomb exploded on an aircraft. The stewardess was Sue Cramsie who was on the course with me, and she behaved with exemplary coolness and courage. But I had left by then.

CHAPTER TWELVE

THE WATER JUMP

My Earls Court lodgings were as zany as the Ruislip bungalow, but in a different way and totally benign. The tall Victorian house was in Redcliffe Gardens. Its neighbours had fared worse than it had in the war and the next two houses were now the rubble of a bombsite.

Within and without the house, maintenance had been minimal. Water pipes leaked, there were large holes caused by dry rot in the floors, the staircase balustrades wobbled, gas was piped to every room but it had been fitted by amateurs. The house smelled of gas and mice.

It was owned by a venerable old lady, who was letting it out into bed-sitters. She always wore a black mantilla, lived in the cellar and never emerged. She was surrounded by sporting newspapers and engrossed in backing 'the gees'. She was reputed to be one of the society belles of the pre-World War One era and with what little money she now had was supporting two impecunious army colonels who had been in her late brother's regiment. When they wanted a night out, they would come round the bed-sitters unlocking and emptying the gas pay-meters.

My bed-sitter consisted of one and a half rooms in the attic, plus the use of a squalid kitchen and bathroom on the floor below and here David came every time he flew into London. He always brought food and nylon stockings and once, for some reason, the most beautiful straw hat, extravagantly garlanded with red roses from Fifth Avenue; and most importantly, more chapters of his novel.

He had stuck steadfastly to his writing in the Montreal public library despite the attractions and hospitality laid on for the aircrew by their Canadian hosts who had taken them to their hearts. He did however go up to Sainte Agathe and learn to ski. It was a fashionable resort. There were skating and ski parties in the Laurentian mountains with film stars and pop groups, parties at the restaurants and in the hospitable homes where they were billeted.

The captains then on BOAC were mostly from the old Imperial Airways and were known as The Barons. Some of them behaved accordingly. Others, like Charlie Pentland, Bill May, Denis Peacock, O P Jones, Alan Andrews, Jim Percy, already a million-miler and Jerry McGinnis were natural pilots from whom the ex-RAF learned a great deal.

David was flying with one of the most intransigent and autocratic of the old barons, when, after take-off from London Airport, the captain complained furiously that his R/T set was dead. David, glancing sideways, saw that it was switched off, so leaned over as he would have done in the RAF and switched it on for him. Only to have his hand smartly smacked. 'I'll tell you when to touch anything, Mr Beaty!' the captain bellowed. 'Till then, sit on your backside, stay still and shut up!'

Inwardly seething, David sat in silence all the way to Prestwick where the captain, also seething, made a remarkably rough landing.

This time he left the flaps down.

Still obeying orders, David waited till the captain was about to clamber out of the aircraft. Then he asked, 'Shouldn't you raise the flaps, sir?'

The captain came back and hit him again.

Other of the ex-Imperial Airways captains liked to reminisce during those long cold hours over the Atlantic, about the old days when the Master, particularly of a flying boat, really was king. A guard of honour of station staff saw him on board.

'If things were not to his satisfaction there was hell to pay. One flying boat captain turned back to his point of departure because milk for his tea had not been put on board,' David wrote in *The Water Jump*.

The old Liberators had to fly through the weather, not above it as aircraft do today. But the pilots learned to cope with the Atlantic storms and learned from flying with the veterans. David's log reads like a roll of honour of pilots who made the water jump of the Atlantic as easy as it seems now.

He flew too with a much admired ex-RAF colleague, Squadron Leader Terry Bulloch DSO and Bar, DFC and Bar, the U-boat sinking ace of Coastal Command. Terry Bulloch, famous for saving the large convoy HX 217 by attacking, with the help of only one other Liberator, thirteen U-boats lying in wait for it.

In 1947, there were more courses to be undergone. Conversion to the Lockheed Constellation and training to first pilot, more hours in the Link trainer doing ADF let-downs and then preparing for more exams. There were never enough aircraft and instructors together and for much of the time the pilots kicked their heels impatiently, while David sat in Westmount Library either studying for his exams or writing.

The Constellation *Balmoral* over the Atlantic.

David wrote in his diary that he was thinking of dedicating his novel, if it were ever published, to BOAC without whose inefficiency it would never have been written. In summer it was written and he flew to London with it in his briefcase and sought out ex-F/Lt Green at Curtis Brown.

He went alone because I had left BEA and was now a hospital almoner (the modern equivalent of which is a medical social worker, except that we handled the money too) at St Leonard's, Shoreditch and hard at work.

Curtis Brown's office at 6 Henrietta Street, Covent Garden was opposite the Market, through a narrow doorway next to a cafe and then up a twisty creaking staircase. There he was told that John Green had left, but that his work had been taken over by a Miss O'Hea.

She was a tall, neatly groomed lady in her late thirties, very beautiful in a severe way and she received him cautiously, even discouragingly. She indicated that a vast number of people thought they could write when frankly they couldn't, that war books were very unfashionable and singularly hard to place and that all publishers were suffering from a shortage of paper. But she accepted his manuscript and promised that it would be read.

Several weeks later, while David had been working on Constellation conversion and command courses, Juliet O'Hea wrote to him at the Donnelly flat. Fearful that her letter might be as discouraging a letdown as her reception of him in London, he took the letter outside, to swallow his disappointment in private. He sat on a bench under the plane trees and opened the letter with trepidation.

The tone of her letter was quite different – warm, even friendly. She had included copies of two reader's reports, one of which said, 'Mr Beaty's manuscript is a dog's breakfast. But boy, can he write!' The other described David's novel as 'brilliant', the characterisation as 'outstanding', the suspense 'well maintained'. The only criticism was that the novel might be improved by an extra chapter to round off the end.

David agreed that an extra chapter might improve the book and wrote a letter to Juliet O'Hea setting out how he would tackle it. His friend Tom Collier, an ebullient ex-Bomber Command Radio Officer, who was about to leave on a trip to London, promised to deliver the letter in person. In the flat, the Donnellys celebrated in true Irish style.

David successfully completed his command course, and in the icy winter of 1947–48 became a junior captain under supervision doing route training before being given his full command.

For route experience two of the junior captains shared command. On the eastbound flight, one would be captain, the other the first officer. Westbound, their roles were reversed. Several times David shared command with his friend Jack Nicholl who was a first class pilot and who later became a very popular and effective training captain and after his retirement, manager of Kidlington Flying School.

Events were moving on the writing front too. Juliet O'Hea, having sent his manuscript to be professionally typed, was, she wrote, pondering over which publisher it should first be submitted to. David would have liked to send it to one of the large publishers such as Cape or Collins or Hodder and Stoughton, but she advised that they were very short of paper and that possession of adequate stocks of paper in these days of post-war shortage was the most important qualification.

She strongly recommended a firm called Werner Laurie who were, she said, bracketed with Hatchards and the best bet both for production and circulation. The fact that Werner Laurie was run by a notorious financier called Clarence Hatry was disturbing, because some time before he had been concerned in a very much publicised financial scandal, but that, Juliet O'Hea assured David, was a thing of the past; and anyway the scandal wasn't as the newspapers had made it out to be.

So to Werner Laurie the novel was sent.

On 16 February 1948, David flew Liberator G-ANYB from Montreal to Gander, Prestwick and London, and scarcely had he

Right: A Lancastrian tanker above David's Liberator whilst being refuelled over the Atlantic.

Below: David taking part in in-flight refuelling trials.

flown more than four further trips when the subject of Flight Refuelling arose. The Corporation had agreed with Sir Alan Cobham of Flight Refuelling to conduct refuelling trials over water for the first time with passenger carrying aircraft. By flying UK to Montreal direct, refuelling stops at Gander and Keflavik (necessitated by the strong headwinds) could be dispensed with. This, the Corporation considered, could be a possible selling point to passengers, enabling a much faster crossing.

Consolidated Liberator G-AHYG, an aircraft often flown by David, at Dorval airport, Montreal.

BOAC asked for volunteers. The response from the Barons was swift. They would have nothing to do with it unless they were paid danger money. David knew something of Sir Alan Cobham's unsuccessful attempts to sell Flight Refuelling during the war. He also knew that had the British Government accepted Flight Refuelling then, Coastal Command would have been able to close The Gap in the Atlantic in which the U-boat packs wrought such carnage and thus the lives of many sailors would have been saved. He volunteered.

He occupied another of his niches in history, when in March as the captain of one of the first passenger-carrying airliners he successfully rendezvoused over the Atlantic with a tanker aircraft. David's Liberator had been modified with a nozzle in the tail. This was connected by a hose to a Lancastrian tanker flying above and behind. At the given signal, fuel was sucked on board the Liberator through the hose.

There was at the time, a westerly gale blowing and the Liberator lurched downwards towards a sea full of white caps. David, never fond of formation flying, found it an extraordinary experience and somewhat alarming. He had visions of the hose parting and gallons of fuel falling. But he was impressed with the skill of the refuelling captain, who followed the gyrations of the Liberator meticulously. In a short time, refuelling was completed and the tanker wound in the hose.

David left the flight deck and went down to inspect the tail. There was a powerful smell of fuel, some of which was sloshing around the fuselage. But the refueller reported everything satisfactory and under control.

The next day a small paragraph in the *Daily Mail* recorded the flight as part of aviation history, and David did four more refuelling trips without incident. Of flight refuelling, he wrote, 'It was a novelty not to have to stop at Gander or Keflavik. To climb on board in the UK or Montreal and get out twenty-four hours later meant easier flying. It was exciting waiting for the first glimpse of the tanker emerging ahead of us and to call, "There she is!"'

When it was suggested that they should try refuelling at night over water David volunteered again. But the Corporation drew back. The Barons continued to oppose the whole idea of Flight Refuelling. No fare-paying passengers, they declared (probably rightly) would put up with another aircraft so close to them, in spite of having a shorter flight.

In any case, bigger aircraft with longer ranges were being built which would preclude much of the need to flight refuel on the Atlantic.

Meanwhile the Liberators were routed via Gander or Keflavik. The schedule was a long one; eighteen and a half hours eastbound, twenty-four and a half hours westbound via Keflavik, departing in the late afternoon from Montreal and the evening from London, in order to arrive at a reasonable time in both places. Of those trips, David wrote:

> 'Often, when the weather was bad, we would have to go up to 25,000 feet. There the heating was never adequate, the frozen-stiff passengers would be bedded down on the flight deck floor, and hour after hour everyone would suck oxygen. Cannonballs of ice slung off the propellers would crash against the metal sides. Sometimes the up-currents were so fierce that both pilots would be needed to level the wallowing wings. Mist often awaited us in London, and fog or snow was the usual Gander weather. Sometimes it was difficult to get in – particularly into Keflavik.'

He goes on to say that despite all that, those hours on the Buttercup route were some of his happiest of his flying life.

> 'We were given almost total independence. The little silver kingdom of the Liberator might lack many comforts, but it really was our world. Nobody ever questioned our decision. The mail and the cargo remained silent, and the staff passengers shivered but smiled. Every hour we would report our position, the wind and the weather. With the automatic pilot in and the four Pratt and Whitneys sweetly turning, the rest of the time was ours.
> 'Always before I had been scanning the seas for U-boats and the sky for

fighters. Now there was time to look around me, at the cloud cauldrons, at the dawns and the sunsets, at the icebergs polka-dotting the sea, at the eternally changing white-flecked greys and greens and blacks of the North Atlantic. Even the storms had grandness. Then the clouds were like dark caves which the blunt nose of the Liberator explored – sometimes setting off an avalanche of snow, or releasing a torrent of diamond hailstones, or a reservoir of rain, to come flooding down on top of us, making the engines sputter like damp matches and turning the view from the windscreen into the porthole of a bathyscaphe under the ocean, the Perspex covered with the phosphorescent eels of electric rain. Those were the days best to appreciate both the dangers and the beauty of the North Atlantic sky – when you were right there in its intestine.'

Those were the days, too, when he could appreciate the danger to which crews and passengers were being exposed by the sheer fatigue of the pilots, and the need for the study of human factors and fatigue became all too apparent to him. We used to discuss fatigue, what it was, how it affected people differently and how it could be guarded against, using the Earls Court bomb site next door as a garden where a pink ash of willow herb had grown over the shattered walls. We sat on broken steps, which made useful garden seats, and stood our drinks on the shelf of an old fireplace.

Then in October, back once again at the Donnelly flat in Montreal, David received a letter from Curtis Brown giving the news that Werner Laurie had made an offer, albeit a small one, for *The Take-Off*, and, full of excitement, he bought a car, a Mercury, and in this he drove to New York to seek out Curtis Brown and try to sell the American rights.

As with their English counterparts, their reception of the manuscript was cool, cautious, and totally unenthusiastic. But on that trip, mindful that he had set himself the task of becoming a captain before we were married, and that now he had achieved his goal, he bought yards and yards of thick oyster satin for my wedding dress.

*   *   *

My parents had by this time moved to Cheshire, so I had the material made up by a dressmaker in the village and we were married at St Philip's Church, Alderley Edge, on 29 April 1948. My sister, Jessie, was matron of honour. Tom Collier, David's close friend in Montreal, was the best man. It was a spring day. The sun shone, the blossom was out and we walked across the churchyard down a pathway edged with cherry blossom to a small country hotel for the reception.

David had booked a room at the Green Park Hotel in London for

Our wedding.

our first night before we flew to Ireland for our honeymoon. To his delight, the hotel was opposite the offices of Werner Laurie, and in the morning off he went to make sure they had his novel well in hand. After the rest of our honeymoon in Ireland, David had to return to Montreal for a navigation course, and to find somewhere for us to live.

As soon as there was an aircraft seat available, I joined him. The pilot was the famous Captain O P Jones, whose old hat David had been given when he joined cash-strapped BOAC, and which he wore with pride. David described him as 'well known for his piercing blue eyes and torpedo beard. He had been with Imperial Airways from the beginning and was already The Grand Old Man of Civil Aviation.'

The aircraft was a Lockheed Constellation. After much argument BOAC had been allowed to buy five of these in 1946. They were very beautiful, graceful aircraft and capable of reaching 350 miles an hour.

London Airport was still stuck in its birth pangs. Mud was everywhere. The departure lounge was still a marquee. The Operations office for the Atlantic service where Minnie Mann was still in charge had graduated to a wooden hut.

David met me at Dorval airport, with the news that he had rented a super duplex for three months in the town of Mount Royal, a suburb of Montreal. He was accompanied by Tom Collier and his pretty wife, Kathy, tall like Tom and very slim, an ex-police car driver now turned model.

We all drove off then in David's new Mercury, of which he was intensely proud, the first car apart from the £5 wreck in Ireland which he had ever owned. We raced along what seemed unbelievably wide smooth roads and in hot sunshine to inspect our first home.

The duplex was well designed and furnished with every comfort and every gadget. It was the first time I had seen a washing machine, the first time I realised that people in Canada expected to own a refrigerator, that constant hot water was something they took for granted. The plenty after the years of rationing and war was a revelation. I shopped in the first supermarket I had ever seen. I spent most of my housekeeping money sending food parcels back home to David's family and my own – joints of gammon, rich fruit cakes, tinned butter, sliced bacon and, of course, nylon stockings, and then gorging myself on banana splits and strawberry milk shakes.

Being on a course, David was studying all day, but there was still time to explore the magnificence of Ontario and to meet the famous Donnellys and the families of BOAC.

We joined the BOAC families in making hay while the Dorval sun shone. There were all kinds of parties, trips to the lakeshore, to night clubs, drives to New York, to the Laurentian mountains and, for the wives especially, Aladdin's caves of shops with no coupons required and nothing rationed.

But after a while a rumour began ruffling the feathers of those families. Another dollar crisis had burst upon Britain. The Treasury had cut the grant to BOAC. It soon became clear that the whole North Atlantic base would have to move from Dorval back to the UK. Filton, just outside Bristol, was named. There would be a cut in income for the staff because the dollar allowance would cease. The staff, who had taken to the Canadian way of life like ducks to water, did not want to go home.

When the three months in our duplex was up we found a white clapboard cottage, with a little verandah, high in the Laurentian mountains just outside the tiny village of St Sauveur des Monts, a close neighbour to the skiing resort of St Agathe. It smelled deliciously of new wood and was comfortable, but there were very few gadgets. Cooking was on a wooden stove which either died a death or blazed away at the whim of the mountain breezes. Heating was by another wooden stove with the same characteristics, but the setting and the views were stunningly beautiful. Below lay the village with its little blue and white

The Constellation G-AHEL flown by David. The photo was taken by him in May 1952.

The wooden cottage at St Sauveur in the Laurentians and our first car.

alpine houses and its dark clumps of pines. Behind us surged the maple-clad Laurentian mountains, turning each day into an ever richer red. The air was clear and cold and utterly quiet. Climbing to the rocks on top of one of the easier slopes, there was perfect unbroken silence, the loudest sound, the rasping of a dead leaf over the surface of the rock on which we sat.

The social life however continued. BOAC was its own community. Our house, near enough to Montreal to be quickly accessible, but far enough away to be like a holiday, became a handy drop-in centre for off-duty aircrew. A frequent guest was a like-minded first officer, Peter Gaskell, a good looking ex-wing commander, who loved books and

149

music and philosophy and was stimulating company. In appearance, he was almost the double of Princess Margaret's Group Captain Townsend. Like Johnny Martin he too had been stationed in the Bahamas and coincidentally, like him, he too had found favour with the Duchess of Windsor. Another frequent visitor was Tom Nisbet, a serious Scot, who as David forecast made it to the top of the civil aviation tree, another, a red-faced rumbustious engineer Ray Hodgson, known as Trader Horn for his intricate business dealings *en route*.

Then too, we found we were near neighbours to a well-known name in civil aviation, Captain Mike Carroll and his beautiful, witty Canadian wife, Natalie, and at the end of October, their baby daughter, Diana.

Mike Carroll had, during the war, been on the Return Ferry Service and so had invaluable experience of the vagaries of the North Atlantic. He had checked David out on the route and they frequently reminisced about hairy dos trying to land in Iceland and Newfoundland.

During the war, Mike Carroll had also flown on what was known as 'the ball-bearing route' flying Mosquitos from Leuchars to Sweden and collecting urgently needed ball-bearings. On his last trip to Stockholm on 6 May 1945 he had been instructed to refuel and fly the Mosquito to Gothenburg. There he was met by the British consul and introduced to an ageing courier from Denmark who was dressed in flying suit, helmet and carrying a brief case chained to his wrist. Mike was then told that the German armies had surrendered to Field Marshal Montgomery and Count Bernadot had brought the peace proposals across to Sweden in that briefcase. It was now Mike's job to get them safely back to the UK so that peace could be announced the following morning. This he did.

The German surrender was duly announced by Winston Churchill in the House of Commons on 8 May.

David was still flying the Atlantic on the old, cold Liberators, though a conversion course to the Constellations was looming. Looming too was the proposal to base slip crews at Gander to relieve the fatigue from which they were all suffering. And at almost the same time, the rumour of the move became reality. The Base really was returning to the UK. The reluctant staff was advised that they must leave by the end of 1948, after which the base would operate from Filton. The staff were promised that when they arrived, Bristol Council would allocate council houses for everyone.

As David was now studying on the Constellation course, which was still being held at Dorval, I travelled ahead of him to London in a

Constellation and thence by train to Bristol with Tom and Kathy Collier to lay claim to the promised council accommodation. We duly reported to the Bristol Housing Department, but because David and I had no children I was not allocated a house on the council estate at Brislington with the rest of the crews. The Colliers managed to scrape through for a house because Kathy had just discovered she was pregnant. But not I. The housing officer was very apologetic when he offered me just a flat instead. But secretly I was delighted. I knew David, who loved his privacy and had had enough of living in a community, would be too.

Our accommodation was the garden flat in an imposing semi-detached early Victorian house, 1 Downside Road at the top of Pembroke Road. (Later the house was used by the Bristol Old Vic Company as an acting school.) It looked out over Durdham Down and was in monkey-calling distance of Bristol Zoo. The monkeys and the peacocks could be heard like an extended dawn chorus every day. There was a semi-circular front garden bounded by a holly hedge and a crab-apple tree stood in the middle of a lawn.

The entrance was up a formidable flight of stone steps through double glass doors to an enormous lofty hall. The rooms were sparse in number but generous in size, with high ceilings corniced with vine leaves and grapes and, in the dining room, birds' nests full of fledglings with perching parent birds. All were filled to the brim with the dust and grime of a century.

It was extremely difficult to heat and there was no central heating. No hot water system come to that. There was a gas geyser in the bathroom, so I did the washing in the bath. But we had an interesting mixture of neighbours. We discovered to David's consternation that our neighbour in the garden flat in the next house, was Captain Andy Anderson, the flight captain, a dour Scot who was very much a management man, his attractive aristocratic-looking wife and a sturdy twelve-month-old son.

The tenants of the basement flat were a hot tempered ex-army prisoner-of-war who had been badly injured at Dunkirk, nursed and hidden by nuns, and then betrayed to the Germans by a pious nonconformist minister who believed it was wrong for the nuns to deceive the Germans. Our friend still seethed with resentment. He had a sprightly, good humoured wife and a querulous old aunt, with whom they were both incredibly patient. While in the top flat were a family who were the source of considerable interest.

Professor C F Powell of Bristol University was a nuclear physicist of the very first rank, who was deep in his work on the observation of mesons. A charming and compassionate man, he was a keen hill walker, a skilful cook and a relentless reciter of epic poems, his favourite being 'The bargee, 'is wife and 'is 'orse.'

On the frequent occasions when the Powells were entertaining students or staff or visiting scientists, Cecil Powell would be persuaded to give his recitation. Because the flats had been hastily converted from this lofty Victorian house and the top of our hall soared up into the Powell flat, we could hear each others' voices only too clearly. What touched us was that always it was Isobel Powell who loyally led the gusty mirth which this poem engendered. She had a very infectious laugh and our flat and theirs rang to the laughter that she led. We marvelled because she must have heard that poem scores of times, yet still her laughter was fresh and spontaneous as if hearing it for the very first time. That, David said, was true love.

Cecil Powell's sympathies were quite a way left of centre. Isobel's were the deepest red of the spectrum. She was the daughter of a World War One officer in the Austrian army. She was a forthright, kind woman and a committed communist. They had two very attractive and very lovable teenage daughters.

When we arrived at the flat in the winter of 1948–9, it had already begun to snow. The flat was freezing cold. The wheezing gas geyser that was supposed to heat the water failed to produce more than a tepid dribble. We had no furniture, not even a bed. Worse, we had no money to buy any.

BOAC in its wisdom had overlooked the necessity for sterling to be available to the staff it had just moved from Dorval, where they were paid in dollars, to Filton. An attempt to borrow money from colleagues was unsuccessful because all the staff were in the same boat and no one had any, so we eventually pawned David's silver cigarette case, which I had given him, and a few other items to tide us over.

In the next weeks BOAC lent us truckle beds and after several weeks arranged for sterling to be available.

That first Christmas David was rostered to take out the London to Montreal service on Christmas Day. The weather was appalling. At 17.20 on Christmas Day, while Heathrow was swept with a hail-storm, David took off in Liberator G-AHYB. They landed two hours twenty minutes later at Prestwick, and there they were stuck until New Year's Eve when they continued to Iceland, then Goose Bay and Montreal.

He continued flying the route throughout the winter and spring. The weather was wild. I used to hear it rattling the ill-fitting doors and windows and once when I went to church I heard it banging away dementedly at the west door, the west wind that outward-bound David would have right on his nose.

The Liberators were getting very old and suffering from such punishment that twice he had to return with engine trouble. Mindful of the problem of crew fatigue, he became active in BALPA and, elected onto the Filton branch committee, became secretary, hammering away at the subject of crew fatigue. A scheme had been introduced to slip crews at Gander; one crew took the aircraft as far as Gander where they handed over their passengers to the crew already there. They themselves rested until the next aircraft arrived when they took on their load of passengers. But this 'slip' was not popular because there was nothing to do at Gander except drink and play poker, thereby losing a lot of money, and when both those consolations became too expensive, to stare out at the snow.

Slipping at Gander was so much disliked that often crews would overfly the airfield, saying the weather was too bad to land, leaving the slip crew helplessly shaking their fists, before dejectedly returning to their drinking. There was a well-known ailment called 'The Gander Clangers', which afflicted the thus deserted crews; and if they didn't get the Clangers, they played too much poker and the more innocent sometimes lost the rest of their month's salary to more cunning players.

A distressed radio officer, newly married, confessed to Captain Pentland that he had lost all his savings in a game at Gander with a notorious poker expert. Captain Pentland, true to his rough diamond image gave him short shrift. He practically threw the radio officer out of his office, told him he had no sympathy and it served him right.

A few weeks later, Captain Pentland, himself an accomplished poker player, put himself on the roster and made it his business to have a game at Gander with the poker expert in question, soundly beating him, and winning back every penny of the radio officer's money for him.

It was David's knowledge of the character of Captain Pentland and his great respect for him that years later convinced him that the verdict of pilot error in the crash that killed Captain Pentland was unjust and needed much more investigation.

Then in April as winter storms were giving way to more benign Atlantic weather, David had to undergo a seemingly minor operation. The very elderly surgeon who performed it promised him that all was now well and David should have no more trouble.

But he did have more trouble and spent a week in hospital, though he was back on the route again immediately afterwards. The elderly

Liberators had been giving trouble too, twice David had to return to the ramp with Liberator YG because of engine trouble.

But 1949 was memorable for two events; the publication of his first novel *The Take-Off* to excellent reviews and, in September, the birth of our first daughter Susan. But some weeks later David had to go into the Bristol Infirmary for a series of very grisly operations.

CHAPTER THIRTEEN

THE HEART OF THE STORM

The medical care at the Bristol Royal Infirmary did not live up to the standards I had seen at St Leonard's, Shoreditch, in my almoner days. David's dressings were rarely changed, the nursing was haphazard, some of the nurses spoke very little English, the food was awful and, after his operation, he was put in an orthopaedic ward with the risk of cross infection. I contacted the BOAC doctor, Kenneth Bergin, a brilliant man, whose genuine concern for the pilots was only exceeded by his ambition.

David had been in contact with him several times on BALPA business, especially on the question of crew fatigue, and he liked him. Dr Bergin had a suave manner, a soothing smile and a keen interest in psychology. He had been a medical officer in the RAF and flown on several trips with the bomber crews over Germany. However, his ambition was to be Chief Medical Officer with a seat on the Board and so sometimes he found it difficult to stick up for the well-being of the crews and at the same time placate the penny pinching management.

On one occasion when a pilot was in Dr Bergin's office discussing a personal problem, the doctor's secretary interrupted to whisper urgently that an important member of the Board was on his way down to see him. Immediately, Dr Bergin leapt up, seized the bewildered pilot by the arm and bundled him into a large stationery cupboard where he locked him in. There the pilot stayed in some discomfort until Dr Bergin had got rid of the Board member. The doctor mumbled afterwards in explanation that it didn't do for the Board to think he was too friendly with the pilots, otherwise he would not be able to plead their cause.

But Dr Bergin immediately went to see David at the Royal Infirmary. He was horrified at the standard of treatment and brought considerable pressure to bear to have the nursing practices improved, for David to be moved to another ward and to have regular dressings of his surgical wound.

Those were not the days when much thought was given by airlines

Just landed! *Berwick II*, one of the BOAC Constellation fleet at Heathrow.

to the well-being of the crews or indeed any of the staff. The only communication David received from BOAC management was a circular to all pilots informing them that because of the need to economise there might be a number of pilot redundancies.

David needed more surgery and hospital treatment for several weeks. We found the very strict and very sparse visiting times irksome. But luckily an ex-WAAF friend of mine, Barbara Appleton, had become the warden of the nurses' home and she showed me the entrance to a disused underground passage which led from the nurses' home under the main road to the cellars of the hospital. So when David was allowed out of bed, on the pretext of needing to stroll down the corridor and stretch his legs, he would get himself into the service lift and we would meet for a few precious moments each day in the hospital cellars.

Once he had been discharged, and after a brief convalescence at home, David completed a Constellation command course and then began operating as a Constellation captain under supervision.

In July 1949, BSAA merged with BOAC, and David was sometimes rostered onto the long and arduous mid-Atlantic route. This was from

London to Lisbon, across to Santa Maria in the Azores, Bermuda, Nassau, Havana, crossing the infamous Bermuda triangle. Its infamy had not then been highlighted by popular mythology, but it was regarded as a challenge because of the headwinds and the hurricanes and the fact that it required considerable navigational skill to take off from the small island of Santa Maria, cross the Atlantic and pinpoint the even smaller island of Bermuda.

Once, approaching Bermuda from Santa Maria, David was so far blown off course by a hurricane and so short of fuel because of persistent headwinds right on the nose that he doubted he had enough fuel to land at Bermuda. He therefore sent out a Mayday. It was answered from Bermuda. Out came two aircraft carrying life rafts, which formated on either side of him until, with almost dry tanks, he managed to touch down safely in Bermuda.

The route was also sometimes extended to Caracas, Lima and a frequently smog-bound Santiago. Because of the length of the flight and the problem of fatigue, and because they were now carrying fare-paying passengers, a scheme was introduced to slip crews on this route too in the Azores and Bermuda, so that the crews could rest for two or three nights while the passengers were taken on by the next crew.

There was bitter argument over this arrangement. As with the Gander slip, the scheme lengthened the time away from home and, as most of the pilots by now were married with young children, they wanted to get home as quickly as possible.

It was while flying this route, at times so bedevilled by hurricanes, that David conceived the idea for his second novel, *The Heart of the Storm*. The plot was to be the shape of a hurricane, the circling winds encompassing the lives of the characters. It was a complicated plot that he had all worked out in his mind. But because he was a conscientious captain, and because the route was punishingly long and he was too tired in between trips, he didn't try to write it. The most he felt able to do were short stories, which the magazine *John Bull* regularly published.

But the novel remained there to be told, and all the time he was living the background to it. There is a sentence in Richard Ellmann's *James Joyce* which is particularly apt. 'The life of the artist differs from the lives of other persons in that its events are becoming artistic sources even as they command his present attention.'

Meanwhile, to add to the problem of crew fatigue and the arguments over the Gander and Azores slip there had been an argument among the pilots and between the pilots and management about North Atlantic pay.

The management, ever mindful of cost cutting and aware that North Atlantic pay was very unpopular with the crews who didn't receive it, let it be known they were intent on abolishing it altogether.

There was an immediate storm among the pilots on the North Atlantic route. Pay was very close at that time to the pilot's heart. Compared to that of pilots in some other countries their pay was pitifully small, and pitifully small compared to the pay of airline pilots today. It was said that pilots' conversation always comprised the three Ss. Salaries, Seniority and Sex. In that order.

So a BALPA representative from head office bearded Sir Miles Thomas in his office and received his assurance that North Atlantic pay would remain. They had his word for it.

Time went by. Then suddenly, BOAC announced that North Atlantic pay would be scrapped. Urgent meetings were again convened. The pilots were belligerent, but stopped short of a strike, which in those days they felt was unthinkable and even ungentlemanly.

Instead, they hit upon the idea that they would paralyse the airline by resigning. It was agreed that the first pilot to land after a trip into London Airport would immediately hand in his resignation. The next one would do the same. And the next, until all the Atlantic pilots had resigned, forcing the management, they hoped, to climb down.

As luck, or lack of it, would have it, the first pilot to land was David, and as promised he duly resigned. The next pilot did exactly the same. But so overcome was he by the enormity of what he had done that he went home and drank heavily. The next morning, still drunk, he was phoned by the management, who persuaded him to withdraw his resignation. None of the other pilots resigned, which left David holding the baby.

He asked to see Sir Miles Thomas. The management did their best to prevent this and instead, to pour oil on the waters, they offered David various inducements – interviews with intermediate officials, and when he refused these, Atlantic pay for him, but not the others. He indignantly refused and went on insisting that he see Sir Miles Thomas face to face. Eventually the interview was granted.

Over our kitchen table we rehearsed the interview he was likely to have; every conceivable question, answer and argument. Then David boiled down his argument to one single sentence. He refused to work for a man who promised one thing one moment and then did the opposite.

Spruced up, he presented himself. The interview lasted all of three minutes.

Sir Miles expressed utter astonishment. He could not recall his own exact words. But if he had really promised that . . . really promised Atlantic pay, then, of course, Atlantic pay must remain. There was no argument. He was a man of his word. So would Captain Beaty now withdraw his resignation?

Having found his position of one man against the whole of BOAC rather lonely, David was delighted so to do.

Other events were taking place on the home front. In the autumn of 1950, our neighbours, the Powells, told us that the professor had been chosen to receive the Nobel Prize for Physics. But there was one snag. Apparently a rule of the Nobel Prize award was that the prime minister or equivalent of the winner's country must approve the award. A Socialist government was then in power and the prime minister was Clement Attlee. But because of Professor Powell's pinkish politics, together with his humanitarian sympathies (he had flatly refused to work on the Bomb) and his wife's declared communist sympathies, left-winger though Attlee declared himself to be, he hesitated.

The press scented a story and moved in. They sniffed out that the Powells had some politically incorrect friends such as Nunn May, who had given (not sold) atomic secrets to the Russians when they were our allies and had been tried and imprisoned for it.

So the reporters surrounded the house. They hid in the shrubbery. They repeatedly rang the Powell's front door bell and ours, and wherever the Powells went they followed.

They had their minor uses. Whenever I pinned out the nappies, whenever I put Susan in her pram, whenever I tried to pull the pram up the steps, a couple of reporters would appear from the shrubbery to assist, in the hope of gaining access to our distinguished neighbours.

The Professor was due to address a small meeting of the Peace Pledge Union and he asked us to go along to support him, which we did. Professor Powell had expected an audience of about forty peace-loving people. Instead the hall was packed with reporters. Flashlights punctuated the entire proceedings and he was mobbed on his way to our broken-down old car, which we bundled him inside.

After that he was holed up in his flat, virtually unable to come out and late one night David had to act as intermediary. The reporters had said they would not leave until they got a statement, that they would sit it out all night if necessary. So upstairs David went and persuaded the Professor to write a short note which David took downstairs, stood on top of the steps and waved vigorously. Out came a hand, plucked the note from his fingers, and off the reporters went. At least for a while.

159

Finally, Clement Attlee came off the fence, approved the award, and the Professor, who was a superb cook, made us a celebration supper of pheasant and sausages and all the trimmings. There was also, of course, to be a university celebration, but in that we were much less popular.

When we first moved into our flat, Isobel Powell had allowed us to share the storage space in her large attic. Into it we had placed, among other things, David's old RAF uniform. We have never been the most careful of people clotheswise, and unbeknown to us, moths had been feasting on the uniform. Unfortunately the Professor's best academic gown was also stored up there and the moths had moved into this superior eating house.

I returned to the flat one afternoon from pushing the pram around Durdham Down to see the strange sight of a black, lacey, academic gown dancing on the clothesline. I thought it strange, but nothing to do with me.

Isobel Powell quickly disabused me. Hardly had I put Sue into her playpen than our door bell rang furiously. An enraged Isobel pointed behind her at the holey gown and promptly told me how it had become so chewed up by moths, how she had discovered the source of them in David's uniform and how the Professor would be publicly humiliated in his hour of triumph by my sheer carelessness, and why, for heaven's sake, did I have to keep the damned moth-eaten uniform?

I could think of no answer, no excuse, and no reason why. I was cornered. My dismay must have shown on my face, for suddenly her own expression completely changed. Now she was the one to look dismayed and apologetic. 'Don't tell me!' she sighed, putting a hand on my arm. 'You don't have to. I know. I've guessed. That was the uniform David was wearing when you fell in love with him.' Her eyes filled with tears. 'Of course you must keep it. Don't worry about the Prof. He can wear a patched gown. Forgive me for not realising!'

The gown was never mentioned again. The university celebration was a great success. So was the presentation in Sweden. We saw a photograph of Cecil Powell at the award ceremony, seated at the front of the stage flanked by fellow Nobel Prize winners, including Bertrand Russell. But happily then they were wearing dinner jackets, not academic gowns.

*　　*　　*

David continued to fly the route. Sometimes London, Prestwick, Keflavik, Montreal, sometimes London, the Azores, Bermuda, Lima,

Santiago. Sometimes flying to New York and then flying a shuttle service to Nassau and back.

On one occasion two engines failed on the flight to London, but the Constellation, whose engines were known to be marginal, was just able to maintain height on two engines and, with priority from Flying Control, David didn't need to divert and was able make a safe landing at Heathrow.

At the end of October 1951, he arrived back on election night from a particularly rough and stormy and lengthy Santiago trip just in time to drive me to the nursing home where our second daughter, Carole, was born. Those were not the days when fathers were encouraged, or in the case of that particular nursing home, allowed, to stay. David was sent home, and he was too exhausted after his trip to even wake when they telephoned to tell him the great news.

There was no fathers' leave either. He went out on service again a week later, a very long one this time to New York, then flying a shuttle between New York and Bermuda. While he was away my mother died. And due to the insistence of our neighbour, the seemingly stern Captain Anderson, BOAC flew out a replacement captain and brought David home as a passenger, for which I was infinitely grateful. David drove straight up to Cheshire, brought the children and my father and me home. But for Christmas David was out on service again.

My father had suffered a stroke the previous year and could not live alone, so, for a number of years, he spent half the year with us and the other half with my sister, Jessie. David's father had not yet retired. In the New Year, he wrote to say that the Reverend Small had heard from Edgar who, having come safely through the war, was keen to join Lufthansa when it was established. There were rumours in Germany that this would take place in the spring. Edgar had spent much of the war flying on the Eastern Front, and the two clerics in their innocence believed that this was because the Nazis didn't wish to make him bomb his compatriots in England. However, we later discovered there was a different reason.

Meanwhile David's first novel, *The Take-Off,* had now been published in America under the title *The Donnington Legend.* The change of title was purely because Thayer Hobson, the virtual owner of William Morrows, loved to name the books he published. It was rather like being their godfather, which in many ways he was. As with the British newspapers, the reviews were excellent. Reviewers like puns and catch phrases and one of the sound bites was, 'A brilliant novelist cleared for take-off.' David's American publisher, Thayer Hobson, wrote frequently asking when they could expect another novel.

David always wrote back to say that he had no idea, because, although he had the next novel very much in mind, he found he needed all his time and energy to fly his aircraft safely from A to B.

Finally, early in 1952, Thayer Hobson and his wife flew into London and took a suite at Claridges. They invited us to dine with them. Over a lavish dinner Thayer Hobson made a proposition. If David would give up flying for two years in order to concentrate on writing, he would pay him his BOAC salary. At the end of two years, David could either go on writing or return to flying, and if by any chance in that two years he did not succeed in writing anything at all, then there would be no debt.

It was a generous offer, but David hesitated. Writing was what he wanted to do more than anything else. He was desperate to write this second novel, and as Thayer Hobson pointed out, to build on the strong foundation of his first novel. But he now had family commitments. He had been in hospital for a series of operations; and like Saint-Exupéry with whom he is often compared, he loved flying, its challenge and its beauty and was interested in all its aspects, especially in the psychology of those who flew and how it influenced air safety.

We discussed the offer over the next few months, and finally David decided that Thayer Hobson's offer was one of life's opportunities which he shouldn't miss.

He extracted from BOAC the promise that he could re-apply to them should he wish in two years' time, and they would, all things being equal, take him on again. But understandably, it would be as a first officer not as a senior captain. They would not allow him to continue paying into his pension, so he had no financial net if anything went wrong.

Having resigned at the end of the summer, David threw himself into the completion of this second novel. It was a challenging one to write, but he was spurred on by the sound of aircraft engines above him, as his successor was trained to take over his command.

I kept the children as quiet as possible while he worked at the big mahogany partner's desk in the otherwise unfurnished dining room. That desk had only become his by the kindness of Mr Phillips of the famous antiques firm. We had seen it at the preview to an antique auction held by a different firm and it was one of the few things David had ever said he would like to possess. We therefore went to the auction, deciding to go up to what was a very high price indeed for us – £30. Once the desk went under the hammer, the bidding was brisk. Our chief contender was Mr Phillips and the £30 limit was rapidly reached.

David immediately stopped bidding. I promptly jumped up and bid £31. David, mindful of our financial situation, leapt up furiously and shouted, 'No!' Oblivious of the crowded auction, we argued fiercely and volubly.

Then it was the turn of Mr Phillips to get to his feet, and with a grandiloquent gesture, he smilingly bowed out of the bidding and the desk was ours.

David and I had always talked freely together, exchanged ideas, and experienced an almost uncanny mental telepathy. Occasionally, as he struggled with his novel, I made the odd suggestion. Once I made a suggestion at the wrong time; in exasperation, as Constellation engines thundered above him, David snapped, 'If you know so much about writing, why don't you do it yourself?'

Stung, I put the children to bed and reached for my pad and pencil. In the heat of the moment, I wrote a short story. When David had finished his writing for the day, I asked him to read it.

David was a man totally free of malice, jealousy or revenge. A lesser man might have said it was no good or damned it with faint praise. He didn't. Instead he was generously enthusiastic, and offered immediately to send it to Curtis Brown, his agents.

In the course of a couple of weeks, we received a letter from Dorothy Daly, Curtis Brown's short story editor. She too, was enthusiastic and confident of a sale.

The short story, *The Frosty Friday*, was sold immediately. It was a great moment. The buyer was the formidable Miss Biddy Johnson, editor of *Woman's Weekly* and *Woman and Home*. She was the only woman on the board of IPC and wielded considerable power. She told Dorothy Daly to get me to write more stories, and there being nothing like success, this I did.

Then, with the Powells' daughter's permission I wrote a story based on her complicated but beguilingly innocent love life. Dorothy Daly sold it to the *Toronto Star*, which meant that it couldn't be published here in the UK until the *Toronto Star* had used it.

Miss Johnson was incensed. She wanted to publish it at once, and she was used to having her way. So that this would never happen again, she offered to pay me the going rate of Canada and America (roughly three times that of the UK) if she could always be allowed to publish first.

This was agreed. The underpinning of our budget by these magazine short stories was very welcome, because David's novel was long and intricate.

Miss Johnson, who was becoming like a fairy godmother, appearing at exactly the right time, offered more. She offered to commission a full-length serial, each instalment to be paid at the American rate. It was generous pay indeed. And as Miss Johnson had a predilection for medical stories, and as I was familiar with a hospital setting as well as an aviation, she asked for the hospital background.

David was now finishing his novel, *The Heart of the Storm*. The background was of the mid-Atlantic route which he knew so well. Set to the swirling vagaries of a hurricane, the real storm capturing the tangled lives of those who operated the aircraft, it was a powerful story. But of importance to David was the fact that it illuminated the scandal of pilots being allowed to fly when they were too tired to fly safely because of no limitation on their duty hours.

BALPA was still struggling to agree Flight Time Limitations with BOAC. To make matters worse from the safety angle, the management were again considering turning the crew rest compartment into a mail locker to increase the payload, a possibility which David had always strongly opposed and which he wove into the novel.

This second novel, once completed, was under option to Werner Laurie, the publisher of his first. But, Juliet O'Hea informed David, the firm teetered on the edge of bankruptcy. They would be sure to turn it down but nevertheless it must go to them. Sure enough they turned it down and shortly afterwards the firm of Werner Laurie disappeared.

Again, David would have liked to submit the novel to one of the big houses, but Juliet had been asked by David Farrer of Secker and Warburg, to find him a really first class author, and in David she felt that she had found one. *The Heart of the Storm* was therefore sent to Secker and Warburg. David Farrer read it with delight and made an immediate offer. So did Thayer Hobson at Morrow.

Not so my serial. Miss Johnson had asked for a first instalment and a synopsis. I had never read a women's magazine serial before, let alone written one. But foolishly I had a go. I was not pleased with my first instalment, but I felt the plot would work out. It centred on a typhoid epidemic caused by faulty drains at a large general hospital very much like the one where I had worked in London.

A hugely disgusted Miss Johnson smartly sent my effort back by return of post. She described it with that worst and most humiliating of all adjectives, boring. Miss Johnson followed her terse rejection with another terse letter, which she ended with the advice, 'Remember! My girls want to read about young men, not smelly drains.'

Two days before Christmas, David received a cable from Morrow informing him that The Literary Guild was interested in *The Heart of the Storm*, but that they would require a change to the ending.

This was the beginning of a heated exchange. At that time a Literary Guild Choice was worth a great deal of money to both author and publisher, but David was unwilling to alter his work at the behest of a book club or a publisher. When he cabled back that he was satisfied with the novel as it was, and didn't intend to alter, Morrow cabled back immediately increasing the suggested advance.

Furthermore, they told him, they had gone to the trouble of working out the alterations. To wit, the whole of the last chapter should be scrapped; substituted would be a chapter of Morrow's devising, which allowed for a completely happy ending. That it was both psychologically and technically impossible mattered not.

David hit the roof. He refused to discuss it further. He was not going to have his final chapter written for him nor what it should contain dictated. This was as bad as RAF censorship. William Morrow were incredulous. They telephoned repeatedly with more suggestions and persuasions and daily increases to the advance.

Finally and mercifully we were given a breathing space when our telephone was cut off for non-payment of the bill. With a young family, money was short and we had no income other than the payment for my short stories and what was promised from Morrow, which hadn't yet come.

But Morrow and The Literary Guild had not given up. A cable arrived to say that Frances Philips, their Editor-in-Chief, would be flying over from New York especially to see David and discuss the matter.

At that news, for the first time, David paled. And when Frances arrived, I could understand why.

CHAPTER FOURTEEN

CONE OF SILENCE

Although over the years we all became more tolerant and gradually friends, Frances Philips was a formidable lady. Placing her large feet ponderously and firmly, she took command of any place she entered. She smiled frequently but her smile was not reassuring. It was wide and sharp toothed and her pale eyes didn't smile. She had a high intelligent forehead and silver-grey hair set incongruously in little curls. She had a habit of expressing disapproval by a disconcertingly loud sniff. She gave one of these loud sniffs as she slowly and disgustedly settled herself into our car, a very old Austin, whose once handsome leather upholstery was leaking at all seams and which refused to start until David pushed it and I steered it down the slight slope from Bristol's Temple Meads Station.

Frances had clearly thought out her strategy during what had been a bumpy flight over. She must separate us and soften each one in turn. With each of us, she became both the friendly and the tough policeman of well-known police strategy. She alternately expanded on the wonderfully warm place David occupied in his publisher's heart. 'We all love you, David,' frequently fell from her lips. When I repeated this to Juliet O'Hea, she retorted, 'They would love anything that would make them forty thousand dollars.'

Frances went on to describe the success that accepting this alteration would mean – the minor book clubs that would follow, the worldwide translations, and most of all pleasing Thayer Hobson, who after all, (getting tougher) it had to be said, was financing David. For David clearly had no money of his own. One only had to look at the decrepit car, the modestly furnished council flat, the ancient geyser in the bathroom.

Frances then produced yet another alternative ending for the novel. It too was totally unacceptable and technically impossible. David refused to put his name to it. We appeared to have reached an impasse.

Finally, the night before she was due to fly back to New York we

166

David shortly after leaving
BOAC.

returned to our flat after a mournful dinner with Frances, during which
we at least elicited the fact that the Literary Guild were still very keen
on the book but were chiefly worried about their Roman Catholic
readership. Would Roman Catholics read the ending as the heroine
having committed suicide and therefore be religiously affronted, they
had been asking themselves.

Together David and I sat down and re-wrote the last page of the
novel, not altering the facts, only the way they were expressed, making
the ending clearer and a little less subtle. We were working on the
principle that Frances should not be made to return totally empty-
handed. Her flight over had been bruited around the publishing
world in New York, and to return with nothing at all would, we knew,
humiliate her.

So as David drove Frances to the station to catch the train for London
and Heathrow, he presented her with a single sheet of paper on which
was typed the only alteration he was prepared to make. She read it in
stony silence except for her loud disdainful sniff. But she did at least
place it in her brief case.

The house rented in the main street of Tossa where David wrote whilst on the roof.

Two days later, another cable arrived. The Literary Guild had suddenly decided they would now accept *The Heart of the Storm* without the whole chapter being altered and with just the minor amendment David had typed out. And sure enough, as Frances Philips had promised, other book clubs followed. The novel was very successful worldwide, and so world coverage was given to the scandalous fact that there was no limitation on pilots' flying time. The book gave a boost to the demand for Flight Time Limitations which eventually came into being.

In fact, when the BALPA representative was negotiating Flight Time Limitations with John Profumo, the then Secretary of State for Air, he presented a copy of *The Heart of the Storm* to the Minister telling him that this set out the pilots' brief and the problem of fatigue better than anything else.

John Profumo took the novel home. Not only did he read it, but his wife Valerie Hobson, the film star, also read it. She was very enthusiastic and thought it would make an excellent film and set about trying to get one made.

Unfortunately she was not able to organise it before John Profumo was involved in the famous scandal involving Christine Keeler, Mandy

Rice-Davies, the Russian attaché, a psycho-therapist called Stephen Ward and the Cliveden Astors, in which Stephen Ward and John Profumo were the fall guys; and in which Valerie Hobson supported her husband most loyally.

Two options were taken out by American movie companies on the novel, but it was never made into a film.

When the novel was published, the reviews were gratifying. The *New York Times* said of it, 'Written with love and precision, the plot has the stamp of truth on it. The skilful shuttle of the four elements gives it greater depth. And Beaty transcends Neville Shute in that the ultimate concern is with human fatigue and frailty rather than mechanical failure . . . transporting his readers into the magic and separate world of flight,'

The reviewer in the *New York Journal* wrote, 'Aviation has come of age and here is a novel about it which also is mature and beautiful.'

The British reviews were equally good and the novel was translated into every European language and into Japanese.

With now a substantial amount of money, and due to leave the rented council flat in which we were living, we decided to seize the moment, find another background and try living in Spain.

We bought a new car, took the ferry and drove down through France in a cold but still sunny November. We had no clear idea of where we were going, except south. We had seen very little of Spain except Gibraltar, where David had landed several times, and we had both enjoyed a brief stay in Madrid, courtesy of a cheap BOAC fare on an old and rattling York aircraft.

As we drove southwards the weather improved. It was warm enough to picnic by the road. But as we crossed into Spain, those roads were hazardous. This was before Spain became a tourist Mecca and the road from Perpignan to Barcelona was reputed to have three hundred and sixty-five hairpin bends. The road desperately needed repair. Minor landslides littered the surface with debris. But having embarked upon it there seemed no choice but to continue even though the afternoon light was fading, and each corner seemed to disclose, like mountain climbing, a yet sharper bend.

But David was a skilful driver and we drove into the Costa Brava, which really was a wild coast then, as night fell. We decided to stay at Tossa, which was just a tiny seaside village with a beach enclosed by little rocky outcrops. There was also a small hotel almost on the beach. We booked a couple of rooms, pending a search for a house or flat to rent.

We found one tall precarious-looking house on the sand track that was the main street. It was owned by the widow Fabriguez, a sturdy deep-voiced lady whose face was always half-hidden in her shawl. She agreed to rent the house to us. She lived in a small shack at the back, from where she watched us like a hawk. She let herself in every day to inspect the kitchen and see if any dish had been broken and to march upstairs to find out if either child had wet the bed. The house had no bathroom and in Tossa at that time there was no electricity three days a week. Cooking was on an oil stove. But two doors further down the street was a bakery which made delicious bread, and every day in the tiny square was a fresh fruit and vegetable market where luscious fruit could be bought and creamy white cauliflowers for as little as a halfpenny. We persuaded the hotelkeeper to allow us an occasional bath and we drove regularly into Barcelona for more baths. David colonised the flat roof of the tall house for a precarious study, dragging up a table and chair and perching himself high above the street. The sun shone warmer than a British summer and life was good, with certain exceptions.

Spain had not fully recovered, either from its devastating civil war or Franco's fondness for the Axis powers. There was acute poverty. Wherever we went, as in a Third World country today, we were followed by beggars. We were told by a retired English nanny who had made her home in the little hotel, that further south it was even worse, with people dying of starvation.

Medical care was primitive. A youthful doctor, who, as the children pointed out, looked like a picture of Enid Blyton's Noddy, and lived in a house exactly like his, was the medical practitioner for Spain's nascent health service. He told us he had qualified at twenty, and his main medical interest lay with animals. He was responsible for their care, too. He couldn't understand how British doctors filled their time without animal patients.

And the third exception, life being more simple and yet much more time consuming, we had little opportunity to write.

Then one morning we heard a strange soft shuffling sound. From our high windows we saw that the sandy street below was filled with a seemingly endless procession of black-clad men carrying candles. The procession filed silently past, the men not looking to the left or right, the only sound the tread of their feet in the soft sand.

The Widow Fabriguez enlightened us. It was the funeral procession for a girl of thirteen who had just died and, as was customary, every man in the village was attending. The little girl had suffered great pain. The widow described the poor child's death of what would appear to have been acute appendicitis. The doctor had sat with her all day

170

consulting his medical books and finally sent her on that rough road round all those hairpin bends to the hospital at Gerona. There they had found she was menstruating and therefore refused to operate on her. She was unclean, the Widow Fabriguez explained. So back over that awful road they sent her to die painfully at home.

Feeling quite appalled – frustrated and guilty that we hadn't somehow known of this girl's plight, and mindful of the inadequacy of the medical services, we decided to take our family home.

*   *   *

Back home in England, we rented a furnished house from the monks at Worth Abbey.

We had come across the house by scouting around the various estate agents while we stayed with David's middle sister Margaret in Kent. She was married to the local doctor in West Malling and had two daughters of similar ages to our own.

Worth Abbey was the preparatory school for Downside. Many of the staff were monks, but they kept a furnished house, Worth Court, at the gates of the Abbey which was divided into two dwellings meant to accommodate lay masters. One half of this was vacant.

Number one, Worth Court, was a pretty, gabled house, tile-hung with a wide terrace at the back and a garden. The garden and the central heating boiler for the house were looked after by Jim, a home-less man whom the monks had taken in as a teenager and who in middle age had become a real power in the land. He was a meticulous gardener and stoker of the boiler and a kind, wise man. When the warmer weather came he would hose down our girls along with the garden. Another attraction was a racehorse called Honeymoon, owned by one of the monks which he grazed in the field at the bottom of the garden and which the girls were allowed to help groom. The monk, the racehorse, Jim and the girls formed a happy partnership.

And it was a good quiet place to write. Furthermore, at the gate was a tall octagonal tower converted to a house for an elderly gardener who had retired after many years at the Abbey. He invited David to make use of his attic for writing. There, David established himself with a view of the Sussex countryside on all points of the compass.

David had already begun on *The Proving Flight*, and at the same time, because this informed all his writing, more exploration of what he was to call human factors, and how those human factors were frequently exacerbated by fatigue.

171

Walking up from the lily pond at Woodside.

I wrote in the dining room. Miss Johnson had mercifully decided to give me another chance after the debacle of the hospital serial. She was tactful and thoughtful. She commissioned a longer short story with an aviation background. When she bought this, she suggested that I further develop the characters into another story and then having bought that, she suggested I make the characters into a full length serial. It was like teaching a child to walk, step by step. And she did this with great skill and patience. *Maiden Flight* was serialised in *Woman's Weekly* and immediately Miss Johnson commissioned another serial. Then another.

Our stay at Worth was a fruitful and happy one. The monks were courteous and kindly landlords. They had established a club in a building just outside the grounds for the benefit of the workers at the Abbey and for the village. They held sherry parties and occasionally dances in the hall of the Abbey to which their tenants were invited.

David was fascinated to read the history of Worth Abbey and discover, ironically, that the wonderfully peaceful lake had been used to test submarines and torpedoes before it passed into the hands of the Pearsons, of publishing fame.

David had finished *The Proving Flight* by the time our lease expired and we had to leave Worth Court because the house was required for a lay master.

After searching in a twenty-mile radius, we found a small house in several acres of garden, woodland and paddock, built in Kentish brick, with tall chimneys, oak-framed windows and bonnet tiles. Close to the house, but not too close, was a single-roomed wooden building with a verandah which the blurb referred to as a bothy. This David immediately colonised for his writing.

And as spring came, the verandah roof was colonised by swallows which delighted him.

Another unexpected delight sounded on a summer night. The rough woods of hazel and alder just beyond the end of the garden were filled with the unbelievably beautiful song of nightingales. They went on singing for several summers, then they must have fallen victim to the song-bird disease which was destroying so many at that time because we never heard them again.

Later on, the girls discovered to their joy that there were horsy people living opposite, and eventually, Patsy Richardson, the most plucky of riders and the most beguiling of blondes, opened a riding school just across the road. While our neighbour to the north, who had been a very correct, stiff ex-major in MI5, sold his house and land to a White Russian, an expert in icons, who made many mysterious trips to the USSR and whom the girls considered was clearly a spy.

Some time later, we acquired the pear orchard from our Russian neighbour. He sold it to us mainly because he had a problem. He had declared war to the death on the jays that damaged his fruit, making ugly beak marks when the pears were almost ripe; he had caught one of the miscreants in a large wire-netting trap which he had specially built. He swore to kill it, but when he came face to face with the bird he hadn't the heart so to do. He couldn't leave it to die slowly, so he fed and watered it; but he felt that to let it go would be a blot on his manhood. Caught in that dilemma, he sighed with relief when the land transfer was complete and said to David, 'Now the problem of the jay is yours.'

That was soon solved. David opened the cage door and out the jay flew, and on the land he had a large wooden hut built overlooking the fruit trees. Here he was far away from all household noises and disturbances, and here in the quietness he could sit at his desk and watch a family of foxes at play. They played safely. We didn't allow the Hunt over our little bit of land; a refusal of which, contrary to the recent

173

Above: David, Sue, Carole and Betty in the wooden hut where David wrote his third novel.

Left: David and Carole airborne over Walkenburg in Holland.

propaganda from the hunting lobby, the local farmers strongly approved.

Meanwhile David Farrer of Secker and Warburg had not greeted *The Proving Flight* with unalloyed delight. Having made a very healthy sum indeed out of *The Heart of the Storm*, he was, like most publishers, looking for something exactly the same with which to follow it. He wanted a weightier novel than *The Proving Flight*, although he acknowledged it to be well written, and the characters exactly right for the exciting plot. Not himself overly fond of women, he confessed to disliking having any women at all in the novel, and even suggested that David might like to re-write it cutting out the women. This David refused to do.

David Farrer's doubts were ill founded. *The Proving Flight* was very successful and was serialised here and in America. 'Mr Beaty understands humanity under extreme stress, and his prose has economy and poise. He can even keep you taut as he inserts sheer satire or a bit of underplayed comedy.' – that from the Book of the Month Club. The reviewer in the *Hartford Times* wrote, 'suspenseful, taut . . . even more satisfying for the reader, he understands the men who build and fly the giants . . . this surpasses his other novel of flight.'

David was particularly pleased that Elizabeth Bowen devoted a whole page in *Tatler* to *The Proving Flight*, describing it as the most exciting book she had ever read and praising his insight and masterly story-telling, finding him quite unique, '*sui generis*'.

Despite their difference of opinion, David Farrer continued to be a staunch ally and friend of David's and an excellent editor. David Farrer promised that he would never let David's books go out of print, for those books supported Secker and Warburg.

A fact of which Fred Warburg was not unaware. He expressed himself as a great fan, as did his wife, Pamela, a very dramatic lady in both looks and utterances. She declared that David was one of the very few male writers who really understood women. But Fred and Pamela Warburg hankered after the esoteric and sought it for their publishing house, and their great love was for foreign translations. Gunther Grasse was their ideal author.

However, they welcomed David's fourth novel, *Cone of Silence*. All David's novels had a well-spring of his insights and experience, but this novel came closest to David knowingly pursuing a cause and using a plot that was uncomfortably and dangerously near to the actual truth. It was especially uncomfortable for the makers of aircraft and the powers-that-be of airlines with the commercial aspect too much at heart, and dangerous for David because of the laws of libel.

Commercial aviation was still in its youth and those running it short of cash. They neither understood nor explored the impact of its technology on human beings. David's novels, gripping stories though they were acknowledged to be, had the supreme value of illuminating this impact in a way no other contemporary novelist succeeded in doing.

One of the results of this was that other pilots tended to come to him with their problems and grievances. He was already developing the theory that most aviation mistakes were due, not to lack of skill or training, but to basic human factors, that is, tendencies and weaknesses due to our genetic inheritance. The misnomer 'pilot error', which was nearly always bruited in the press after a fatal accident, was a particular anathema to him and one which he fought against all his life. When unjustly fastened onto a pilot, it was an excruciating burden for that pilot to bear. There was an old aviation saying, 'If the accident doesn't kill you, the Inquiry will.' And thus it had seemed so unjustly to work out.

The particular injustice which inspired David in *Cone of Silence* and which also enlightened him on yet another human factor, that of conformity, was the Inquiry following the Comet take-off accidents (the Comet explosive decompression accidents had a different cause).

In his book *The Naked Pilot*, David wrote of conformity in chapter 13 and names it 'The Three Headed Hydra', describing the first head as obedience to a possibly mistaken authority; the second as going along with other people's views rather than our own; the third, the excessive desire to please.

He writes: 'It was the first head of the Hydra, obedience to a possibly mistaken authority, which precipitated the Comet accident at Rome on 26 October 1952.'

*   *   *

At 17.56 that evening, Captain Harry Foote released the brakes of the brand-new, fully laden G-ALYZ for take-off at Ciampino airport, Rome, and opened up the engines to full power.

The Comet was the new wonder plane, the first civil jet aircraft in the world. At last, the British were ahead of the Americans in the aviation race, and already millions of pounds of orders had been placed with de Havilland by the world's airlines. The BOAC Comet fleet was an élitist group, and Captain Foote was a member who attended ritual monthly get-togethers at the local pub to foster good relations between pilots and management.

David at Gatwick in 1960.

Foote himself was a quiet, modest, soft-spoken man. After a distinguished career in the RAF where he won the DFC and Bar, Foote was to become an instructor – a job for which he was well suited, for he was very deliberate and methodical and did everything by the book. On long holiday trips through France, when his wife was driving as he rested, he would tell her the exact speed she should drive at and would immediately point out to her when the speedometer needle had fallen below or risen above that speed.

The Comet training manual on which he had been instructed had told him that on take-off the Comet's nosewheel should be lifted off the ground at eighty knots.

That evening it was pitch dark and raining. The wipers clanked across the windscreen to reveal muzzy blobs of runway lights, but there was no horizon. Slowly, into the damp darkness, the heavily-laden Yoke Zebra moved and began gathering speed along the slippery runway, bound for Cairo.

The needle on the airspeed indicator crept round the dial: 60, 70, 75 knots, 80 knots – the speed laid down in the manual to lift the nosewheel. Just as he had been instructed, Foote eased the control column back. The nosewheel came off the ground. The speed built up to 112 knots, the already correctly calculated unstick speed. Again Foote moved the stick back, this time to lift the aircraft off the runway.

Yoke Zebra inched off the ground. Foote called, 'Undercarriage up.'

At that instant, the port wing dropped violently. The aircraft swung left, then began juddering. Instead of rising, Yoke Zebra bounced back onto the runway. Everything appeared normal, *just the aircraft would not fly.*

The Comet appeared not to be responding to the controls. Its speed was not building up. And now the aircraft was rapidly approaching the red boundary lights at the end of the runway.

Foote's only thought was to save his passengers. He slammed back the throttles and tried to stop. Seconds later, Yoke Zebra was sliding over rough ground. Both main undercarriage legs were wrenched off. The wing broke. The aircraft came to an abrupt stop.

There was sudden silence. The reek of kerosene was everywhere. Although the first officer was injured, the crew shepherded all the passengers out safely and there was no fire.

The wonder plane was a write-off, yet Foote had obeyed the manual to the letter.

Following his description of psychological experiments on conformity, David goes on:

> 'After the accident there was an immediate outcry. Nothing could be wrong with the wonder plane. Hardly had the pieces been picked up from the ground, let alone examined or an Inquiry held, than the Ministry of Civil Aviation produced an interim report and BOAC and de Havilland issued a joint statement – all to the effect that they were satisfied that neither engines nor aircraft were to blame for the accident. They maintained that Foote had lifted the nose too high – there were tail skid marks on the runway to prove it – thus preventing the aircraft becoming airborne.
>
> 'Yet one of the things that does come naturally when flying an aeroplane (perhaps inherited from flying animal ancestors millions of years ago) is *not* to get the nose too high. It is possible that a pupil might do so, but it would be impossible for an experienced airline captain with 5,868 flying hours to do so *unless there was a very good reason.*
>
> 'The Ministry of Civil Aviation Inspector wrote to Foote saying that, as a result of BOAC's Inquiry, "blame for this accident has been attributed to you." The verdict was "pilot error".
>
> 'Foote was asked to sign a government form accepting the total blame. Wanting it over quickly and quietly, Foote signed.

'Retribution followed. Foote was formally admonished and posted to Yorks, the oldest BOAC aeroplane, used for carrying freight and exotic animals such as leopards and monkeys. Vast publicity in the newspapers highlighted his punishment. The Comet had been vindicated and could continue to be sold worldwide untarnished.

'Foote remained worried as to how he could possibly have got the nose so high, spending most of his time doing endless graphs and calculations.

'Behind the scenes, BOAC and de Havilland were worried too. The manufacturers had been doing further tests and a new take-off technique was introduced. The nosewheel had to be lifted off the ground at eighty knots, but afterwards it had to be placed on the ground again – a most extraordinary manoeuvre. When he returned from Rome, Foote found amended and undated instructions in his locker, but the training manual had mysteriously disappeared.

'On 12 February 1953, Captain Charles Pentland who had instructed me and my generation of pilots on flying the Atlantic, arrived in England to take delivery of a new Comet, *Empress of Hawaii* for Canadian Pacific Airlines. Like Foote, he was a book pilot. At de Havilland he received his training on how to fly the Comet. He was even trained how *not* to fly it by a demonstration of "the Foote take-off".'

'On 2 March 1953, on a hot, dark night at maximum all-up weight, Pentland tried to take off from Karachi – and crashed, killing all eleven people on board. It was a repetition of the Rome accident. Pentland, too, had implicitly obeyed.

'You would have thought that now there would be a vindication of Foote, but the Comet sales potential was too valuable for that. Instead, the Inquiry blamed Pentland, bringing in another verdict of pilot error. But now other people were voicing doubts. *The Aeroplane* stated that with two such similar accidents, such a mistake as lifting the nose too high "must be presumed to be easily possible".'

Frantic modifications were being made to the Comet. Pilots were calling for more efficient brakes and stall-warning devices. A question was asked in the House of Commons about the change to the Comet take-off technique. An inquiry was called for, but not granted. Foote tried unsuccessfully to explain to the Vice-Chairman of BOAC that he had discovered that the Comet could stall at higher speed near the ground than in free air.

Captain Jackson of the International Federation of Airline Pilots threatened to call a worldwide strike of 15,000 members every 3 March (the day of the Karachi accident) unless de Havilland, who had so far refused, now released information on the take-off accidents.

From the beginning, Captain Foote had sought David's help both to try to understand what had happened and to clear his name, meeting on numerous occasions to discuss the accident and that of Captain Pentland. Harry Foote asked David to write about the accident and the blank wall he had met afterwards in trying to get at the truth.

This inspired David to write his novel *Cone of Silence*, the title based on the radio range. A pilot flying to a destination receives radio signals telling him when he is to one side or another of the target. When he is exactly over the target, there is perfect silence, and this, the coning of the beacon is known as the cone of silence. When the pilot splits the silent cone with his aircraft, he has located himself. This was a theme very close to David's heart. Professor Forsberg quotes David as saying in an interview with her that for him the cone is truth, and on every level one knows truth by silence. And on a philosophical level, it is love that takes one into this circle where truth is found, where 'the tumult dies away'.

Similarly, in many situations when one arrives at the truth, there is silence. As Harry Foote found. So it seemed a particularly apt title for the novel that they both hoped would help clear the names of Harry Foote and Charles Pentland. Ironically, Captain Foote had an opportunity to demonstrate his superb flying skill on 1 September 1955.

David writes:

> 'He was piloting a York freighter to Bangkok when there were two sudden bangs and the aircraft swung to the right as both starboard propellers disappeared into the Bay of Bengal.
>
> The York plunged towards the sea. All freight, mails, tools and loose gear were thrown out in a desperate attempt to remain airborne, but Harry Foote, correct and calm as always, refused to jettison his suitcase, remarking that he always liked to change after a flight, particularly in the tropics. With no starboard engines and half the starboard elevator torn off, it was Foote's skilful airmanship that brought the stricken York safely down at Rangoon. This time BOAC could do no other than give him a commendation.'

CHAPTER FIFTEEN

VILLAGE OF STARS

David and Harry Foote continued to meet and ponder the cause of the accidents. Why, they asked themselves, had other pilots not experienced the same difficulties?

David eventually concluded:

'The conditions of high weight, high temperature, darkness and lack of horizon had been rare during the four months that Comets had operated before the accident. The only clue to correct attitude without a horizon was minute movement on the artificial horizon, not normally regarded on take-off, and the controls had only an artificial "feel" incorporated in them.

'Pilots have an intuitive idea of how to fly an aircraft. Other Comet pilots had realised that there was a ground-stalling problem. Finding it impossible in such circumstances to judge the angle of attack for take-off, they had not lifted the nosewheel, keeping it on the ground until almost at unstick speed.

'Richard Leakey, in *The Making of Mankind* writes: "The most notable characteristic of primates is opportunism." Here it was used for just that, and was stronger than conformity. The other pilots had *not* obeyed authority, trusting in their instinct. Not so the very correct instructors Harry Foote and Charles Pentland.

'Eventually a guarded statement was publicly issued to the effect that tests had "revealed a hitherto unrecognised feature that the stalling speed near the ground was higher than the corresponding figure in free air, and that the disparity increased as the aircraft weight increased. The safety margin at the highest take-off weights were thus found to be smaller than that indicated by the certification flight trials."

'Pentland was not cleared of pilot error. Neither was Foote.'

David was now more than ever convinced of the need for studying the human factors that lay at the root of aircraft accidents, a study that even pilots at that time greeted either with derision or with open hostility.

Cone of Silence had been accepted with enthusiasm by both Secker

181

and Warburg and William Morrow. When it was published, the press immediately leapt onto its similarity with the Comet take-off accidents. The press also contacted de Havilland. They and the aircraft lobby were very powerful. The government was behind them. It was rumoured that Churchill himself had decreed that the Comets should not be grounded, but should continue flying before the cause was clearly identified, because so many orders, so much money, so many jobs rode on the success of the Comet. Our telephone rang constantly with reporters anxious to make David say yes, this novel *is* based on the Comet take-off disasters, and David had considerable anxiety that de Havilland might try to sue him for libel.

They didn't. For although his explanation was not acknowledged, it was in fact the correct one. The novel was enthusiastically reviewed. It was a *Reader's Digest* choice which meant it would have a wide public. It was serialised in America and there was considerable film interest on both sides of the Atlantic.

There was also interest from Ted Willis, then the most prolific film and television writer of his time, who had produced *Woman in a Dressing Gown*, a very successful play and film starring Sylvia Syms and Anthony Quayle, *The Blue Lamp* and many other films. Ted was, of course, the creator of *Dixon of Dock Green*. Besides being a playwright and novelist he founded The Writers' Guild and fought vigorously for authors' rights. He approached David with a view to making *Cone of Silence* into a West End play. He had some intriguing and very innovative ideas for the adaptation, but it would all cost money. West End productions were notoriously risky and generously he advised David that if he could get a film sale then that would be better for the book and for David. And although the play idea did not come to anything, it began a lasting friendship.

The film rights of *Cone of Silence* were bought by Aubrey Baring, and he sought David's help to find someone in civil aviation who would hire him or lend him a suitable aircraft for the film. David had several helpful contacts in civil aviation including Sir Peter Masefield, who arranged for the loan of an aircraft called the *Ashton*. The story line fell neatly between the two Courts of Inquiry, and George Sanders accepted the role of President of the Court, a role he played to perfection. Gort, who was loosely based on Harry Foote was played by Bernard Lee, and the young training captain by Michael Craig. Elizabeth Seal, who was enjoying a great West End success in *Irma la Douce* was cast as Gort's daughter. Peter Cushing was the press-on flight captain and André Morell, the line manager. The film was directed by Charles Frend of *The Cruel Sea* fame. The screenplay was by Robert Westerby.

David visited the set. As a pilot who had learned the hard way to memorise difficult pieces of information thrown at him from Flying Control, he was appalled that the actors, in particular George Sanders, didn't know their lines, and remarked upon it vociferously.

Other matters were more urgently engaging his mind. After finishing *Cone of Silence*, David, before beginning on another weightier book, had written for light relief a wry novel, based on true events, about a young pilot's attempt to get his command, entitled *Call Me Captain*. It had caused an intellectual frisson at Secker and Warburg.

'Frankly,' David Farrer solemnly pronounced, '*Call Me Captain* would sit ill upon our list.' At the same time, David Farrer made very clear that Secker and Warburg did not want to lose David and of course if they declined any novel, contractually David could leave them.

In the background, Juliet O'Hea assured David that in the event of his leaving Secker and Warburg, there would be no problem. She had several publishers who were waiting in the wings to acquire his novels, and in retrospect it might have been better if he had.

But David decided to be generous. He would put *Call Me Captain* under a pseudonym, send it to another publisher, and still stay with Secker and Warburg for his David Beaty novels. Secker and Warburg were much relieved.

They were considerably less relieved when *Call Me Captain* was snapped up by Michael Joseph and by Morrow in America and serial rights sold, and their relief turned into hostility as the sales grew.

However, another interesting situation was developing. David had been approached by a very senior RAF officer, with an intriguing proposition. David had once worked under this officer so he was known to both David and me, but only as someone in a position of authority and not as a friend.

This officer told David that he had followed his career with tremendous interest, had read all his books, admired his writing enormously and shared many of his opinions. In particular, he shared David's opinion, one which David had written and spoken about, on the danger of nuclear testing, and the need for nuclear disarmament.

This officer had been in the RAF at Woomera and had been appalled at the dangers to which servicemen were being exposed, and further, at the very real danger of some of these nuclear devices malfunctioning, threatening a catastrophe of unimaginable proportions. He then went on to say that he could, if David wished, give him details of such an episode, one he had actually witnessed, when a device had malfunctioned and disaster had hung on a thread.

He himself had not the skill to write a novel on the theme and as a recently serving officer, now on pension, he would not be allowed to, but would David consider building a novel around that idea? With the success of David's previous books, such a novel should reach a wide public. He himself wanted nothing for the idea. Just that, for everyone's sake, it be written.

David and I talked this over at considerable length. Although we knew we could work and write together, neither was eager to take on an idea from anyone else. At the same time, the nuclear danger was close to David's heart and this officer's account of an episode so recent, an awful warning. Already in his mind David had the idea for a novel which explored the nuclear theme. He had often pondered what would have happened if he had accepted the permanent commission which he was offered at the end of the war. What would have happened if he had had control of a nuclear device? What would he have done if he had been ordered to use it?

Like many of his generation, he had a profound hatred of war and a determination to try to ensure that succeeding generations did not have to fight one. He felt that world governments were irresponsible, politicians too power hungry, that man's moral growth had not kept pace with his technical advancement and that the public were largely ignorant of the dangers that threatened them.

When the atomic bombs were dropped on Japan, many servicemen and women as well as many of the civilian population had been instinctively troubled. David's father, then a minister near Birmingham, had preached a sermon, especially courageous in that his three younger children were all on active service and his eldest was married to a naval padre. The text of his controversial sermon was that we had won the war, but we had won on a foul.

In the end, David decided to accept the senior officer's idea and to develop it into a novel. But only on condition he as author had an entirely free hand to write what he wanted, without alteration or suggestion or any interference from the officer in question. In fact, he would not even show him the manuscript until it was finished. When it was finished he would market it through Curtis Brown.

Then David, being always generous, added that although the officer had declared several times that he wanted no financial return whatever, David would give him half the royalties if the book were published. They then shook hands on their gentlemen's agreement.

Some time later, when David was obsessively deep in the novel, he received a hand-written note from the senior officer, asking if he would be kind enough just to sign this enclosed piece of paper, saying half the royalties would indeed come to him. It was merely to keep his accountant happy and of no importance. David, always vague on business and anyway totally engrossed in writing his novel, signed it blithely without even reading it.

*   *   *

David decided to call the novel *Village of Stars*, because the world at night looks like a village from the cockpit of a high flying aircraft and in this nuclear age, the world is a village.

David used a quotation from Antoine de Saint-Exupéry on the flyleaf.

> 'Only too well he knew them for a trap. A man sees a few stars at the issue of a pit and climbs towards them, and then – never can he get down again but stays up there eternally, chewing the stars . . .
> 'But such was his lust for light that he began to climb.'

Then David decided that, as the idea for the actual nuclear emergency had come from someone else, it wasn't a purely David Beaty book and that he would use the same pseudonym, Paul Stanton, which he had used for *Call Me Captain*. (He had adopted the name Stanton because it was the local railway station for RAF Oakington where we met.)

It was a very difficult novel to write. Much depended on the characters. The parameters of the plot were necessarily confined by the technicalities of the subject, and yet the moral implications were wide. But David possessed in his writing an acknowledged gift for explaining technicalities to the lay person and the novel came over graphically. This was confirmed by the two loyal part-time typists who, always giving an honest reader's opinion, helped us so much in those years – Joan Long and Billie Cooper.

Billie and her husband Joe, who had both come over from Argentina at the beginning of the war to join up, lived in the next house to us down the lane. Billie typed in her spare time, while Joe commuted every day to the Foreign Office where he worked in Accounts. They and their family, Peter, Jonathan and Helen were great friends.

Joan Long, who also did a heavy load of typing, struggling patiently, like Billie, with David's very tiny handwriting and his many alterations, also acted as a trustee for a small, and in retrospect rather pathetic little trust which we established for our daughters lest, in the way of so many writers before us, we fell on hard times and went bankrupt.

Coincidentally, the day after the complete and final typescript of *Village of Stars* was ready, we were visited by Sam Lawrence of Morrow, come to see how their author was doing. Sam was at that time Morrow's blue-eyed boy, a big handsome drawling socialite, comfortably rich, a close friend of the Kennedys. He regaled us with scandalous stories of the Kennedys, which we in our ignorance didn't at first believe, and which now years later have emerged as possibly the truth.

Although the following year Sam abruptly but catastrophically fell from grace, he was pleased that day to take the manuscript back with him. And within days, David had an ecstatic reaction from Morrow.

Michael Joseph also reacted promptly and enthusiastically. A *Reader's Digest* choice was almost certain, and in those days that was very valuable.

David immediately telephoned the good news to the senior officer in question, and was surprised that he who had said he didn't want any monetary reward, simply asked two questions, 'How much?' and 'What else?' He made no other comment.

But David was not unduly disappointed, and when later both his accountant and Juliet O'Hea, his agent, chided him for being absurdly over-generous in offering half of his royalties when David had done all the writing, he said he was happy with the arrangement, he wanted the subject bruited, and anyway by being possibly over-generous, he had done the officer in question a good turn and he would be another friend for life.

Those were famous last words on a subject over which for several reasons, a veil must be drawn. The acquisition of anything, least of all money, had never been one of David's priorities in life. Brought up in a frugal Methodist household, sufficient unto the day was indeed sufficient for him. And insightful psychologist though he was, he never anticipated finding greed or dubiety in other people.

Besides, there was now the excitement of a strong film interest, from Hollywood and here the Curtis Brown film agent, Hettie Hilton, came into her own.

She was a tiny black-haired, combative, and very clever woman who knew the film world and its wicked ways. She lived in a flat with several cats opposite Harrod's which was her corner grocery and was constantly wined and dined at all the best restaurants by hopeful film touts and publicity people, but she was not deceived.

She told us that Twentieth Century Fox and Paramount were both keen on *Village of Stars*, the former especially so because Alfred Hitchcock wished to make the film and had told them to acquire the rights. In fact, shortly afterwards he announced in the press that he would indeed make it his next film. Paramount and another film company were also very interested and Hettie, in her element with such a set-up, suggested an auction.

Twentieth Century Fox won the auction and paid a good price. David, once again joyously phoning the officer, received the repeat questions in reply, 'How much?' and 'What else?'

But worse followed. The officer then went on to tell David that he possessed half the copyright of the book, that he could say yea or nay to any deal and that for his own financial reasons he would if necessary exercise such power.

This was appalling news to David, who under no circumstances would ever knowingly part with the copyright or a share in the copyright of any book he wrote. His creativity and independence of spirit were too precious to him. A book and therefore the copyright of it, were parts of himself.

Then, it was discovered that in the handwritten little note, which he hadn't bothered to read, he had parted with half the copyright as well as half the money.

Next came even more disturbing news. The officer declared his intention of leaving Britain and taking up residence in Switzerland so that he paid no tax on whatever share he got. Apparently the Swiss government levies no tax on authors.

Hettie Hilton was visibly alarmed. She pointed out that any argument over copyright or tax would certainly put off the film company and the matter must be resolved immediately or the deal lost.

Matters got worse. David consulted his accountant and solicitor and finally the Inland Revenue only to be told that if the officer in question did leave the country, David would be liable for all the officer's tax as well as his own, even though he himself only received half of the money for the book which he had totally written. The solicitor advised getting Counsel's opinion.

The matter was still dragging on when the film of *Cone of Silence* was ready and had passed the censors with a U rating, which pleased the producers.

More encouraging still, David Farrer was told that Lord Rank was very keen on the film and wanted it for the Royal Command Performance. He had seen it several times and liked it better on each viewing. But, according to David Farrer, it was customary to alternate British and American films and this year was the turn of the Americans. So in the end, after coming very close, *Cone of Silence* was just the runner-up.

The film *Cone of Silence* at the Odeon, Leicester Square in London.

However, the Odeon, Leicester Square, was booked for its first night and it was a very glittering occasion – names in lights, cars and taxis drawing up with the cast in dinner jackets and beautiful gowns. There was only one discordant note. Fred and Pamela Warburg, mortified by the fact that such a successful novel had not been published by Secker and Warburg, refused to attend, and when Fred came to write his memoirs, cut David and his part in literally supporting Secker and Warburg throughout their difficult years completely out of them.

The reviews of the *Cone of Silence* film were good and plentiful. It was described by the *Sunday Express* as 'breathtaking', and by *Flight* as 'one of the best aeronautical films', although David considered it to be rather tightly packed and needing to be a half-hour longer. It was very well made and very exciting, with outstanding camera work, and even now appears from time to time on television.

One of its exciting moments was when the aircraft suffered from explosive decompression. The mask was torn off the pilot's face, everything flew around the cockpit and the whole crew were temporarily blinded by the force of the inrush of air.

A week after the first night, Aubrey Baring, to his horror, received a vociferous complaint from a firm making such masks threatening to

188

sue him for libel. Such are the dangers of film and novel producing.

Shortly afterwards, by painstaking argument, David and his advisers managed to rescue the other half of the copyright of *Village of Stars*, and although David naturally had to pay the income tax on his half of the royalties and the film deal, the officer in question departed for the kinder tax climate of Switzerland to enjoy his gains.

David returned to his writing of the novel which he had conceived before he was persuaded to write *Village of Stars*.

This novel, to be entitled *The Wind off the Sea*, embodied much of his philosophical thinking and of his own experience. It was also written around a human factor he had discovered because he had suffered from it himself and noticed it from time to time in some of his fellow pilots – laterality confusion, mixing left and right. In this novel he develops that confusion into moral choice. The book also relates to his own old imagined dilemma, what would he have done if he had stayed on in the RAF and been told to launch a nuclear attack?

Professor Forsberg, professor of English at Whittier University, the author of several books on David Beaty and Antoine de Saint-Exupéry wrote: 'David's powerful communication is here infused with a sense of urgency, of crisis in the affairs of men which is not basically due to the nuclear weapons. The crisis is the result of man's growing confidence in his own powers.' She compares the strength of his story-telling to Conrad, the lyrical beauty of his descriptions of flight to Saint-Exupéry and his social comment to that of Chaucer.

As he was writing the novel, our two daughters Sue and Carole tried to persuade David that the paddock which adjoined the garden was the perfect place for a donkey. A very loving father, he had already succumbed to numerous pets – cats, dogs, hamsters, rats, guinea pigs, rabbits, doves – all of which had appeared instantly to multiply and that being the time when the film of Dodie Smith's book, *A Hundred and One Dalmations* was hugely popular, he had threatened to write a book called A Hundred and One Damnations.

In the end, David compromised by unwisely entering into a game with the girls, the prize for which would be a donkey. The game was also designed to keep the girls quiet in the car without that dreaded litany – 'When do we get there? I want the potty, I'm hungry, I feel sick. I'm thirsty. She pinched me.' The game had only one rule. And one prize. They had to spot a full-size motorbike driven by a girl with a man hanging on behind. This was 1960, and although this might often happen now, it was very unlikely then. David assured me that the girls could not win. No man would be fool enough to ride pillion to a girl on a motorbike.

For several glorious months they didn't, and our daughters' behaviour in the car, eyes glued to the traffic on the road was impeccable and almost totally silent, except for the breathless question, 'Is that a man or a woman?'

But in the end, only a couple of miles from home they spotted the phenomenon, and David honoured his obligation.

Sue and Carole had a day's holiday from their school for the Feast of St Peter and St Paul and off I took them to Tonbridge market, where the girls chose for its sheer pathos and unmarketability, a forlorn grey donkey, with its bones sticking through its matted hair, clearly needing a vet and a good home. We acquired her against little opposition even from the meat men for the sum of sixteen guineas.

Unfortunately, she had been mistreated for too long and if she was grateful for a warm stable, a grassy paddock and plenty of oats and carrots, she had an inverted way of showing it. She kicked, she bit, she chased the children head down like a young bull; worse still she was a born escapologist; she could squeeze herself through the tiniest space to trot up the road and eat our neighbours' prize flowers and fruit and vegetables which were being nurtured for the Horticultural Show.

In the summer, we were persuaded against our better judgement to bring Honey to give rides at the summer fete at the Convent school. We warned Reverend Mother of Honey's wicked ways but she simply smiled seraphically and refused to believe us. All would be well. Donkeys were especially beloved by Our Lord and His Holy Mother. Honey would not misbehave. She herself would lead her.

It was a difficult journey, walking Honey to the Convent. She resisted every inch of the way, butting us, taking sideways kicks, nipping our arms. But once in the charge of Reverend Mother, she was all sweetness and light. All that hot afternoon she walked up and down the Convent pathways giving rides, without a bite or a kick or a butting, just gently nuzzling her nose into Reverend Mother's voluminous habit, giving her one and only demonstration of affection. At sixpence a time, the donkey rides were most successful money-spinners.

We discovered later that Reverend Mother had a large bag of aniseed balls in the pocket of her habit and that by the end of the afternoon the bag was empty. But when we tracked down and bought a large quantity of aniseed balls, they didn't work for us at all.

Honey's behaviour and how she became Public Enemy Number One in our normally tolerant village, David later chronicled in a book called *Milk and Honey,* which for some reason became very popular over here and in Germany and is still appearing there now under the title *Keep Smiling.*

190

Inevitably, donkeys were not enough, and abetted by our glamorous riding instructor neighbour, the girls graduated onto ponies and then horses. David was not very keen on horses, but he gamely rode out with the girls, through the woods and along the country lanes, returning one day with two black eyes after Sue's big Irish mare had taken exception to a milk lorry.

He made another concession to fatherhood. Having been a heavy smoker all his flying life – there being nothing else to do in twelve-hour stretches on the flight deck – he gave up smoking literally overnight. No patches, no nicotine substitutes, no withdrawal symptoms. He did this partly because of Professor Doll's researches but mostly because he wasn't going to smell disgustingly of stale tobacco when he kissed the girls goodnight.

Meanwhile all David's creativity was engaged on *The Wind off the Sea*. When it was published in 1962, *The Wind off the Sea* was a Book Society choice and the sales were excellent. It was several times top of the best-seller list and the reviews were enthusiastic.

The *New York Times* hailed it as 'magnificent'. The *Los Angeles Times* said, 'there is perhaps no one writing of flying today with more authority and understanding than David Beaty.' 'Sweeps us along to the bitter denouement,' wrote Martin Levin.

And like its predecessors, it was widely translated into German, French, Italian, Spanish, Dutch, Norwegian, Icelandic, Yugoslav and Japanese.

I had graduated from writing magazine serials to straight novels under a pseudonym. My first novel was published by Jonathan Cape and my second, set in the wartime WAAF and published by Michael Joseph, appeared later that year.

But both those events were outshone in the birth of our third daughter, Karen. And with her arrival, there came a change of step and a desire for further change.

CHAPTER SIXTEEN

HUMAN FACTORS

David decided that, having written consistently for the magic seven years, now was the time to return to the world. He was wary of the ivory tower syndrome wherein writers keep themselves apart, or establish themselves in writers' cliques, and concentrate on their creations, only to find themselves out of touch and out of communication with their readers. Besides, he had a complex personality. He had always said he was a mixture of a creative writer and a man of action, and this in many ways was his strength, the source of his understanding of his fellow pilots, and his ability to interpret them and their environment for people who had never left the ground.

As he was considering his re-entry into the world, he saw an advertisement for Lecturer in the Humanities at the Hamble College of Air Training. He applied and was offered the job. And there, as he was often to say, he learned far more than he taught.

We rented a furnished house at Dibden Purlieu on the edge of the New Forest, and David drove his battered old Land Rover every day to the College. It was in some ways an idyllic time. Our Dibden Purlieu house was comfortable and airy and had a lovely garden. The College was situated close to the river. But the set-up of the College shocked and alarmed David. What he saw hardened his resolve to study and write about human factors.

The selection process for would-be pilots was antiquated and, at a certain level, racist. They had difficulty, they complained, in recruiting the 'right sort' of student. The wistful story was told about the perfect student who had applied. He had an excellent education, an engineering degree, a private pilot's licence and wonderful references. But when he turned up for interview, horror of horrors, the man was black. Naturally they had to turn him down.

They also seemed to try to choose the students for their conformity, the very human factor which in his mind, David had identified as the precipitating cause of several accidents including Foote's and Pentland's Comet take-off accidents.

Then having chosen the students, the College set about confirming them in conformity. The students had to wear caps and blazers like overgrown schoolboys. Argument was discouraged. They lived in fear of failing the course, 'getting the chop'. Some of them were convinced there was a book where minor infringements and failures were written down, adverse marks recorded and when they reached a certain total, they were out. The students were meant to gobble up knowledge and when called upon at examination time, regurgitate it.

One of the staff remarked to David, 'The trouble is you can't get them to say boo to a goose.'

However, there were some excellent students and in the very limited way he could at Hamble, David tried to remedy this bias towards conformity. He tried to get the students to think for themselves, to evaluate a situation to take decisions and carry those decisions through, if necessary, against opposition.

He had, over the years read a great deal on psychology and as I had studied psychology at Leeds University, we talked about it constantly. David obtained copies of Civil Aviation Authority Accident Reports and studied them minutely. He had also kept in touch with several of his BOAC pilot friends including Johnny Willett and Jack Nicholl with whom he had shared command flying the Atlantic. He had great respect for them both. Jack became a BOAC training captain before taking charge of the Flying School at Kidlington. Johnny, the line manager, before becoming the Chief Pilot at Qatar. He learned a lot from them. He had also made contact with the Chief Psychiatrist to the Norwegian Forces, Professor Rolf Gerhardt, who endorsed David's ideas on laterality and conformity. Armed with his research, David gave lectures and seminars on psychology to the students, tried to get them to study themselves and their own weaknesses to prepare them for the unexpected emergency.

But it was not unlike the situation of the Dutch boy with his thumb in the dyke. The whole set up needed re-thinking and re-organisation. This was hardly surprising, since those running the airlines gave no credence whatever to psychology or the study of human factors. Accidents which did not appear to have been caused either by the weather or mechanical failure were deemed to be due to 'Pilot Error', a blanket term which David strove all his life against.

David began on a novel loosely based on such an establishment as Hamble, called *Sword of Honour*. But at the same time he took a very important decision. He needed to explore the human causes of accidents. As a novelist, many of his theories would be dismissed as flights of a novelist's fancy. He needed to return to university and study psychology and add academic reinforcement to what experience and intuition had taught him.

As he already had an MA in history from Oxford, he was allowed to apply for the psychology conversion course at University College London, open only to mature graduates. He managed to secure a place. The fees, of course, he had to pay himself and have enough money left over for his research and to support the family. He didn't attempt to get a grant. The money came from the royalties on our novels.

There were seven students on the course. Most were vividly diverse. All had degrees. All were clever or slightly mad. David was the oldest and the most iconoclastic, not hesitating to say that he found some of the teaching bad. The staffing suffered from the fact that some of them had obtained their degrees during the war while their colleagues were in the services, and David and his fellow students suspected that they had been allowed through their exams rather easily.

There were, however, exceptions, like Professor Drew and Professor Norman Dixon. Norman Dixon was a brilliant teacher and an imaginative researcher into psychological processes and an inspiration to David. He had certainly not obtained his degrees during the war. Far from it. He had been serving in the army on bomb disposal, had lost an arm in a serious incident and for his bravery received the MBE. He wrote brilliant books on the theme of our worst enemy being ourselves, others on military incompetence.He and David found a real meeting of minds and formed a close and continuing friendship.

He also formed friendships with three other students, a young, very intelligent and very outspoken young man Ben Hogan, who was an engineer with scathing opinions on motor industry mis-management, Ahmed Akhbar, who was to be the Professor of Psychology at Baghdad University, and who wrote down every lecture verbatim, translating each word into Arabic with a ponderous slowness which infuriated the lecturer, and Kerry Rice, a tiny, beautiful girl, exquisitely dressed, who was the daughter of the film star Gene Kelly and the step-daughter of Carol Rice, the film producer. She, David always said, was the cleverest of them all.

David found the course immensely difficult. The conversion course students had to sit exactly the same examination after nine months tuition, as the Honours Psychology students sat after three years full time lectures. There was no concession to age or experience.

A further difficulty was that University College's Psychology department was at that time in the grip of the Behaviourists. Times have now changed. But then, little that couldn't be experimented with and proved on rats, was held to be of value. Human reactions were off the map.

Furthermore, they spoke another language. David found as much difficulty in getting used to their specialised terminology as he had done repeating back Flying Control instructions on his first trip to New York. But he learned. Like his fellow mature students, he mastered the terminology and the Behaviourist teaching. He realised that they had consigned certain words to the semantic dustbin, that to use them was as offensive as a four-letter word at a Methodist meeting. Then for the final exam he had to resurrect his Matriculation French and to answer, as was required, one of the major questions entirely in French.

Having passed the final examination, the next step was to study for and write his M.Phil. thesis. As he was thinking about this, he was offered the job of psychologist to an Air Ministry team at long last studying fatigue in pilots. No assignment could have been more appropriate, been more to his liking or been more helpful for his M.Phil. thesis which he decided to call, 'Errors made on the flight deck. How far can fatigue be considered a factor?'

By an unhappy coicidence, some years after David had published *The Heart of the Storm* (in which an accident is caused by the pilot's fatigue, the rest compartment on board having been converted to a mail locker and the pilot having been on duty for over twenty hours without a rest), such an accident, similar in all those details, actually occurred in Singapore to one of David's ex-colleagues.

It had been a particularly harrowing accident. Most of the passengers had died. The stewardess, who could have escaped through a hole torn in the fuselage, nevertheless went to the back to help her passengers and was burned to death along with them. Most poignantly, if the passengers had gone to the front instead of trying to get out of the rear door, many more would have been saved, but shock had narrowed their vision. They had developed a mind set.

This same novel was the one the pilots had given John Profumo to read so that he might grasp the fatigue which the pilots had to suffer.

Although David had left BOAC he remained a lifetime member of BALPA and a lifelong contributor to air safety magazines. Now, through the Ministry of Civil Aviation, facilities were given David to test pilots for fatigue as soon as they landed from a flight. But, of course, at that time no means existed either for defining fatigue or testing for it.

Again David was allowed a free hand to devise tests which he considered appropriate.

This was where training and intellect and imagination met. David spent hours devising his tests for diminished alertness and other aspects of fatigue. The tests which he devised have themselves survived the test of time. Not only are his books being used as the basis for much Cockpit Resource Management, but his tests too. And now they are being widely used in this very year in Education.

At the time, however, the pilots accepted the tests with considerable reluctance, and at times, hostility. Wary of losing their licences and their jobs, they were suspicious of anything that might be written down and used in evidence against them, maybe at their six-monthly medical or simulator test.

But one bright eager pilot, having sailed through his tests with flying colours, then turned to David, announcing with relish, 'And I can also tell you – I have observed the hidden trick.'

'What trick is that?' David asked him warily, disguising his astonishment.

'You know! The one you don't ask us, but which we'll spot if we're really on the ball.'

'Which is?' David asked even more cautiously

Triumphantly, the young man pointed to David's ankles. 'That you're wearing one diamond patterned red sock and one plain blue one.'

David had not the heart to tell the eager pilot that it was my erratic dealing with sock washing and pairing and his own indifference to dress. He complimented the young man on his alertness and pulled down the turn-ups of his trousers to disguise his shame.

But of more significance than the acute observation of the clever young man the tests revealed an interesting pattern of diminished alertness in certain pilots. Furthermore, a diminution of which they were, in most cases, quite unaware. Another interesting fact was that fatigue also seemed to exacerbate the effect of other human factors such as laterality, mind set, conformity and the desire to please, and that clearly there was a whole vista to study.

Meanwhile, worn out by the frustration of being wrongly blamed for his Comet take-off accident, Harry Foote's health deteriorated. He died of a massive heart attack at the age of fifty-three. 'His memorial is now carried,' David wrote in *The Naked Pilot*, 'in jet aircraft throughout the world in the lights, horns and stick-shakers of the stall-warning devices.'

After David had finished his thesis and had it accepted, he decided to sit the examination for the Administrative Civil Service, that being supposedly one of the most difficult examinations one could take.

He had in mind that, if he passed, he might well be offered a job at the Ministry of Civil Aviation where he could continue his work on fatigue and human factors and make a significant contribution to airline safety.

He passed the examination, but in the unfathomable way of the Civil Service he was not offered a place in any Ministry of which he had prior knowledge. He was offered the post of principal at the Overseas Development Administration, an offshoot of the Foreign Office.

*   *   *

Although David knew nothing about Overseas Aid, he had seen enough of the Third World to be deeply concerned about its problems and felt this was another interest he could pursue with enthusiasm. The ODA office was conveniently close to Victoria. There was a reasonable train service on what was known as 'the push and pull' from Hever to Oxted and then Victoria, so he began commuting.

He found the Civil Service a revelation; as indeed he found all aspects of life, revealing, challenging and of unfailing interest. Perhaps the only thing in life he wasn't interested in was making money or any kind of self-advancement.

But because life at the Ministry was more leisurely and less responsible than flying, less difficult than the psychology course, it allowed him the time to continue his human factor study, and the salary allowed him to replenish our severely depleted finances.

Some time before he took up the job, he had finished *The Siren Song*, for which Pamela Warburg, who was very enthusiastic about the novel, had designed the dramatic jacket, the shadowy profile of a woman. William Morrow described it as 'a game of love played three ways', and Professor Forsberg comments, 'All comfortable amenities and eye-fooling beautifications are inexorably stripped down in order that the reader may see in their naked horror the amoralities with which modern man operates individually and socially.'

Secker and Warburg, and especially Pamela Warburg, had been delighted with it. David was forgiven for their not publishing *Village of Stars* and it came out to good reviews, as David was finishing his novel, *The Gun Garden*, a tribute to Malta. He was still studying human factors and amassing material for the book on them that he would shortly write.

Neither the RAF, nor civil flying, nor his psychological studies had prepared David for the Civil Service mentality. In one sense he found it more praiseworthy than popular programmes such as *Yes, Minister* would have one believe, in another sense, less.

Once, challenging his superior about the glaringly misleading minutes of a meeting which they had both attended, he protested, waving the minutes indignantly, 'This was not what X said. And certainly not what Y said. Nor Z for that matter!'

His superior pressed his hand gently on David's shoulder and replied soothingly, 'Well, no. That isn't what any of them said. But think of it this way, that is what all three would like to have said.'

At the same time David developed a quirky liking for the civil servants. In their own way they did their best, and were in the main incorruptible, conscientious and humane.

Working in foreign aid meant that he had some money to hand out. What amused David was how, now that he had this small cache at his disposal, the lobbyists and seekers-after-grants carved a pathway to even his modest door.

There were only small pickings that he could have handed out even if he had been minded to, which he wasn't. His responsibilities at the Ministry were varied. They included charities and town twinning plus a portion of overseas aid, which involved the sending out of experts on aid projects. David bitterly complained that he had been given a lot of old boots and wanted something to get his teeth into.

He was sent out to Africa to inspect some British Aid projects and returned angry and frustrated. He had seen television sets at schools in the jungle where pupils simply stared hopefully at the screen because there was no one who knew how to operate them or service them, and even if they had known, there was probably nothing being transmitted. He inspected the sites for the building of dams, much needed but held up by corruption, and the building of dams where they weren't needed or wanted except by the contractors making money from them. Despite his admiration for the youngsters Britain sent out to help, he felt that the aid, hamstrung as it was by being tied to trade, manipulated by big business and bedevilled by local corruption, rarely reached its target without much of it being devoured in the process.

After his visit to Africa, David was then requested to assess certain charities, with the object of getting these charities, which were supposed to specialise in overseas aid, to part with some of their cash and to work in tandem with the government. His cynicism deepened. One small charity in particular, which had been a one-off – i.e. it had come into being because of a much publicised human disaster – had amassed capital, the interest on which was just enough to pay the comfortable salaries of the administrators. Parting with any money on any project would mean those administrators would have to take a drop in salary. So they simply sat tight on their money.

Inspecting British aid projects in Latin America.

Shortly after his stern assessments of the charities, David was assigned a more congenial task – that of amalgamating the Centre for Educational Television Overseas, the Overseas Visual Aid Centre and a straight Educational Organisation into The Centre for Educational Development Overseas. For this project he had to find in himself considerable organisational and persuasive skills.

The government promised to find a large proportion of the money to underwrite the Centre and charities were asked to chip in. Next it needed spacious, but not too expensive premises, not easy to find in central London, a Board of Governors, a distinguished Chairman, an ethos, and most of all, a dedicated staff.

In preparation for it, David read and researched with his usual thoroughness and enthusiasm, especially on African topics, where much of their education would be directed. In the Foreign Office files he discovered a treasure house of information. He was in his element. It was not unlike allowing a chocoholic a free run of Cadbury's.

For CEDO's headquarters, David managed to rent some excellent accommodation from the BMA. Gradually a board of governors under the Chairmanship of Sir John Russell was appointed and an expert staff recruited. A film studio was equipped and set up in the basement. And the Centre was running by the time he had to return to ODA to take over the Latin American desk there.

The time setting up CEDO had been one of personal sorrow. David's father died in the summer. Vigorous and dauntless to the end of his eighty-seven years, he had taken a service at the local Methodist church the night before his sudden death. In October, David's sister, the closest to him in age, who had always been his great friend and champion in childhood, died, and the following January, his mother.

In what spare time he had, David threw himself into his writing.

The results of his study and research for his M.Phil. formed the basis for *The Human Factor in Aircraft Accidents*, which was published on both sides of the Atlantic. Strangely enough, as David often remarked, the reviewers and reporters were quicker to seize on the immense potential of its ideas, than were the managements of the airlines and indeed the pilots themselves.

David was asked to come on various radio and television shows. He was never a showman and disliked appearing. He disliked too, the fact that the interviewer always wanted the programme to be confrontational. To that end they usually recruited rather hidebound pilots whose contribution was to say flatly that pilots never made mistakes, and they most certainly did not want to probe their psyches.

Or if it wasn't a confrontational interview, then David was asked to come at very short notice onto a programme following some crash, in the hope that he would give a snap opinion on the cause. Again, something that was anathema to him. In no way would he presume to say why an aircraft had crashed.

Usually he simply refused these invitations. But some time after *The Human Factor in Aircraft Accidents* came out, he agreed to be interviewed by David Dimbleby, who had also invited a BOAC doctor and a captain from an independent airline. This pilot had declared himself totally unconvinced about the importance of human factors and all set to challenge the Beaty theories.

The first thing David saw when he went into the studio, was 'a black decapitated aircraft nose'. David Dimbleby introduced him to this monstrosity with the words, 'At enormous expense, the BBC have hired this Trident cockpit, so that you can sit in it and point out how easy it is to misread instruments and turn on wrong switches.'

Watched by the airline doctor and the other pilot, David duly climbed inside. He had only been inside a Trident cockpit once, but, bearing in mind that aircraft instruments were fairly standard, he wasn't worried.

Then he started to look round, and was immediately horrified. 'I couldn't recognise a single dial, switch, lever or gauge. It was as though I was in some Wizard of Oz aeroplane with wonky numbers and crooked needles.'

Meanwhile the Dimbleby programme was about to go on air. The cameras were moving in.

> 'I was wondering what on earth I was going to say to the watching millions, when suddenly I saw a knob on the instrument panel. Looking over my shoulder, the airline captain saw it too.
>
> On the knob were the words 'Bomb Release.'
>
> Suddenly enlightenment dawned. This was certainly no Trident cockpit. This was a theatrical prop from some film.'

In considerable indignation, David climbed out. He and the airline captain refused to have anything to do with the counterfeit contraption.

After that bad start the programme never quite recovered. David tried to explain that pilots made mistakes. The airline captain, also considerably put out by the start to the interview, simply said flatly that they didn't. Periodically the airline doctor chimed in to keep the peace.

But David was irritated and stressed by the interview. He hastened to the hotel where he was to stay. The desk clerk told him room 53, and handed him the key. Up David went to the third floor, put the key in the door – and couldn't turn it.

Even more irritated, he went down to the reception desk to complain. A porter duly accompanied him to the lift, clutching the offending key. Only this time he pressed the lift button for the fifth floor, marched down the corridor, put the key in the lock of room 53, and opened it smoothly.

David in his irritation, anger and fatigue had reversed the room number from 53 to 35. It was a small incident, but it reinforced David's experience that under fatigue, a hidden laterality asserts itself. Not too dangerous, though potentially embarrassing in a hotel, but possibly fatal on a flight deck.

Already he had discovered several aircraft accidents where the pilot had reversed the digits of a vital number, such as height above the ground, with fatal results.

In the chapter entitled 'Left Hand, Right Hand' of *The Human Factor in Aircraft Accidents*, David cites just such a reversal when the first officer of an aircraft flying to Nairobi asked for the setting to put on his altimeter for the aerodrome height at Nairobi (QFE).

Control told him 839 millibars.

The first officer set it reversed on his altimeter – that is 938.

Nairobi is 5,500 feet above sea level. By setting up a level almost 100 millibars higher than the true one, the pilot raised his height indication by 3,000 feet. Being three thousand feet lower than he thought he was, he hit the ground nine miles from the threshold of the runway.

A further accident in which both laterality and conformity were factors was the Kegworth disaster in January 1989, when a British Midland B737-400 bound for Belfast developed a fan blade failure in the port engine.

Asked by the captain which engine it was, the first officer replied, 'It's the le . . . it's the right one.'

So the starboard engine was throttled back, and later, to calm the passengers, the captain broadcast that there was trouble with the right engine and they were diverting to East Midlands airport near Kegworth.

Yet horrified passengers had seen the smoke and sparks coming out of the left, port, engine, but not one of them brought the vital discrepancy to the attention of the cabin staff.

CHAPTER SEVENTEEN

LATIN AMERICA

The Human Factor in Aircraft Accidents was enthusiastically received, especially in America. It had many reviews, numerous book clubs and write-ups in aeronautical journals. Gavin Lyall in the *Daily Telegraph* described it as 'A fascinating and frightening book'.

Of it the *New Society* reviewer wrote:

> 'Novelist David Beaty is a kind of Wilkie Collins of the air age. But this time Beaty's spine-tingling prose isn't fiction. His catalogue of air disasters all the more chilling for an avoidance of sensational adjectives is enough to send even a jet travel enthusiast by slow boat the next time . . . anyone who flies should be grateful (if also petrified) that Beaty, himself a former senior airline captain, survived his thousands of airborne hours to issue this warning.'

The *Morning Star*:

> 'His book attacks the official opinion that such human error accidents are inevitable. He provides an absorbing, cool but somehow exciting study of air accidents from psychological concepts.'

John Evans in the *Manchester Evening News* wrote:

> 'Although fatigue, frustration and decision-taking dilemmas are known to be part of the airline pilot's job, the psychological stress remains an almost totally unexplored area of understanding. The first attempt comes from David Beaty, a former senior captain with BOAC . . . his book provides a cool and often scientific appraisal of the human factor in flying. He suggests that if psychological factors were better understood and properly investigated, a considerable cut would be noticed in the now rising accident rate.'

David was given membership of the Royal Aeronautical Society, and in America made an honorary member of the Association of Aircraft Accident Investigators. He was invited to do a coast-to-coast promotion and become the Ralph Nader of civil aviation. Never fond

Flying round Latin America for the ODA.

of publicity, David baulked at this. But he continued his research for his next human factor book.

In 1972, an accident had occurred which was of particular concern to David. Trident Papa India of BEA took off from Heathrow. Take-off had been preceded by an argument in the crew room and communication on the flight deck was strained. The first officer was a very conscientious young man, a graduate of Hamble. The captain was, unbeknown to himself or anyone else, suffering from a severe heart condition. A number of factors then came into play. At some point, the captain suffered a heart attack, the stall-warning system was not working or had been switched off. The aircraft crashed at Staines a few minutes after take-off.

Geoffrey Lane, who had shared the same hut at Bibury during night flying training, was appointed Commissioner of the Inquiry. David sent him a copy of *The Human Factor in Aircraft Accidents* and they met and talked. Sir Geoffrey subsequently indicated not just one cause but twelve salient factors.

Meanwhile David continued with the administration of aid to his Latin American countries. He went on a trip to Latin America to find out the conditions for himself.

And because his remit was widespread, from Colombia to the tip of

Peru, the ODA allowed him the hire of a light aircraft. Strictly speaking he hadn't the licences to fly it himself, but as David had often flown Constellations over Latin America, the Peruvian pilot was kind enough to allow him occasionally so to do. David admired that pilot whose navigation was as instinctive as a bird's, finding his way along dry river beds between mountains, and who, undeterred by low cloud right down on the deck, always gave the same answer to any request, 'No Problem'.

Once again, David returned appalled by the size of the problem, the mixture of wealth and poverty, all exacerbated by the corruption – not only the corruption of individuals, or overt business corruption but the covert corruption of governments, including our own.

When David returned and was regaling me and the family with his account of Latin America, he suddenly said with great concern, 'We'll have to do something about the Falklands. If we don't, Argentina will invade.'

The family replied with a question. 'Where are the Falklands?'

A question that many people in this country might well have asked in the early 1970s and which was only too painfully answered at the end of that decade by the Falklands War. But why, one asks, didn't our so-called experts and our politicians realise that?

The foregoing was an example of David's acute clarity of vision. Another example of it was his great interest in Idi Amin of Uganda. Foreign Office files, an Aladdin's cave to David, had disclosed in his opinion, a potential monster. But the received wisdom among the civil servants and more emphatically among the government and the politicians was that Idi Amin was a thoroughly good chap and best of all *on our side.*

A delegation of MPs had visited him and been lavishly entertained, and very favourably impressed. One susceptible lady MP had gone so far as to nickname Idi Amin, 'The Gentle Giant'.

The fact that the bodies of Amin's innumerable victims were even then floating down the river as the delegates consumed Amin's food and drank his drink was neither mentioned, nor in all probability known.

David would later feel compelled to write a novel based on such a regime as this but there was other writing and other work that he had to do.

Firstly, a brief holiday visit to Ceylon, now Sri Lanka, had re-awakened his love for the richness of its culture, and sparked off a flying novel set there entitled *The Temple Tree.* As always with his novels, suspense and excitement with a vivid evocation of people and

David (extreme left) representing Her Majesty's Government at the Pan American Conference in Quito, Ecuador.

places, past and present, superstition and so-called scientific truth overlay a deeply felt philosophy. He placed centre stage the brilliant spectacle of the Perahera with its outer trappings of devil dancers, Kandyan chiefs in gorgeous robes, elephants clad in scarlet and gold, tom-tom beaters, conch-shell blowers, and milling crowds with, at its heart, simplicity and stillness.

The novel was a success both here and in America and was a *Reader's Digest* choice. The *Sunday Mirror* described it as 'A distinguished thriller, beautifully done.'

David was still at ODA. One of his next assignments was to be part of a three-man team representing Great Britain at the Pan American Conference in Quito

He decided to take me with him for a holiday. Sue was now working as an editor for Guinness Superlatives on a team with the famous McWhirter twins and Francis Mason, the authority on the Battle of Britain. Carole was finishing at college, and Karen, our youngest, was to stay with a schoolfriend and her family, who were also our friends in the village.

The afternoon, before the flight to Ecuador, as David prepared to leave his desk at ODA in reasonable order, suddenly there was panic.

It had been discovered that the diplomatic bag with the instructions on how the conference was to be conducted from the British point of view had not been sent to the British Ambassador in Quito who was to lead the team. The panic increased when it was discovered that the diplomatic bag was not ready and flared into shock/horror when it was realised that there was now no Queen's Messenger available to take the bag in time.

'There's only one thing we can do,' said David's superior officer, taking command. 'You must be made a Queen's Messenger. At once! Come along! We'll swear you in.'

Down the corridor went David, thinking all this was wonderful grist to his mill, and was duly sworn in as a Queen's Messenger.

When that was done, he was instructed almost on pain of death never to part with the bag, and never to let any unauthorised person read the highly confidential instructions therein. So valuable and secret was this bag that HMG would be paying for a special seat for it on the aircraft and there it had to sit. It must not be put in the over-head locker.

The empty diplomatic bag was then deposited in David's office, and all afternoon a procession of department heads and desk officers came in, discreetly and silently dropping into the bag their secret information. The last one would be the most important and over-riding one, the official Foreign Office instructions for David himself, the Ambassador and the other civil servant forming the three-man British team.

When all the instructions and information had been put in, the bag was sealed three times. The seals must remain unbroken until David delivered the bag to the British Ambassador in Quito. Then David's and the team's final instructions would be revealed to them.

Meanwhile as the flight was in the morning from Gatwick, David must take the bag home to our house at Hever and sleep with it beside him.

Five-thirty came on a wet, dark, blustery evening. David enquired if, because of the importance of the bag, HMG would now allow him the cost of a taxi all the way home to Hever. But no, that was not allowed. Would they allow a taxi to Victoria station, he asked? But that too, was vetoed. He must walk to Victoria station as usual and carry the bag onto the commuter train.

As usual the train was packed to the gills. It was difficult to find room to stand; certainly there was not a seat for a man, woman or child, let alone a diplomatic bag. Jogged, jostled, elbowed and banged, its bulk glared at by fellow commuters who vociferously demanded that it be put up on the rack, the bag arrived safely at Hever station.

Here I usually picked up David in the car. That night, he was not the only passenger to alight. Out of the next compartment stepped our neighbour, the Russian icon expert whom the girls suspected of being a spy. As he had no one to meet him, I naturally offered him a lift, and off we all drove. Disappointingly, he showed no interest whatsoever in the bag sitting beside him. Safely home, the bag slept beside us that night on the bedroom floor.

The twice-weekly British Caledonian flight from Gatwick did not go direct to Quito. It only flew as far as Bogota in Colombia where we must stay overnight and then board the local Avianca flight to Quito. For this flight, British Caledonian had overbooked. There was a near riot when it was seen that a bag was occupying a seat that could have been used by an about-to-be-bumped passenger.

Peremptorily, the frazzled stewardess told David to remove the bag at once from the seat and put it in the overhead locker like everybody else. He refused. She was vociferously supported by would-be passengers. The captain was asked to intercede. He sided with David. The bag remained where it was.

The flight over the mid-Atlantic was comfortable, and familiar to David, who had flown it many times, though then he had had to fly right through the weather, not comfortably above it as we did then. He knew Colombia and had touched down there. But he had not before landed at Bogota as escort to the diplomatic bag.

Immediately he stepped onto terra firma, the anti-terrorist, pro-security precautions swung into action. David was met by the Head of Chancery from the British Embassy, who earnestly advised him to keep his eyes open and let no-one approach too closely. Difficult advice to take in a crowded airport.

He then conducted us to a reinforced Land Rover drawn up at the kerb immediately outside the terminal. A driver sat hunched over the wheel. The engine was still running. He hustled us inside. One last look over his shoulder to make sure we weren't being followed, then he told the driver to move off.

On the way to the Embassy, the Head of Chancery explained that Bogota was one of the most lawless cities in the world and foreign visitors, especially those considered to be of diplomatic status, at some considerable risk of kidnapping. If they were carrying the diplomatic bag, then the risk was even greater.

Arriving at the Embassy, the Land Rover didn't simply stop at the front door. The driver pulled it right onto the pavement. There were searching glances to left and right to make sure the street was empty. Then iron gates beside the main door were raised, and in we drove to a compound.

There were more iron gates inside guarding Chancery, and marching through into this inner sanctum, David was invited to hand over the bag and witness it being safely stowed in the indestructible safe. He was given instructions to collect it in the morning.

Meanwhile now it was the First Secretary who escorted us to the Land Rover and thence to our hotel. He stayed with us for a welcoming drink and then left us to have dinner. After dinner, as usual in an unfamiliar city, we went out to explore. Possibly it was because of David's London briefing or the Head of Chancery's description, the city certainly seemed to emanate an aura of menace. It was like a film set where the audience awaited a burst of gunfire, or in those dark deserted and dusty side streets, a knife between the ribs.

But the hotel rooms were comfortable and unremarkable, and after breakfast the same Land Rover conducted us to the Embassy where the bag was formally released from Chancery and we were driven once again to the airport to board the little Avianca aircraft in its brilliant red and cream livery.

Other passengers boarded carrying shopping bags and wicker baskets imprisoning clucking hens. The atmosphere was wonderfully relaxed. No one else bothered about seat belts. Pre-flight checks were minimal. A dark-eyed stewardess handed out delicious hot savoury patties, soft drinks and bars of bitter chocolate.

The only dicey moment was on the approach to Quito when the pilot seemed to head straight for the Andes as if waiting for them to get out of his way. Finally a gap opened, to which he had been apparently heading all the time. But even so, an immovable mountain sat on the end of each wingtip, which, when we were on the approach, moved over just enough to let him slide through and land with surprising smoothness.

The air at Quito, ten thousand feet above sea level, induces, if it doesn't knock you out, an immediate euphoria. Here we were met by another First Secretary. The bag was ritualistically, but more relaxedly taken into Chancery, and then we were installed in a luxurious hotel in the centre of the city.

Late that afternoon, David was summoned for a talk with the Ambassador and a Foreign office representative who had arrived via Miami. The three of them comprised the UK team for the conference. David was to be responsible for the speech and any questions, though the speech would be delivered by the Ambassador.

The diplomatic bag was then opened. All was now to be revealed. David was agog for his secret instructions, which had been so earnestly, if clumsily guarded,

The final note was unfolded. The instructions thereon were brief. Four words – *Keep a low profile.*

*   *   *

It was not easy to keep a low profile. All kinds of international currents were swirling. Latin America was rich and getting richer and the big powers jockeyed for influence. Refreshingly, the overwhelming feeling among the delegates was pro-British, but anti-American. The Yanks were suspected of having far too many fingers in the Latin American pie and the American hegemony far too close for comfort.

The most extraordinary mix-ups were made in the accommodation of some of the delegates. Chief ministers, prime ministers, foreign ministers of tiny countries, who were hyper sensitive about their rank and importance, found themselves in very unsuitable and undignified accommodation, one even landing up in the red light area.

Eventually the accommodation was straightened out. The conference began with a glittering reception. More lavish receptions were given at all the embassies. The Russians and the Germans were to be seen at them all, chatting assiduously and with great charm to the delegates and each other, scorning one another for the so-called aid, which had massive strings attached, or which was totally inappropriate. The German Ambassador loudly complimented the Russian on their kindness in donating their surplus snow ploughs to Nigeria, and other Russian howlers. The Ambassador's daughter, one of those who seemed really to care, talked to any that were interested about her work with the myriads of little boot-black boys, who darted around Quito polishing shoes.

The conference at least served the purpose of the delegates talking to one another and glimpsing each others' problems, but it also gave glimpses of irreconcilable differences and troubles to come.

But apart from grumbles about the accommodation, the conference was pronounced successful. Though there had been some near misses, no one had stormed out, not too many gaffes had been made and the

Ambassador, an accomplished speaker, sewed it all neatly together and his speech went down well.

When it came to the return journey we had an example of the fact that although the Americans might be resented for their interference they also possess a great capacity to cut through red tape and get things done.

David and I arrived at Quito airport for the return British Caledonian flight, only to discover that it returned via Miami. We therefore needed an American visa. Both David and I had recently had our passports renewed and hadn't yet obtained American visas on them.

Firmly we were told by the airline representative that we couldn't return on that flight and must wait three days for the next one which would be via Antigua, and therefore wouldn't need an American visa.

David had an important meeting for which he had to get back to ODA and I had to get back for our daughter. In vain we protested and pleaded.

By chance the Ambassador arrived to wave off his wife on home leave and he stepped forward and said he would do what he could.

He phoned the American Ambassador, and in the winking of an eye the whole visa franking machine was transported from the Embassy in the centre of the town out to the airport. We were each given an American visa on the spot and we boarded the aircraft only a few minutes late.

David had seen at first hand yet more vast problems which as a humble Foreign Office representative he was powerless to do anything about. The experience served to reaffirm that it was in writing that he could make his talents and insights most effective and that in writing he could and must express his vision of life.

Before he finally decided to leave ODA and return to full-time writing he made one last trip on behalf of ODA to Africa, heading north and this time arriving in Ethiopia.

He found it a strange but interesting country. From the air, it looked a desolate landscape, much of the country covered in rocky outcrops, cinder fields, or scrub the colour of the surrounding stone. Dry water-courses meandered through the crusty surface, dotted with shanty villages and a few small towns originally built to subsist on the railway.

Addis Ababa, with its wide streets, once-gilded statues and palaces was a mixture of the Middle East and the crumbling edifices of the west, once the dream of the venerated but now departed Emperor Haile Selassie. In one of these fine crumbling edifices David met a young man who had been originally sent out by ODA and had stayed

David receiving the Malta Medal from the President.

on without any more financial support from them because there was so much need.

The young man had taken over the once beautiful Austrian Embassy and converted it into a shelter for homeless boys. Apparently, as soon as boys were old enough they flocked into Addis Ababa under the false premise that there was plenty of work, plenty of shelter and food.

They found otherwise.

When David visited the old Austrian Embassy it was full to bursting with boys, whom the young man was feeding and sheltering. He was also trying to teach them some basic skills in the hope that they could earn a living for themselves. The young man himself had no money, no possessions and was dressed in a torn T-shirt and shorts. He said that what basic things he had possessed when he arrived had all been stolen from him by the boys. He was quite philosophical about it. Now he had nothing, so there was nothing for the boys to steal. He bore them no ill will whatever. They stole because that was their way of survival.

When David arrived, the young man was preparing a meal of grain and vegetables, gifts of which from time to time mysteriously appeared on his doorstep, and thus he managed to keep going.

212

In David's opinion, that young man did more than all the conferences and expert advice and loans-with-strings, and on David's return to London, he made strenuous efforts to organise an ODA or charitable grant for him. But his efforts seemed to fall just outside the rules of giving for all of them. In the end, David sent the young man what he could from his own pocket. And now he knew it had to be back to full-time writing. The pen was indeed mightier than not just the sword, but governments and organised charities too, and it reinforced his belief in the power of one person.

However, his time as a commuter had not been wasted. Pressed cheek by jowl with his fellow sufferers in the crowded compartment from Hever to Victoria, listening and observing and thinking as always, he conceived a novel called *Electric Train*. In fact, so intent were his observations on those commuter trains that his elder daughters said they were too embarrassed to travel with him, as notebook and pencil poised he wrote down the travellers' words hot from their lips.

Those travellers lived intriguingly tangled lives, and David saw that many of them had a world at one end of the line which was home, another at the other end which was work, and one in the middle on the *Electric Train*. Within all these theatres, the travellers formed exciting and fascinating relationships.

David found the climax of the plot in the tunnel itself. It had been cut in the nineteenth century through the chalk of the North Downs. Noticeably after heavy rain, the train tiptoed with extreme caution through this Oxted tunnel. And as it tiptoed, rivulets of water could be seen cascading down its mouldering Victorian brick. Nervous gossip among the commuters said that there was a lake on the Downs immediately above and that too much vibration might collapse the tunnel and bring it down, hence the train's slow passage through the danger area.

And while the tunnel crumbled, while indeed our railways crumble now, the powers-that-be dithered, as they dither now, about how much money should be spent on upkeep and who should spend it and when, if ever. Nothing changes. Now we have Railtrack.

The Brisbane Courier Mail reviewer described *Electric Train* as 'A good example of a modern literary work, very strongly reminiscent of classical Greek tragedy . . . It is this feeling of impending doom which Beaty so skilfully develops, moving his narrative along to the monotonous almost malevolent clackity-clack of the electric train between Ocklington and London, the iron wheels tapping like a hypnotic metronome.'

213

Meanwhile David had already conceived a non-fiction book which he wanted to begin describing the history of transatlantic flight, called *The Water Jump*. He chose that particular title because of the analogies between flying and riding. For just as aviation adopted some of the terminology of the sea, so it also did of riding and many pilots likened the handling of an aircraft to that of a horse. There is no higher compliment to rider or pilot than to say that he or she has 'a good pair of hands'. The water jump in a race was usually the most difficult. And so, in the early days of civil aviation, was the flight across the Atlantic.

David had by now so many ideas for books that he knew the time had come again for change. He couldn't both write his books and do a decent job at the Ministry, so he bade farewell to the comparative security of the Civil Service and returned with renewed zest to full-time writing.

BOAC were very helpful in making their records available for *The Water Jump*. David found that he was writing it just in time, for many of the documents and photographs of the early years were about to be destroyed. A stay of execution was granted until he had acquired prints of them, and then they were gone.

Thus some of the illustrations in *The Water Jump* are the only ones extant. Many of the aircrew who pioneered the Atlantic are no longer alive and gathering their first-hand testimony then was invaluable, as was the debunking of a well-known Churchill story.

The story arose in 1942 when Prime Minister Churchill decided to fly back to Britain on the Boeing 314 after his conference with Roosevelt in Bermuda, instead of travelling back aboard the battleship that was waiting for him.

Churchill was accompanied by Martin, his private secretary, Charles Wilson his physician, Dudley Pound, the First Sea Lord, Charles Portal, Chief of Air Staff, Beaverbrook, Minister of Aircraft Production and Hollis, Secretary to the Chief of Staff Committee.

A member of the airline staff was moved to comment that they thus had, 'All the baskets in one egg.'

Churchill describes that flight aboard *Berwick* in detail in Volume III of *The Second World War* as after 'a merry dinner', he had slept soundly in 'a good broad bed in the bridal suite at the stern with large windows on either side.'

While still west of Ireland, weather at Pembroke Dock, the designated terminal, deteriorated badly, so Captain Kelly-Rogers, one of the most experienced and skilful pilots on the route, decided to divert to Plymouth, which was only a little further. He made the necessary alterations of course to starboard, sent his Estimated Time of Arrival as 09.00 and actually alighted in Plymouth Sound a minute early at 08.59.

Churchill's account of that flight was completely different and much more dramatic.

Captain Kelly-Rogers had invited the Prime Minister on to the flight deck as they approached the English coast and recalling that visit, Churchill wrote that he immediately sensed a feeling of anxiety all around him, a feeling that 'we did not know where we were'.

Astonishingly, Churchill goes on to claim that had they held course for another five or six minutes before turning north, 'We should have been over the German batteries at Brest.'

Brest was the main German U-boat base and one of the most heavily-defended fortresses in Europe, with a balloon barrage, numerous anti-aircraft batteries and fighter squadrons. To take the British Prime Minister over it by navigational error would have been a blunder of appalling magnitude and such an account was a great slur on the captain's reputation.

A least four of the distinguished passengers subsequently wrote their memoirs and, describing that flight, drew heavily on Churchill's account.

General Sir Leslie Hollis in James Leasor's *War at the Top* said they were within minutes of coming into 'a clear sky over Brest, the most heavily defended French occupied port in the Channel. We were so low and so slow that the German gunners could not have failed to bring us down. I seriously considered tearing up my report and burning the whole thing in the aircraft kitchen rather than risk capture.'

David, however, never liked to use research material at second hand. He contacted Captain Kelly-Rogers, whose report, handed in after the flight, had shown it to be perfectly normal. Furthermore the flight was under radar surveillance for the last part and according to the Control Officer, nowhere near Brest.

Captain Kelly-Rogers was only too eager to re-affirm his own perfectly normal and unexciting account. He had written to Churchill and then to the other four memoir writers correcting the accounts; he had had a letter published in the *Daily Telegraph* in which he wrote: 'Mr Churchill displays exceptional skill in navigating the Empire through the uncharted seas of war, but in the course of this and subsequent flights over the Atlantic with me, I have to say he appeared to take no more than the layman's interest in the art of aerial navigation and was inclined to dismiss the whole thing as a bit of a mystery.'

Yet Captain Kelly-Roger's protests were to no avail. He felt that

Churchill's account was a stain on his own professional competence. But that stain was never removed. Churchill's motives for the fictional drama were unclear. Creative writer that he was, perhaps he was simply carried away by what he conceived to be a good story. It was well known that he liked to finish a book on a high dramatic note.

Captain Kelly-Rogers was delighted to see the correct account appear in print at last.

Throughout the book, there were many other accounts and pieces to check, and for the actual writing of *The Water Jump*, we retreated to a small holiday house we had bought in an unfashionable corner of Sidford in Devon. All the jigsaw parts of the manuscript and its accompanying photographs were spread in every corner of every room, even on every tread of the staircase.

The manuscript when finished, but unbound, was still determined to be scattered. It was sent to America, and was given straight to Frances Philips, now retired but still a power behind the throne. She was so fascinated by it that, although now very elderly, she took it with her on an aircraft and disembarking, dropped it on the tarmac from where the pages were blown by aircraft engines to the four winds.

However, another manuscript was prepared. Publishers both sides of the Atlantic were enthusiastic. A publishers' party was given at the RAF Club in Piccadilly, BOAC co-operated, and it was attended by David's old protagonist Sir Miles Thomas, besides other distinguished aviators. BOAC lent a magnificent model of Concorde and pictures to line the walls.

The Water Jump was widely translated and some time later, after we had returned to Hever, David received a request from a Belgian television team saying that they would like to make a series of it for Belgian television and could they send photographers over to take shots of David in his home and workplace?

This was arranged. The house was made tidy.

At the end of the recording, David, always vague about the money side but knowing that television rights on a book commanded a substantial fee, asked the team leader, 'Have you arranged to buy the book?' Meaning, of course, had they been in touch with his agent and bought the television rights.

'Oh, yes. We've bought it,' he replied, waving his copy. 'I flew over specially last week to buy this from Hatchards.'

And that was all they ever paid. They simply took the book without paying anything for the television and radio rights.

Unfortunately, the writer is wide open to theft of his property. Some years later, the BBC was advertising a programme called *Diamonds in the Sky*, featuring Julian Pettifer. The final instalment was to be on the conquest of the Atlantic.

Not normally a television addict, David was reluctantly persuaded to look at this instalment as it should be of particular interest to him. So down he sat in front of the television, prepared to relax and be entertained, only immediately to hear his own exact words being spoken back to him.

All David's books were from the heart and he could recall every word of them. Besides, the conquest of the Atlantic both in war and peace had been his own hard-won experience.

He wrote down as much of that instalment of *Diamonds in the Sky* as he could. But he needed the script which the producer had worked from.

So the next morning, he telephoned the BBC and asked them for a copy of the *Diamonds in the Sky* script.

'Not corporation policy, old boy!'

He wrote to them asking again and voicing his complaint.

An indignant Julian Pettifer telephoned him, exclaiming, 'But of course the script wasn't taken direct from your book! Of course they weren't your words! That would have been plagiarism!'

But it was, although Julian Pettifer was the entirely innocent party to it. He simply read aloud what he had been given to read aloud. The BBC still refused to part with a script.

David wrote to Mark leFanu of the Authors' Society. Mark approached the BBC, who were at that time having to deal with another complaint, this time involving Desmond Wilcox. They were rather on the ropes about that, so they were more malleable.

The BBC gave in as far as producing a copy of the script. Then they had to give in altogether because when we carefully went through the script comparing the relevant chapters in *The Water Jump*, the plagiarism was abundantly clear.

It was also clear to Mark leFanu and the BBC. At a hastily arranged meeting the BBC settled for a sum to be paid to David in compensation and for new credits to be run on all subsequent programmes including David's name.

An ominous note for writers and the safeguarding of copyright was sounded by the producer. As he bade farewell that day to Mark leFanu and David, he remarked regretfully to the latter, 'It all happened because we were so rushed. We simply didn't have the time to alter your words so that you couldn't recognise them.'

With *The Water Jump* launched, David went on researching and writing on human factors. He wrote articles and gave lectures and he was still being contacted by pilots in difficulties. But he needed to write his novel on Africa, inspired as he had been by his Foreign Office researches into Uganda and its most ungentle dictator.

The novel that arose was *Excellency*. The jacket was simple but dramatic; the feathered hat of His Excellency splashed with blood from a panga knife beside it. David Farrer remarked cynically that unfortunately he had found that the better, the more restrained the jacket, the worse the sales. But *Excellency* was popular both sides of the Atlantic and was a *Reader's Digest* choice. It was described as 'A brilliant story full of colour and movement that brings Africa to life.' And by the *Daily Telegraph* as 'An excellent example of the British thriller at its best.'

But it communicated much more than thrills. It gave an insight into coming events in Africa.

CHAPTER EIGHTEEN

THE BLOOD BROTHERS

Over the years we had enjoyed a close friendship with Audrey and Ted Willis, and we were actively supporting Brigid Brophy and Maureen Duffy in the cause of the Public Lending Right whereby authors would be paid a small amount per library borrowing. Much in the campaign was rightly made of such fine authors as S D P Mais, extremely popular in the forties and fifties, whose books were still borrowed on a large scale but who were now living in straitened circumstances and received no financial reward from the library borrowings. The campaign for a public lending right had been originally started by John Brophy, Brigid's father, and on his death had been taken over by Brigid Brophy and Maureen Duffy, supported by Michael Foot and Norman St John Stevas.

There were many frustrations and setbacks. In one attempt to pass the Act in the House of Commons, it was filibustered by a group of MPs. Ted, who had worked tirelessly for it through the years and who had now been made a Lord, threatened to lie down in the Chamber.

Finally opposition was overcome and the Public Lending Right became law in 1979. Norman St John Stevas and Michael Foot hosted a small party to celebrate success in the Cabinet Office. Talking to Ted at that party, David and I decided to write a family saga together about the interweaving lives of two families, both in their vastly different ways devoted to aviation. We enjoyed working and writing together and had established a telepathic communication with one another, feeling at times that we could walk in and out of each other's minds.

Before we embarked on the saga, David finished *The White Sea Bird*, a gripping RAF novel that described operations in Coastal Command, and which became a great favourite especially with the ex-206 crews. 206 Squadron had been re-formed very quickly after the war and, was distinguishing itself in its operations, being known as the premier maritime squadron. A 206 Squadron Association flourished with retired Squadron Leader Alan Smith as its indefatigable secretary, and David felt honoured to be a vice-president.

Shortly after *The White Sea Bird* was published, David was surprised to receive a letter from his old playmate Edgar proposing a visit to us at Woodside. He had changed his name to Kloppinger and he gave the news that his mother had survived the war, although she had lived throughout in Hamburg which Bomber Command had literally set ablaze. She had recently died and now, after visiting us at Woodside, Edgar was going to stay with some of his father's relatives in England. He, like David, had gone into civil aviation and was now flying as a pilot for Lufthansa.

David, curious to see his childhood friend, was watching from the kitchen window as Edgar's car drew up in the drive. About to go out and welcome him, David paused as the stocky muscular man leapt out of the car, then immediately subsided onto the gravel doing rapid press-ups. Then he ran up and down the drive half a dozen times and finally rang the doorbell, bowing and smartly clicking his heels when David opened it.

But here was no regimented Nazi. The two friends talked late into the night. Edgar the Lufthansa pilot was keen to hear much more about human factors and to discover how the knowledge could be used in Lufthansa. He had been in charge of Lufthansa pilot training, and still acted in a consultative capacity so could put David's knowledge and experience to good use. He told David how eventually he wanted to found a group to live on environmentally friendly principles. Both friends were still dedicated to a more just society, to peace and to the abolition of nuclear weapons.

Edgar told David that his father was still living in Sri Lanka, now devotedly looked after by the Buddhists, who revered him as a holy man. Edgar also recounted the story of how he had ended up on the Russian front. It was certainly not because the Nazis in their kindness had wished to spare him bombing his compatriots. In fact he *had* bombed British cities. He had been sent to the eastern front because his father had tried to contact him. The Reverend Small had become anxious having had no news of him for some time and he had begun to fear that Edgar was dead. In desperation the Reverend Small had sent a letter via a Swedish missionary in Ceylon who was going back to neutral Sweden on furlough.

The letter was intercepted by the SS and, despite the fact that Edgar was one of the *Luftwaffe*'s crack pilots, he was thrown into gaol for attempted contact with the enemy. Two things saved him. He had a courageous squadron commander who spoke up for him and the *Luftwaffe* was acutely short of pilots on the Russian front. So he was released and sent there and survived.

The two friends had fought a fierce war on opposing sides. One of Edgar's British targets had been Sheffield, where I, then a student, had shivered in a cellar during the six-hour bombing. Edgar had captained one of the bombers. On the other hand, his mother had endured the relentless RAF bombing and then the dreadful firestorms of Hamburg.

David had for some time been nurturing a plot based roughly, but not too exactly, on his friendship with Edgar, but at that time we were still writing *Wings of the Morning*, the saga of the two aviation families. The title was taken from the 139th psalm: 'If I take the wings of the morning; and remain in the uttermost parts of the sea; even there also shall thy hand lead me; and thy right hand shall hold me.'

Juliet O'Hea had retired, so our agent for that novel was Caradoc King, a very astute and business-like young man, who liked the book so much that he decided it should go to auction. Macmillan made the highest bid in this country and Doubleday made a truly handsome bid in America.

When it was finished, David's novel *The Stick* followed. It was the dramatic story of an airliner on fire intertwined with the pilot's relationship to his wife. A taut and deeply moving story, it was based on that fragment of truth which David always felt crystallised the depths of an author's experience.

After *The Stick*, two projects, both non-fiction, fired David's interest. One, *The Complete Skytraveller*, a vade-mecum of flying, in which airports and aircraft were lucidly explained for non-technical readers, the other an investigation into the disaster which had befallen that silver shape he had glimpsed as a schoolboy – the R101.

He found the investigation fascinating, both from a psychological point of view and also as an assay into the world of the paranormal, about which he was both highly suspicious and curious. Then, by investigating the R101, David's self-generated remit widened and he accumulated other fascinating and seemingly inexplicable aviation happenings. Those he put into a book called *Strange Encounters*, and for the R101 he interested the BBC in commissioning a radio serial. Subsequently, the *Reader's Digest* commissioned a full-length book on R101.

Research into R101 opened up a strange world to David; and although he suspected that ultimately its tragedy lay in human factors, in primarily the human factors of conformity, the desire to please, machoism and ambition, he was intrigued by the notion of the paranormal, in which so many people fervently believed, especially at the time of the tragedy. Then mediums, many of them fraudulent, had been preying upon the sorrow after World War One, although the medium, Mrs Eileen Garrett, was highly regarded on both sides of the Atlantic. She had been the medium through which a warning had supposedly come that the R101 would go up like a bomb. Sir Arthur Conan Doyle had added the weight of his reputation to the warnings, accompanying the widow of the famous pioneer aviator Captain Hinchliffe to Cardington to issue his warning.

We went several times to Cardington, a suburb of Bedford where R101 was built, the city to which it had brought prosperity in the nineteen-twenties. R101 was very much Bedford's ship, built by Bedford men. Her crew lived locally; as did her designer, Colonel Richmond, whose design had broken away from the conventional Zeppelin design and incorporated his own patented gas bags, wire braces, Triplex glass windows and a lounge big enough 'to foxtrot all the way to India'.

The Minister of Civil Aviation, the monocled Sir Sefton Brancker, one of the notables to fly on her maiden voyage, was an old boy of the famous Bedford School, while the Secretary of State for Air, Lord Christopher Birdwood Thomson had taken the title 'of Cardington' when created a peer.

After exploring Cardington David set about tracing the survivors and the families of those on board. In this he met a large cast of interesting people. He also uncovered the story behind R101, a Greek tragedy of courage and devotion to duty with two ill-starred love affairs to set alongside the technical failures, the greed, the ambition, the corner cutting and other human factors and frailties.

When David had first begun writing, he was often compared to Nevil Shute, although they were really very dissimilar. But Nevil Shute wrote about flying and was, like David, a man of action as well as a writer. They were both published by William Morrow in America, they were both under the wing of the formidable Frances Philips and they were both acknowledged to be masterly storytellers. They both possessed an uncanny prescience, as Neville Shute's readers may remember of his novel *No Highway*, which hinged on hitherto unknown metal fatigue, and into which he too brought a touch of the paranormal.

Neville Shute, in his capacity of aeronautical design engineer, had assisted Barnes Wallis, the designer of the rival to the R101, the successful R100, a private enterprise airship. R100's achievements kept the designers and administrators of the nationalised R101 on their toes and made them doubly determined to keep the departure date of 4 October 1930.

The captain of R101 was Herbert Carmichael Irwin, always known as 'Bird'. He was a young, strikingly handsome and skilful airship pilot. He was born in County Cork, a strict disciplinarian and a former Olympic athlete, deeply in love with his elegant wife Olivia. Even in old age she had the most compelling sapphire-blue eyes and the aura of a woman who has always been loved and admired. The twenty-three-year-old daughter of rich parents, she was an accomplished tennis player and party giver and a woman of great courage. Together they were a very glamorous couple, the Beautiful People of the late twenties. He was delighted to be given the command of R101 and at first everything in life seemed to be wonderful. But he soon reckoned that all was not well with the airship and that she needed several trials before embarking on her maiden flight.

Especially as, in order to get more lift, her servo-motor steering gear had been removed, a look-out at the top of the ship dispensed with, her Triplex glass windows replaced by a type of light celluloid called 'Cellon' and, most drastic of all, her belly had been ripped open and an extra gas bag inserted making the airship seven hundred and seventy-seven feet in length.

She was now larger than a cathedral and so long that the Canadian air ace, Billy Bishop, pointed out that 'the great machine can be in two kinds of weather at once, the nose of it fighting a clockwise gust, and the tail of it attacked by something quite different.'

R101's seventeen enormous gas bags were made of 'goldbeater skin', which was membrane from the intestines of a million oxen secured to cotton, through which the hydrogen tended to leak. Worse, the engineers had found hundreds of holes in the bags where they had chafed against the nuts and bolts of the lattice-like metal frame. These chafing points had been bandaged on the orders of the Air Ministry, and although the Cardington airship inspector, Frederick McWade, had objected, his objection had been overruled.

While this bandaging was being done, the rival R100 made a successful crossing of the Atlantic to Montreal, and two weeks later flew back again. Private enterprise seemed to have won. The screw tightened on the R101 team.

Another player in this Greek tragedy was Hugh Dowding, who a decade later as Air Officer Commanding Fighter Command and the director of the Battle of Britain would take charge of Britain's aerial defence and save this country.

On the day before the maiden flight, Dowding was supposed to supervise the one and only test on R101 before her much-heralded trip to India. But that afternoon Dowding was tired and the flight so smooth, the seats of such surprising comfort that he went to sleep. But he did subsequently express anxiety that R101's eight-cylinder Beardmore engines (the first diesels to power an airship) had not been put through a high-speed test and he requested that a high-speed test be done on the airship immediately after slipping the mast when she left for India. However, because of the bad weather, this was not done.

Bird Irwin, deeply disturbed by the lack of trials, asked for a post-ponement of the India trip, and even contemplated refusing to fly on the appointed day. But he was up against the most powerful player in this drama, who had strong reasons for that trip to take place at that time. Lord Thomson, the Secretary of State for Air, close friend of Prime Minister Ramsay MacDonald and the besotted lover of Princess Bibescu of Roumania would not be gainsaid.

The 1930 Imperial Conference was about to take place in India and Lord Thomson had promised himself a dramatic entrance there. He had worked out his life plan. He would honour with his presence the maiden flight of R101, be seen as the patron of the newest and, at this point, most successful form of air travel. He would confound the intractable pro-aeroplane lobby and once arrived in India he would make an impressive entrance to the Imperial Conference. After which his close friend the Prime Minister would invite him to be India's next Viceroy. A shrewd politician, he realised that the Labour government was tottering and that he might soon lose his Secretary-ship of State. But to be Viceroy was even better. As Viceroy, Lord Thomson would lay the Viceregal crown at the Princess' feet and live happily ever after.

He carried a silver slipper belonging to those little feet when he arrived late on 4 October for departure at Cardington. His valet also carried for him a magic carpet from the apartment where Lord Thomson had courted his princess, and six cases of champagne – this though all other passengers and crew were restricted for personal possessions to ten pounds in weight.

The Secretary of State's late and laden arrival irritated Bird Irwin as, with his colleague Major Scott, he watched from R101's flight deck. The weather had turned against them and was deteriorating rapidly. Squally winds and rain were forecast. Bird Irwin had tried again for a postponement and even enquired what would happen if he simply refused to go. He had been told that his great friend, Ralph Booth, an experienced airship pilot and regular RAF officer would be *ordered* to go in his place. And Ralph would be unable in his turn to refuse, without being court-martialled.

An insoluble dilemma. It was that dilemma, not the telephone call earlier that day from Lord Thomson accusing him of being an obstructionist and by implication a coward, that had made Irwin go. Ralph Booth and his wife were the Irwins' closest friends.

The events of that fatal flight are now history. Buffeted by squally winds and drenched in torrential downpours, in what was described by a witness as 'a tempest from the west', R101's struggling engines were unable to make headway or maintain height. Having crossed the Channel at less than cliff top height the airship crashed on the ridge by Beauvais in France and, with five and a half million cubic feet of hydrogen on board, exploded into a roaring inferno.

In the aft engine pod, two engineers, Binks and Bell, near to suffocation saw, with horror, the flames licking around. They knew, as they later put it, that in a few seconds they would 'roast instead of suffocate' when the fire reached the petrol for the starter motor. They said a solemn prayer and shook hands with each other. Then suddenly, a miracle. Water cascaded down, as immediately above them the ballast water bag burst, drenching them and the car and dousing the flames.

Painstakingly, David tracked down a number of the survivors. Some of them had fared badly. Despite the fact that the tragedy had caused a public outpouring of grief, almost like Princess Diana's death, and a fund had been opened, in the end only enough was distributed to one victim's relative to enable her to buy a new pair of spectacles.

Eventually David discovered Bird Irwin's widow Olivia living not very far from us in Kent. But she was too ill at the time to give an interview. Air Marshal Sir Victor Goddard, who had himself been an airship captain and a close friend of the Irwins and also living in Kent was very helpful, acting as a go-between. Luckily, Olivia made a complete recovery and in many meetings gave David valuable insights into the R101 tragedy.

As did Sir Victor himself, an important player in several dramas of history. Just before the Second World War he had been contacted by Charles Lindbergh. In fact, the hero of Atlantic flight had interrupted his journey home from Berlin after receiving the Lilienthal Prize, to beg Goddard in all sincerity to tell the British government that they could not possibly defeat Germany and that the *Luftwaffe* would make mincemeat of the RAF.

Then in 1940, Sir Victor had been in charge of the British Air Component in France when France collapsed. He remained with Lord Gort to the last moment and then flew out of France in a bullet-riddled aeroplane with a personal plea from Lord Gort to send everything they had to evacuate the men of the BEF. Goddard had begged that they send 'pleasure steamers, coasters, fishing boats, lifeboats, yachts, motor boats, everything that can cross the Channel.' And so he was the architect of the Dunkirk evacuation and the armada of little boats which turned defeat into something like a victory. Later, he was given command of Allied Forces in the Far East.

Sir Victor had begun his career as a naval cadet at Osborne with King George VI. He told David that the King was left-handed, but had been made to use his right hand. David wondered if this resulted in the King's stammer, in line with Professor Gerhardt's theory that such disabilities as stammering often follow misunderstanding of laterality confusion.

Then, through Sir Victor Goddard, David met Muriel, the Lady Dowding, widow of Lord Dowding, a dazzling woman with violet eyes and rich auburn hair piled on top of her head. She usually dressed in regal purple with a white camellia in her hair. She was great company, deeply compassionate, and being a life-long champion of animal rights she founded Beauty Without Cruelty. She brimmed with ideas and was mischievously full of intriguing anecdotes about the denizens of the House of Lords and the political establishment. She described Dowding's connection with R101, his grief over that tragedy, for which he felt partly responsible, and then how deeply he felt the loss of so many young fighter pilots in the Battle of Britain; his sometimes stormy relationships with Churchill and Beaverbrook and the annoyance he had felt with Bader.

We had lunch with Muriel Dowding the day after the Prince Charles and Diana wedding, which she had attended; she said then that, though an impressive and beautiful spectacle, it was an arranged marriage, that Diana was too young and a virgin and that the marriage wouldn't work and would end in tragedy.

The fascinating story of how Muriel met and married Lord Dowding, David, with her permission subsequently incorporated into his book, *Strange Encounters.*

In the course of time, having been a loyal wife to Lord Dowding, Muriel had since his death fallen deeply in love with the still dashing Sir Victor. It was a romance which we watched with surprise and pleasure. They were both very old but suddenly curiously young, attractive and full of life.

She was a complete law unto herself. She died in her late eighties. David and I went to the interment of her ashes at Westminster Abbey when her remains were laid to rest with those of Lord Dowding and other towering, much honoured and much decorated RAF leaders, the only woman among the high and mighty men. Somehow exactly the right resting-place for her.

Now David turned to his novel based on his friend Edgar and the duel between two boys brought up together, one a German, one British. The characters were similar to Edgar and himself, the RAF pilot serving as he himself had done, with Coastal Command. But because he had experience of fighting submarines and had formed a great respect for the U-boat commanders' courage, he made the German a U-boat commander instead of a bomber pilot.

Some months before he began the final writing we had decided we should sell Woodside, our house in Kent. It had been a fruitful place to write and a good family home. Two of our daughters had been married at Hever church and three of our granddaughters had been born while we were there. Now our family was grown-up and independent. Besides, over the years we had haphazardly bought surrounding parcels of land, mostly to graze the horses and donkeys, but our land had increased so that it was of disproportionate size in relation to our comparatively small house, and as neither David nor I were good gardeners, something of a burden.

Two of the girls' old ponies, now into their thirties, still grazed the paddock, so we kept back sufficient land from the sale to enable them to end their days there, and Karen, our youngest daughter, newly married and living only a few miles away, undertook to look after them.

In January 1986, with *The Blood Brothers* almost completed and Woodside sold, we moved down to our holiday house in Lymington. It was small and warm with a view from the upstairs windows of the yachts in the harbour. It was rumoured that it was already a fruitful place for writing, in that during a previous ownership a round the world yachtsman had written his book describing his epic voyage there.

Settling himself in the attic with his back to the yachts, David finished *The Blood Brothers* and sent it in to Methuen.

The following week we received an estate agent's blurb describing a house in a West Sussex village on the South Downs where, David said, he had heard there were magnificent beech woods. We both liked the description of the house. We went to view, fell in love with it and made an offer.

227

With the offer accepted, we planned to move in on 1 May.

The night before the move, on the last day of April, David had a severe heart attack

There followed a dangerous and agonising succession of medical misjudgements and errors. The GP, a complete stranger, was misled by David's stoicism into discounting his pain. We asked that David see a cardiologist but he said he wasn't ill enough. But he did offer a cardiograph. However the machine, when he hauled it out of a cupboard, was broken so the doctor sent David to the local cottage hospital, a short walk round the corner, but a long walk when your heart is in crisis. The hospital registrar, also misled by David's stoicism, refused my plea to admit him and, saying David's condition wasn't bad enough for hospital treatment, sent him home. David was in agonising pain during the night, but he still wouldn't let me call out the doctor, because we had already been to the hospital and received their medical opinion. But I crept downstairs in the early hours and called the duty doctor. Luckily she was a bright intelligent woman, who promptly came round and sent David by ambulance to hospital, where it was found he had already suffered a severe heart attack.

When David had recovered from that, the cardiologist recommended a quadruple by-pass operation to be carried out immediately. And in a five-hour operation at the Chalybeate hospital in Southampton this was most skilfully performed by Mr Shaw, a bright light on an otherwise very murky medical horizon.

David was out of intensive care, sitting up and making notes for his next book thirty-six hours later. He had seen enough at first hand of medical practice to realise that human factor study should not be confined to aviation but should be most urgently extended to medical practice. There was plenty of dedication and hard work and significant technical advances, but the same dangers pertained in the lack of study of the human beings at the centre of medical practice as had pertained in aviation.

The by-pass operation was followed by a strenuous cardiac rehabilitation course, and a leisurely convalescence at Osborne House on the Isle of Wight, Queen Victoria's favourite house, which had been given by her son, Edward VII, as a convalescent home for officers of the services.

There, in beautiful surroundings, looked after by a dedicated and effective staff, the convalescents flourished.

Back in Lymington, David improved daily, forcing himself to walk, first to the end of the path at the back of the house, then to the end of the road, then to the end of the next. Then finally, triumph. Right down to the Yacht Club, though not inside.

And while convalescing in Lymington, David was contacted by an interesting voice from the past.

CHAPTER NINETEEN

EAGLES

David had first met the film and television producer Brian Dégas years before when *Village of Stars* came out and there had been a good deal of publicity in the States. Alfred Hitchcock had requested the film rights, so these had been acquired for him by Twentieth Century Fox and he had named it for his next film. But as David told Brian Dégas, when Twentieth Century Fox applied to the Pentagon for approval in making the film and hopefully for possible co-operation, they were told they could go ahead and make it. But the Pentagon would not co-operate and furthermore they would ensure that no cinema in the States ever showed it. So the film was never made, although a stage play was.

Brian Dégas was still enamoured of *Village of Stars* but now wanted to interest David in a new project.

So, shortly after David had recovered sufficiently for us to move into Slindon, Brian swept into our house, a puckish figure suitably dressed in a long red-lined cloak and a navy-blue beret. He had an impressive list of successful films and television series to his credit, including *Colditz*, and he was persuasive and likeable. He was director of a firm called Polymuse, and they in turn were hopeful of backing from Coca-Cola who had, Brian said, money sloshing around ready to pour into a suitable television series. But it was what the series was to be about which interested David, not the sales talk or the money. It was to be about the Americans based at Upper Heyford in East Anglia.

David's interest was again based on human factors, particularly that of machoism, an exaggerated male egotism which in some circumstances can border on recklessness. From what he had seen of the Americans during the war and subsequently dealing with them in publishing and in The Overseas Development Agency, that human factor was very relevant.

Furthermore, Brian Dégas appeared to have carte blanche to visit and talk to the Americans at Upper Heyford any time and this David wanted to do. So eventually he gave a guarded yes.

It was conditional on being free to write exactly what he wanted in the script. There was to be no propaganda. And if, as a result, David wanted to write a novel, that was to be his entirely. All was agreed. And then Brian invited me to take part in the writing as well, and that too was agreed.

The next step was to visit the American base at Upper Heyford, where, exactly as Brian had promised, we were received with uninhibited warmth and enthusiasm. We were invited to stay in the Mess, were taken into Operations and other sections and personnel talked freely to us. We watched the F111s taking off, met the crews, heard their anecdotes, in some cases their life stories, and obtained a vivid picture of the station and the men and women who served there. Then we explored the village and talked to the inhabitants and saw the banners hanging from upstairs windows which read 'YANKS GO HOME'.

Other visits followed. We uncovered many stories. A script was written. In fact, two scripts were written. One which had additions from Brian giving it a more pro-American slant. These David had refused to put in, not because he was anti-American but because they were clearly propaganda. The other, a script without the additions.

Polymuse accepted both and paid the agreed sum. But Coca-Cola never came into the picture and the series was never made, largely because the political landscape suddenly changed. Unexpectedly, the villagers were getting their way and the Americans were pulling out of Britain. A series on the Yanks in Britain was no longer the up-to-the-minute series Brian had envisaged.

But the indelible picture of the American station, the F111s, the lives of the crews who flew them, their problems and dilemmas and the hostility of the village inspired David to write the novel *Eagles*. Once again, it was a prescient novel. David felt that they were all so geared up that the station was like a pressure cooker.

The climax of the novel was the use of the F111s against a foreign dictator, and it was published before the American attack by F111s on Colonel Gaddafi's headquarters and home.

David had wanted to call the novel *Cage of Eagles*, as that was exactly how Upper Heyford had struck him. Highly trained, macho youngsters, imprisoned among English villages that didn't want them, raring to go. But when he sent the novel to Methuen, they were worried because a novel by Ken Follett had already been submitted coincidentally called *Cage of Eagles*. So David agreed to cut his title to *Eagles*.

The novel was never published in America. David had formed a high opinion of the crews and the novel was an accurate and not unkind picture, but it was not perhaps as the powers-that-be over there saw their forces.

With his novel about to be published, David turned his attention to gathering all his research and explorations together into a new book on human factors. It was a daunting task.

But the move to Slindon had provided him and me with a most singular stroke of luck. Living opposite were a British Airways captain and his wife, Ken and Bonny Beere. With them, we found an immediate rapport and became firm friends. They have been immense supports to us both and then finally and sadly, just to me.

The two pilots shared long conversations and exchanged ideas and experience. Bonny, who had been a stewardess, was a miracle worker who could turn her hand to literally anything, and turn it with charm and humour and good sense. David fired Ken with his enthusiasm for human factors, and Ken's up-to-the-minute experience, his keen intelligence and sense of humour were invaluable. David asked Ken if he would like to help him on the book he had already decided to call *The Naked Pilot*, which Ken generously and most ably did.

An indefatigable helper, a meticulous researcher and a thoughtful friend, Ken frequently tried to cancel out David's thanks with a shrug of the shoulders and a shake of the head and the words, 'That's very little to do for someone who saved my life.'

Eventually, I asked Ken what he meant by that remark and he told me the story of how he reckoned that David had saved his life without ever knowing it.

'It was the 1950s and I was a young BEA co-pilot flying the last sector of the day from Benbecula, in the Western Isles to Glasgow. After settling on our course, Benbecula airport asked if they could close down for the night and we agreed that we needed no further assistance. We were not to know that the deepest depression in years had skirted the weather ships and was rapidly approaching the west coast of Scotland.

'The first sign of trouble was the onset of turbulence in the heavy cloud, followed by a rapid build-up of ice on the wings. We requested a higher altitude, but it soon became apparent that the DC-3 aircraft wouldn't make it. The influence of the ice on the lift and the extra weight threatened to make the aircraft stall even though we applied full power.

'By now the turbulence was becoming severe and it was taking all the captain's skill to keep the aircraft flying as it rolled forty degrees from side to side. The noise of ice flying from the propellers and hitting the fuselage was deafening, forcing us to shout to each other while electrical interference removed all radio communication and navigational aids. We were on our own in thick cloud.

'A bad situation deteriorated further as the airspeed dropped inexorably back towards the stalling speed. Full power didn't rectify the problem and we were forced to start a descent if we were to stay airborne. There was one problem. Ben Nevis, the UK's highest mountain, was somewhere below and too close for comfort in our present predicament and we were now below the height of the mountain peak.

'It was then that we had our first piece of good news. Searching desperately through the radio and navigational frequencies I picked up the radio range from Tiree, an airfield out to the west. One of the last remaining radio ranges in the western world, it transmitted a narrow beam roughly east-west from the transmitter. Pilots flying along the beam would hear a steady note in the headsets. Stray to the north and they would detect the Morse letter "N" (dah dit); to the south it would sound "dit dah". There was one drawback. There was nothing to indicate whether one was flying towards or away from the station.

'Normally this would not be a problem, but by now we had no idea of our position. The only good news was that if we stayed on the beam we would avoid Ben Nevis. We would have given our pensions for a crosscheck from another station to establish where we were along the beam, but there was nothing else to be heard.

'After an hour of enforced descent, being flung all over the sky, we began to have nagging doubts. Had we passed Tiree? Were we now heading for the North Atlantic? Out of the blue came a possible solution.

'Many pilots, like me, invariably read David Beaty's novels the moment they were published. Tucked away in one of them was reference to an old aviator's trick used when they found themselves in the same predicament. They turned down the volume of the radio until it could barely be heard. If the sound disappeared they were flying away from the transmitter. If it stayed or increased, the station was ahead of them. I tried it and discovered that we were still on course for Tiree. That vital piece of information probably saved all our lives.

'To end the story, the aircraft broke cloud at 900 feet. In the dusk we recognised an island close to Tiree surrounded by a fearsome sea. We made contact with the controller at Tiree who gave us clearance to land, together with the wind strength. As he gave the wind direction of 280 degrees we were relieved that it was blowing directly down the runway. When he gave the strength as eight-five knots, gusting to ninety-eight knots "but that's as high as the anemometer goes", it suggested that the excitement was not yet over. Only the superb flying skills of the splendidly named Captain Jimmy Scotland got the DC-3 on the ground without incident, continuing to "fly" it while stationary on the runway until the ground crew lashed the fuel bowser to it to stop us blowing away. We sat on the flight deck watching hangar doors cartwheeling across the airfield.

David during a visit to
Australia to talk to Qantas
about human factors.

A crew reunion in 1991 at Manchester House.

David demonstrating his dancing prowess with Karen, our youngest daughter, aboard USS *Uganda* on the way to Egypt.

> 'I had known David several years before I ventured to tell him the story and suggest he had probably saved my life. Exactly as I had feared, he flatly refused to believe me.'

David continued flatly to refuse. When I expressed belief in the story, David told me sharply that Ken was just being kind, not wanting us to feel too obligated. Whoever was right, Ken and Bonny were the best things that happened to us in Slindon.

And there was another story about a book of David's and its life-saving application to an aviation crisis. Again David was sceptical, though the account was reported in the American press. The first news David had of it was when he received a newspaper cutting from the senior RAF officer who had left some years before to enjoy his gains from *Village of Stars* in Switzerland. The newspaper cutting contained an account by the captain of an airliner who received an R/T message while airborne above Alaska. The message informed him that a bomb had been hidden on board his aircraft and set to explode at an altitude of 6,000 feet; thus it would go off automatically when he came in to land unless he ordered the handing over of a huge ransom. In the captain's account, some weeks before he had read *Village of Stars* and therefore knew what to do to land safely without the bomb going off and without giving in to the terrorist.

The object of the very senior officer's letter was to get David to write in to the airline concerned demanding a reward, either from the airline or its insurers. But naturally David did not.

Meanwhile Slindon was a good place for work. David had his office overlooking the garden and, visible on the horizon when the day was clear, a narrow glimmer of the sea. I had mine immediately above. Still keeping up his weekly sessions at Cardiac Rehabilitation, David threw himself into his research; more reading, more exchange of ideas, more investigations, more visits to safety departments.

The Naked Pilot was published by Methuen and came out to excellent reviews. It was eagerly read by pilots and the safety departments of airlines worldwide.

Aviation News described it as 'one of the most balanced and erudite books published for some time on the subject'. And of it, the *Daily Mail* critic wrote, 'Soars to spine-chilling, thought-provoking destinations'.

One of the first to read the book was our old friend, Ted Willis, who had early on espoused the cause of human factor study. He immediately passed a copy to Lord Clinton Davies and John Prescott, then the Opposition spokesman on Transport. Had John Prescott read it and absorbed it and in turn passed it on to the railway chiefs, the subject of drivers passing signals at red would probably have been explored before it has become too late for so many.

Ted invited David to come to the House of Lords to talk about human factors to colleagues who ought to be interested in aviation safety, and some time later Ted Willis tabled a question on aviation human factors in the House of Lords which David sat among the sleepers to hear.

In David's opinion the question fell, if not on stony ground, at least on baffled and uninterested ground. The question simply elicited a stock reply that they didn't know anything about the book or human factors, and by implication that they had no burning desire to find out about them.

Ted was bitterly disappointed. He had a supplementary question that he wished to ask if there were sufficient interest and reaction for him so to do. The supplementary question related to the case of Captain Glen Stewart, in which David had interested Ted, who was always keen to pursue a cause.

Glen Stewart was one of the pilots who had contacted David after *The Naked Pilot* was published. This British Airways captain, a quiet but very angry Scot, had come to see David about his extraordinary case.

Glen Stewart admitted he had made a mistake, but one which he felt had brought unduly severe retribution.

Captain Stewart's incident took place in the early morning of 21 November 1989 during a Cat II approach to Runway 27R at Heathrow airport. Low-visibility procedures were in force. In command of a Boeing 747, G-AWNO, BA012, Captain Stewart's aircraft captured the glideslope, which ensured that the aircraft was descending correctly. However, the aircraft was not properly established on the localiser and therefore not lined up with the runway. He continued the approach. A minimum height was recorded dangerously close to nearby buildings (the tallest of which is seventy feet) to the north of the runway before a go-around was initiated. On the second attempt the aircraft landed safely.

The incident, publicity wise, could hardly have happened at a worse time. The roads around the airport, including the North Perimeter Road, were packed with traffic. Some of the vehicles were driven by airline employees, who were terrified as the huge Jumbo roared over the roof of an airport hotel, clearing it by a few feet and so low over the car park that car alarms were set off. There was panic below, as it seemed inevitable that G-AWNO would crash into one of the buildings.

But that worst case scenario was not realised. Captain Stewart managed to land safely. No one was hurt. No damage was done. But it had been a very public and very frightening display, which was swiftly reported.

In the resulting inquiry, the crew was blamed.

There were mitigating circumstances. Captain Stewart cited human factors, including hearing what one expects to hear and not what has in fact been said. Hearing what one expects to hear and seeing what one expects to see were described on page 100 of David's first book on human factors published in 1969, twenty years before Captain Stewart's episode.

Captain Stewart cited other mitigating factors. The crew had been taken ill at Mauritius with food poisoning and the first officer was still sick. Captain Stewart was worried about fuel. There was insufficient communication on the flight deck and with management. The particular autopilot had given trouble before at Anchorage, Heathrow, Vancouver and Delhi and, according to Captain Stewart, the 747-100 autopilot was thought to be less satisfactory than the 747-200.

Unfortunately Captain Stewart had not immediately reported the incident and talked it through with his line manager. Perhaps he was himself in a state of shock. Now too much time had gone by, attitudes had become hardened. Captain Stewart had refused the first punishment handed out by British Airways. There were personality clashes, and the Civil Aviation Authority had taken the drastic step of prosecuting Captain Stewart in the criminal court. So the matter had reached an impasse and the proceedings in the Criminal Court only served to sensationalise something that hadn't, in fact, become a disaster.

In the Evening Standard, there was a banner headline 'A Few Feet From Disaster'.

Had the Jumbo flown at that height for a few more feet, the report said, there would have been a crash causing such death and destruction that it would probably have been among the worst in aviation history.

Captain Stewart was found guilty on the first of the two counts – negligently endangering an aircraft and persons therein.

David and Ted thought there was just a remote chance that Ted might be able to ask questions and get the case re-opened. But it was very remote indeed and Ted's question on human factors disappointingly did not elicit an interested response, merely a bewildered one, and he was not able to ask the supplementary question which he had in mind.

A number of people, including his lawyers, went on trying to help Captain Stewart, and he continued his own efforts to clear his name. But pilots' names are difficult to clear.

In the end, the stress became too much for Captain Stewart. He travelled up to Leuchars where watching the Liberators take off as a boy he had resolved to be a pilot, and there he killed himself.

Justice for pilots has always been slow. Blame for their crashes is still attached to Captains Foote and Pentland. Captain Pentland was killed in his crash. Captain Foote did not long survive the unjust verdict on his. There must be many others.

But although justice is slow, David's philosophy was that one should

David with Sue and his three granddaughters, Tamsin, Zoe and Olivia in the entrance tower at Merton where David had his room.

never give up, but keep on pursuing the truth and keep on writing about it.

When Methuen sold out of the hardback edition of *The Naked Pilot*, Airlife bought the paperback rights. David had done more research in the meantime, so he brought the text right up to date. Airlife made a good production, with a simple but arresting cover. It has had to be reprinted several times, and both hardback and paperback publishers reported that individual pilots from all over the world have kept contacting them, seeking copies.

Thus gradually over the years, through his books and his articles and lectures, David's ideas on human factors have percolated through the aviation establishment.

In 1992, the study of human factors became compulsory throughout the EEC for pilots applying for their licences. And in the same year, David was awarded the MBE for services to aviation. Ted Willis gave the cognoscenti interpretation of what the letters MBE stood for – My Bloody Effort. And never more true than with David, Ted added. Unlike some of the other awards which had much less flattering interpretations.

And upon those once-frowned-upon ideas of decades ago, a huge

The Window at Longstanton church, where upon seeing it, David decided to write *Light Perpetual*.

worldwide industry has now been built in cockpit resource management, communication skills, assertiveness courses, and safety. Furthermore it is still spreading. The fact that none of this was of any pecuniary advantage to David did not trouble him at all.

Another significant development was that now human factors were being recognised in other transport accidents and in other spheres such as medicine. A dean of medicine at a well-known university wrote that he gave his colleagues *The Naked Pilot* to read, and acknowledged that medicine had much to learn from it. Yet another medical consultant said he used *The Human Factor in Aircraft Accidents* when he was setting up a new department at a big general hospital. But these are just a few isolated, though perspicacious individuals. The whole set-up in medicine, David believed, needs human factor study.

Now, following so many medical scandals, the medical profession is being advised by government to seek help from the airlines in the identification of human errors and how to guard against them. David's work has come a long way from when he began it over half a century ago. In Dryden's words, 'Mighty things from small beginnings grow.'

That summer, with *The Naked Pilot* successfully launched, we allowed ourselves the luxury of returning to RAF Oakington where we had first met. We had returned several times in the past and been allowed to wander round the old haunts.

But this time the RAF had left. The Army had moved in, and though the soldiers were co-operative and seemed to welcome any diversion, they could only allow us to wander around if we were accompanied by a small armed posse, and it wasn't quite the same.

So we drove on to our next port of call, the village of Longstanton, the nearest to Oakington airfield. We pushed open the door of the Norman church, where in 1945 we used to go to Evensong, and suddenly there was a blaze of blue light. Sunlight streamed through a vivid blue star-spangled window, offered up in memory of 7 Squadron of the Pathfinder Force which had preceded 206 Squadron at Oakington.

David described it as:

> 'Ever changing blues sweep like the wind across the window, the dark shades of the night sorties merge with the light blues of the day. And in the darkest blue at the top of the window flies the RAF gold eagle, within the quatrefoils below the Pathfinder and Bomber Command crests, while from the left tracery lights fall a myriad stars, symbolic of the lives lost, with the red poppies of remembrance beside them. To the right hovers the Archangel St Michael bearing the squadron emblem

on his shield, his wings and right arm upraised, his finger pointing upwards as Lancasters are caught in the swirls of the sky, and momentarily in the white of a searchlight.'

7 Squadron suffered the loss of 981 airmen and 167 aircraft.

As we admired the window, the churchwarden came in and told us that it had been dedicated a few years ago by an ex-crew member, who had survived the war, taken Orders and become a bishop. Contributions for the window had come from all over the world.

Afterwards we sat in the bar of another favourite haunt, the Pike and Eel at Needingworth. That was unchanged, although there was no longer a ferryman to take customers across the river. But the swans still sailed by, or groomed themselves on the banks of the creek. There was the same polished oak furniture, even the same carpet and doormat. And there we talked of 7 Squadron's impressive window, and the beautiful windows at Kinloss, and other airmen's memorial windows and David's next book was conceived.

He realised it would be expensive to produce, and publishers would be reluctant to outlay money on a highly illustrated book. It would require considerable skill and patience to photograph stained glass. It was asking a great deal of the photographers. And it would also entail a considerable amount of research.

CHAPTER TWENTY

LIGHT PERPETUAL

Almost immediately things fell into place. The book was carried forward on a great wave of help from many people.

The lifelong friend of a good neighbour in Slindon, Roy Haycock, held influential rank in the present RAF. Roy told him about David's project and on an informal basis the RAF officer contacted all the station commanders under him, asking if they would volunteer the services of their photographic sections. The book would be a tribute to airmen and David had already decided he wouldn't want to make money out of it, so he would give his profits to the RAF Benevolent Fund. Every station commander agreed to help.

Research showed that there were still a number of windows beyond the areas where the RAF could help. Professional photographers were needed. But they were expensive as David knew well, in that our youngest daughter's father-in-law, Tony Tester, was himself a professional photographer. Generously he immediately offered to give his services free.

But with so many windows, one photographer was not enough. David's nephew, though a hard-working general practitioner, was also a skilful photographer. He also offered his services free.

Laborious organisation followed. Some incumbents of the churches were difficult to pin down. And when the photographers arrived at the church or cathedral or school or museum, they often found that taking pictures of windows required not only the right weather, just the right amount of sunlight plus skill and patience, but considerable physical agility too.

Photographing the window at Chelmsford Cathedral, David's nephew had to hang on to a perilously high ladder with one hand, while pointing the camera with the other. Frequently the photographer had to sit astride a beam, and once to swing out right over the full drop of the church.

David received great help in the developing and production of the pictures from Karen's in-laws. Tony had been travelling the country taking photographs, and now Mary, his wife, enlisted the services of the firm where she was company secretary and a director (CPL Colour Printing Laboratories). They were both tireless in their efforts, so it was a great family enterprise.

The photographers found it an emotional experience too, as David did in the writing of it. He particularly admired the delicately beautiful windows at Moreton church, which were engraved by Laurence Whistler, and he was intrigued by the mysterious love story behind them involving the RAF pilot shot down over France, and the anonymity of the windows' donor.

David, always keen on reconciliation, ended the book with the story of the memorial windows at East Chinnock, given by the ex-German prisoner-of-war, Gunther Anton.

Gunther was an eighteen-year-old rear gunner in a bomber of the *Luftwaffe*, shot down in 1944 while carrying out a raid on Southampton. He survived the crash and was imprisoned at Houndstone, Yeovil. Like many prisoners-of-war, he was allowed to live and work on a local farm. He came to East Chinnock. He was well treated. But this was the time of the Bomber Command saturation bombing of Germany, when the RAF were targeting such cities as Stuttgart, where Gunther Anton's father, a master glazier, and his mother lived. He had heard nothing from them. He didn't even know if they were still alive. He used to pray in the church of St Mary the Blessed Virgin at East Chinnock where he found comfort.

Eventually, he heard that his parents were safe. He stood in the kitchen at the farm, looking over the fields at the church and resolved that one day he would make a window for that church in gratitude for his parents' survival.

Returning to Germany, he and his father built up the family business making stained glass windows. Before he died, Gunther's father reminded his son of his vow to make a window for East Chinnock church. Gunther did more than that. Over the years he filled East Chinnock church with the colour and beauty of windows in the nave, the south chancel and the north chancel, and a small window over the west door.

Gunther was stopped at HM Customs while carrying one of the windows, because they could not believe that such an expensive item could be a gift. Finally in 1988, Gunther created a screen of glass bricks with the Agnus Dei superimposed to fill in the open arch between the nave and the bell tower. His thanksgiving, he said, for the kindness shown to him by the people of East Chinnock, for his safe return from the war and as an act of reconciliation.

At the RAF club for the launch of the book *Light Perpetual*. Left to right – Ian Jeffery, John Cox, David and Tony Spooner.

The making of the windows took him the last twenty-six years of his life. It was that story which made John Beaton, David's editor at Airlife, suggest the title for the book – *Light Perpetual* – which was exactly right. And Airlife prepared the book in time for the fiftieth anniversary of the end of World War Two. The magazine *This England* made an arresting feature of the book with faithful reproductions of some of the pictures. Then because the pictures were so evocative, Tony Tester made huge enlargements and light boxes to display them. The RAF Museums at Hendon and Duxford displayed a collection of them. Others museums requested them, but all this took money and David had already promised his profits to the RAF Benevolent Fund.

He therefore approached several firms asking if they would make donations and Rolls-Royce, Dowty Undercarriages and British Telecom were kind enough so to do. The British Telecom contribution funded a display of the windows at RAF Duxford together with a tribute to the telephone and telegraph workers who had kept communications going during the war and whose contribution is rarely mentioned.

Human factor study still occupied much of David's time. But one afternoon a week, in response to a suggestion that authors might give a little of their time to teaching creativity in prisons, we went to our nearest prison, Ford. David had always regarded the penal system with a jaundiced eye and automatically was on the side of those who were locked up, for even though this was an Open Prison, a prison it still was. The site, too, was of some significance to David. It had been built on the airfield where in World War Two he had landed in Beaufighters and Whitleys. The prison education block overlooked what had been the runway where, in 1943, having just completed a most secret Vixen test in Wellington 5657 on a device for use with the Mark 2 ASV, he found a couple of Messerschmitts fastening onto his tail.

When we arrived at this education block we were told that the prime need was to teach the prisoners how to read, never mind teaching them creativity. So this we tried to do.

But there was a more basic need. Hesitantly, and with shame, one prisoner confessed that he couldn't tell the time, as well as not being able to read. He was always in trouble for being late. But he was too ashamed to tell the staff and certainly too ashamed to tell his fellow inmates, who would laugh at him. We made a clock out of a cheese box and after he had begun to learn, others came to the classroom too, saying they were in the same boat. One chap also came with a huge grievance. He had bought a watch from a bloke in the market, and clearly, he said, holding it up, he had been done. The watch, when he looked at it closely, had a loose hand which went round and round and didn't behave like the other two hands. He couldn't wait to get released to clobber the bloke.

But there were prisoners there who did very sensitive writing, both poetry and prose, once they learned how. David established a great rapport with them, contrasting their start in life with his own, his freedom with their lack of it. He would like to have devoted some more of his time to exploring prison reform had his health not given out.

Meanwhile, in September of that year, David made a visit to Johannesburg to discuss South African Airways human factor courses, staying at the hotel established by his former CO on 206, Wing Commander Bertie Leach. He had already been to Australia to discuss human factor study with Qantas.

On his return from South Africa, David began on his novel, *The Ghosts of the Eighth Attack*, but halfway through October he was admitted to hospital for a colon cancer operation. When he was referred to the hospital, his GP warned the consultant that David was very stoical and would be in much more pain than he admitted. And he was indeed as stoical about that diagnosis and treatment as he had been in action. Returning home, he resumed his writing on this his last novel.

The plot of the book was one he had long considered. He had always felt an almost instinctive mistrust of twin-engined bombers and all his life he remembered arguing with two of his friends at South Cerney course who were determined to opt for them, only to be killed within a few months.

The novel is set on a Kentish airfield, to which a battered Blenheim squadron is posted. The time is 1940 when the Nazi invasion barges lie just across the Channel poised to invade. The title is taken from the American epic poem *The Ghosts of the Eighth Attack.* The novel mingles a wartime love story with the struggle of that squadron to find itself; the wartime past is cupped within the present and the fates of those who survived. Beneath the excitement and the action lie real human dilemmas which only time resolves. Of it, one reviewer wrote: 'It is as if this was the novel he had lived all his life to write.'

By the time it was ready to be sent to the publisher, David was ill with a second malignant growth and the packaged manuscript was posted on his way to have a CT scan, with the result we had both dreaded.

A second operation was needed. This time, his heart threatened to give out before the operation was finished, but it rallied and he came through. He lay battered for two days in intensive care and then was wheeled up to his room.

There he found a magnificent bowl of flowers and a note from the *Reader's Digest,* saying they were interested to talk about *The Ghosts of the Eighth Attack.* It was the most potent tonic for a writer.

So, still bruised and physically weak, but not in spirit, festooned with tubes, still wearing the silver mob-cap from Intensive Care, David sent for the telephone trolley and began talking to his primary publisher.

I stayed with him until he was ready to come home. The hospital provided a mattress on the floor and friendly nurses kept me supplied with food. David, watching his treatment with a keen eye, wrote the rough draft of an article for the *British Airways Safety Magazine,* 'Who do you trust more, your airline pilot or your doctor?' And another on that human factor which he felt was not yet properly addressed – laterality confusion. He also wrote a short story, a very tender and loving one, *The Unfinished,* inspired by Schubert's 'Unfinished Symphony', David's favourite piece of music.

After David had recovered from the operation, the oncologist prescribed a course of chemotherapy. David refused to let the nausea and weakness it engendered deter him from his new project on human factors in other forms of transport, in shipping, on the railways and roads and in medicine itself. Aware of the number of disasters in all of these, which appeared to have a human factor cause, David was preparing a book which Airlife had told him they would welcome.

He had already done some research on shipping because years before, while preparing *The Naked Pilot*, he had visited the Merchant Navy Headquarters Office in Southampton and been horrified by the lack of attention to safety. But the research was interrupted. Another CT scan revealed a new malignant growth, this time in his lung.

Surgery was suggested, but his cardiologist and the anaesthetist refused to accept him for it. So it was another course of chemotherapy and, at David's suggestion, a course of radio-therapy too.

They seemed to be successful, and to our joy our fourth grand-daughter, Victoria Skye, was born. We spent a happy week at Osborne, the perfect retreat. There, we heard that the Convalescent Home was to be the subject of a special bill in the House of Commons to overturn Edward VII's will, close the Convalescent Home and turn it into a theme park. David joined the campaign to keep the home open.

Shortly after our return, another scan showed that the cancer had spread to David's liver and the growth in the lung had revived.

He took all the news stoically. Leonard Cheshire, when being applauded for his Victoria Cross, remarked that there was even more courage shown by cancer patients than was ever shown on the battle-field. David never showed fear. He had another two weeks in hospital, this time having the fluid drained from his lung. David's sister Margaret, still sprightly and skilful and tender at eighty-seven came to help the immediate family. So David returned home to the house he loved with the view he loved in the care of the family he loved and who loved him. He remarked that although the last four years had been medically painful and daunting, those years had also been tran-scendently happy.

On his last day he could not speak properly but he could hear, and Rosie, the Macmillan nurse who called, suggested I tell him that death was close. So I asked him to go ahead towards the light and keep a place for me.

With what was the last bit of his strength, he raised his right arm, fingers lightly curled in a typical pilot's gesture, 'Will do!' Then he managed to smile and put his arms round me.

David with his family after
receiving his MBE.

In the following hours, he was transformed and ageless, his face that of a young man, his skin smooth, his lips red, his eyes bright.

Later we lay side by side in bed, holding hands. Shortly after midnight on 4 December he simply stopped breathing, leaving behind a sublime certainty of the power of one person to make a difference, of a winged life most marvellously and courageously uplifted and fulfilled. And yet, though fulfilled, like his last short story, going on. Unfinished.

Throughout his life, David had faced sudden death on innumerable occasions, always with courage. But the courage with which he faced death from a long and painful illness was an especial and deeply moving one. So great and so calm was that courage that it rose above death, dispelling fear not only in himself but in all those around him, truly quenching the darkness of death in light perpetual.

Rosie, the Macmillan nurse said to me, 'Your husband has left a priceless legacy.' And so indeed he had.

INDEX